1986

S0-BSC-566

GEN 82
Estrin, Ba
The raven and the lark.

3 0301 00088967 1

The Raven
and the Lark

Wild Folk Family, engraving by Master BXG. *(Courtesy Cliché des Musées Nationaux, Paris, Louvre, Collection Rothschild.)*

The Raven
and the Lark

Lost Children in Literature
of the English Renaissance

Barbara L. Estrin

LIBRARY
College of St. Francis
JOLIET, ILLINOIS

Lewisburg
Bucknell University Press
London and Toronto: Associated University Presses

© 1985 by Associated University Presses, Inc.

Associated University Presses
440 Forsgate Drive
Cranbury, NJ 08512

Associated University Presses
25 Sicilian Avenue
London WC1A 2QH, England

Associated University Presses
2133 Royal Windsor Drive
Unit 1
Mississauga, Ontario
Canada L5J 1K5

The paper used in this publication meets the minimum requirements of the American National Standard for Permanence of Paper for Printed Library Materials Z39.48-1984.

Library of Congress Cataloging in Publication Data

Estrin, Barbara L., 1942–
　The raven and the lark.

　Bibliography: p.
　Includes index.
　1. English literature—Early modern, 1500–1700—History and criticism.　2. Abandoned children in literature.　3. Foundlings in literature.　4. Orphans in literature.　5. Parent and child in literature.
6. Children in literature.　7. Shakespeare, William, 1564–1616—Characters—Abandoned children.　8. Spenser, Edmund, 1552?–1599—Characters—Abandoned children.
I. Title.
PR429.A2E8　1985　　　820'.9'35206945　　　83-46155
ISBN 0-8387-5075-3 (alk. paper)

Printed in the United States of America

820.9
E823

119,407

For Mark

Just so lost children imagine
their parents are lost, not they.
"Where did you go?" they chirp, as if we hadn't been
shrieking, searching,
or, as if our terror had been a game.
It's the season of the mushroom all of a sudden.

Sydney Lea, "After Labor Day"

Contents

Acknowledgments

I wish to thank those whose ideas and labors—from the very beginning and in various subsequent stages—are incorporated throughout this book, especially Ralph Bravaco, Maria Casals, Mark Estrin, Robin Estrin, David Hirsch, Edwin Honig, Wilson Howitt, Peggy Karp, Robert J. Kruse, c.s.c., Thomas Lockery, c.s.c., Ray Pepin, Frank Ryan, Andrew Sabol, and Alan Trueblood.

For her generous help at the very end—in the transition from manuscript to book—I am grateful to Katharine Turok of Associated University Presses.

The Raven
and the Lark

1

The Affinities of Kind: The Literary Formula

The Ambassador. If you're found, you're lost.
Chico. Don't be ridiculous. How can I be lost if I'm found?

Duck Soup

The lost-child plot begins with an exposed aristocrat who is saved by peasants, raised in primitive surroundings, discovered through a talisman or birthmark, and returned (usually at the moment he is about to marry) to his biological parents. He thereby restores a royal dynasty severed by his absence. The stories of most lost children follow the rituals closely in every detail. Like Moses or King Arthur, they are abandoned in infancy and are unaware, until the climactic moment, of their real parents. Characters whose experiences approximate the formula—who are in the same literary genre and whose stories will be included in this discussion— might be called analogous foundlings. Like Persephone and the Joseph of Genesis, they know their parents but are separated from them after infancy, sometimes even as young adults. Though their stories differ either in the manner of their initial exposure or in the form of their concluding recognition, they endure the same separation, the same loss, as formulaic foundlings. Occasionally, they are reunited with their parents but do not produce children themselves. In this respect Christ is an analogous foundling. He finds his Heavenly Father but cannot marry.

Despite the differences between formulaic and analogous foundlings, all lost-child plots present two philosophically opposed goods: the good of art (what man invents) and the good of nature (what god, or some higher power, molds). Art appears in the adoptive sections, in the aspirations of the foster parents who pretend—and who perhaps even come to believe—that the child they find is their own. Nature is represented by the temporary desperation and ultimate exaltation of the biological parents who at first lose and then get back the missing child. The reunion provides the happy ending, the joy of familial continuity replacing the transforming adventure of adoption.

The word *foundling* itself anticipates the eventual finding implied by the initial loss. Otherwise the deserted infant might more appropriately be called a *lostling*. The appearance of such a child arouses in audiences a conditioned expectation for his recovery. The reader of a fairy tale or a novel by Dickens has a generic faith that its orphan hero will turn out to be royal or at least wealthy, that he will discover his legitimate ancestors and reject his substitute family. The theme reflects an aristocratic longing. Because the conclusion predicates that the biological parents are superior to the adoptive ones, the foundling formula suggests that "nature" is better than "nurture."

The mere naming of genealogies establishes a sense of well-being; *knowing* a background is equivalent to *having* a future. In those rare Old Testament passages (Numbers 16:29; Genesis 5:24) where the generational link is effaced, the connective desire is intensified by its actual or threatened severance. Moses intimidates the tribe of Korah with the specter of mass and total extermination:

> If the LORD make a new thing, and the earth open up her mouth, and swallow them up, with all that appertain unto them, and they go down quick into the pit; then he shall understand that these men have provoked the LORD. (Numbers 16:30)

As punishment for their transgression, Korah and his men will be so totally absorbed that no trace of them will be left. They will not die "the common death of all men" (Numbers 16:29). Like Enoch, who "was not; for God took him" (Genesis 5:24), the tribe's past can be taken away and its destiny thereby eliminated; nothing will remain to verify an entire communal life led. In their darkness, these moments contrast to the natural course of events in the Bible. Normally, confirming an ancestry ensures a dynasty. Because a verified past promises continuity, biblical and classical mythology assert that the way forward involves some sort of return. The terror of the Enoch and Korah passages lies in their very uniqueness. Their disappearances are irrevocable. The assurance in the lost-child story is that its interlude—an exposure that seems annihilating—is only temporary. The good of nature resurfaces through a linking of past and future, as in the legends of Abraham, Joseph, and Moses, which obviates any rupture in between.

The good of art appears in the adoptive sections where the supremacy of inheritance is superseded by the idealization of the replacement. Thus the aristocratic court is supplanted by the simple country, the proud king by a modest peasant. During this "diaspora," the lost child absorbs values that his biological parents could never teach him. Principally, the adoptive sections represent a belief that individual differences—even those of race (Moses' rescue by the Egyptian princess) or species (Romulus and Remus's rearing by wolves)—can be overcome. A stranger can sustain the child as well as his parents can.

Even in *Titus Andronicus*, the darkest of his plays, Shakespeare presents as a psychological given the optimism of the adoptive interlude. Just before her rape, Lavinia, pleading with an eloquence denied Philomela in the myth, appeals to a notion of universal motherhood when she suggests that she might replace for Tamora the son Titus sacrificed:

> Yet every mother breeds not sons alike:
> [*To* CHIRON] Do thou entreat her show a woman's pity.
> . . . .
> 'Tis true the raven doth not hatch a lark:
> Yet I have heard—O, could I find it now!—
> The lion, mov'd with pity did endure
> To have his princely paws par'd all away.
> Some say that ravens foster forlorn children,
> The whilst their own birds famish in their nests:
> O, be to me, though thy hard heart say no,
> Nothing so kind, but something pitiful.
>
> (2.3.145–46; 149–56)

Lavinia defends an order transcending the generational cycle—a kinship based on caring rather than consanguinity. In such a kingdom the lion relinquishes his supremacy for love, the raven his family for the wretched. Though the bird of darkness cannot hatch a lark, he might, through pity, adopt one. Lavinia presents a vision of romantic love (the lion as suitor) and earthly fellowship (the raven as fosterer) alien to her world. Her plea in desperation is as absurd as asking, in solicitude, of parents whose child has died, "Are there any other children?" Seeking to be that other child (to substitute her lark for Tamora's raven), Lavinia belies the plot she thinks might save her. The foundling theme insists that there can be no replacement for the missing child. But the compensation of the adoptive interlude presupposes the reparative goodness of art—a goodness that might transcend or alter the evil in nature.

Such a belief constitutes the ethical structure of Malory's *Works*, where the line of adoption—extended from Merlin to Arthur and from Arthur to his knights—forms the happy union signified by the fellowship of the Round Table. The fellowship falls apart when the natural values of familial heritage reassert their primacy on the quest for the Grail and permeate themselves into the final sections when Gawain and Mordred claim their biological rights. Contrarily, in Sidney's *Old Arcadia,* the analogical foundlings, Pyrocles and Musidorus, follow their loves, forsake their knightly origins, assume pastoral poses, and proclaiming the value of transformation intrinsic to art, find (through a deus ex machina) their true selves. In Spenser's work, the theme receives its most complex expression. *The Faerie Queene* has many formulaic (Red Cross Knight, Arthur, Pastorella, Amoret, Ruddymane, the babe Satyrane finds) and analogous (Una in quest, Fidessa in the story she invents, Britomart in pursuit, Lucifera in ambition) foundlings. The audience assumes that all the characters will eventually experience a happiness guaranteed by the mere use of the formula; but that expectation is dashed because the characters' stories are either never fully told or never fully formulaic. In the extant version Ruddymane does not grow up; Artegall leaves Britomart dangling. Una and Pastorella should be reunited with their parents (as they are) and married (as they are not). Spenser's failure to provide the anticipated resolution and his reluctance to endorse the good of nature implied by marriage may indicate that he sides with the good of an art unveiled most blatantly on Mount Acidale in book 6.

In Shakespeare's plays, the art/nature debate (which in *The Faerie Queene* is entertained by what the reader perceives to be a disparity between the author and his characters) is undertaken by the characters themselves. It is pursued in *Richard III* and *Romeo and Juliet* as the heroes deliberately recreate their lives—sever all natural ties—in order to realize a self-determined destiny. It is resolved in *Comedy of Errors* and *Pericles* when the lost children are found through a woman's affirmation of her natural function. In *As You Like It,* Rosalind's willingness both to accept the natural vicissitudes and to risk the transforming ethos of love enables her to enjoy all the triumphs of the plot. She finds a father and a husband. Cleopatra, an analogous foundling who also comes to see the good in nature, experiences a recognition corresponding to Rosalind's and anticipating those of Hermione and Perdita. Similarly, Hamlet and Lear, both analogous foundlings, have ties to characters in *The Tempest* and *The Winter's Tale.* Prospero is a saved Hamlet, Leontes a redeemed Lear. *Antony and Cleopatra, Hamlet,* and *Lear* raise philosophical questions that are answered by Shakespeare's total commitment to the formula in the last plays.

Foundlings appear in the work of virtually every major author of the English Renaissance. When he works within (or deviates from) the established paradigm, the poet's resolution of the art/nature controversy involves *(a)* his choice of literary genres (tragedy, comedy, and romance); *(b)* his exploration of both emotional and philosophical ("womanly" and "manly") approaches to life; *(c)* his juggling of a private passion to forge a poetic—creative—identity with the contravening impulse to contribute to the social—dynastic—mainstream; and *(d)* his weaving (in an effort to achieve balance and reveal his purpose) double or multiple narrative structures (as in *The Old Arcadia, The Faerie Queene, King Lear, The Winter's Tale,* and *The Tempest*). Why, for example, does the return of the lost children accompany the dissolution of a kingdom in *Le Morte d'Arthur* and its salvation in *The Old Arcadia?* What does it suggest about Spenser's attitude toward poetry that, though *The Faerie Queene* abounds in foundlings, only one couple (Marinell and Florimell) marries? Conversely, why does Shakespeare retain every detail of the convention in his four last plays, promoting with Hermione a natural continuity and abjuring with Prospero the artistic alternative? These questions about the formula help determine a writer's purpose. When he uses only part of the theme or manipulates his audience's plot expectations, those uses and manipulations are revealing in themselves. The foundling theme is a mini-genre; its variations provide the same insights into a work as variations in comedy, tragedy, or pastoral convey. Moreover, it is a mini-genre connected to the maxi-genres. Its formulaic closure may involve the comedy of *As You Like It* or the romance of *Pericles;* its failure to be completed becomes one way of defining, for example, Lear's tragedy.

As a literary formula the theme affords the most of all possible worlds. During the adoptive interlude (in the Bohemia of *The Winter's Tale* or the Acidale of *The Faerie Queene*) it yields to the goodness of art. The interlude allows—through the pastoral sojourn—a physical exploration beyond the inherited kingdom and—through the foster parents—a psychological duplication of native parental kindness. With the concluding recognition, it asserts the affinities of kind, endorsing the goodness of nature. The return of the real child surrounds the restoration of what was with the aura of rebirth. What was, even sinning man, seems all at once good enough.

2

The Affinities of Kind: The Renaissance Context

Citing Leonardo's drawings and Raphael's *putti*, David Kunzle argues that the image developed in Renaissance art "belies the impression we have of that era as one largely indifferent to the special characteristics of children and their various stages of development."[1] As a literary formula, the foundling theme—with its wrenching loss and joyous recovery—proved a vehicle for handling the ambivalence Kunzle describes. The writer using it could convey both the idealization of the child circumscribed by certain philosophical and artistic dicta and his neglect in response to still other religious and social pressures. Regarding the twofold Tudor attitude, Ivy Pinchbeck and Margaret Hewitt maintain:

> Amongst the upper classes, bonfires were often built in celebration of a wife's pregnancy: the actual birth might cause a similar conflagration. But having arrived, the child's infant progress was deemed of too little interest or importance to his family to merit record.[2]

Children were to be heard (and seen) principally at moments significant to their parents' sense of continuity. A fiction, like the foundling plot, where they disappear for fifteen years only to surface when they are socially useful, might then express a desire to eliminate the difficulty of raising (without experiencing the guilt of neglecting) the necessary dynasty.

Demographically, children were crucial for a family's perpetuation. They provided a hedge against obscurity. Lawrence Stone describes the Tudor obsession:

> Among the landed classes in pre-Reformation England, nuptiality—the proportion of surviving children who married—was determined by

family strategy. The three objectives of family planning were the continuity of the male line, the preservation intact of the inherited property and the acquisition through marriage of further property or useful political alliances. Given the very uncertain prospects of survival, the first could only be ensured by the procreation of the largest number of children in the hope that at least one male child would live to marriageable age.[3]

Each child becomes a piece of property, a way of holding the already acquired—and extending the still coveted—family realm.

Tudor marriage manuals picture a thread of connection, cemented by the child, between God and man. Miles Coverdale speaks of marriage as a covenant:

> Wedloke is a lawfull knott unto God and acceptable yokynge together of one man and one woman with the good consent of them both to the intent that they two may dwell together in frendshippe and honestye one helping and comforting the tother . . . [bringing up] children in the fear of God.[4]

The knot holding couples together stretches into a collar that includes the raising of children and enforces the teaching of obedience. Imitating their parents in a grand procession stemming from a higher source, children are part of a chain with God at the helm. For John Rogers

> Children (vndoubtedly) is the highest guift, and greatest treasure of this worlde, and maintenaunce of the same. For Children is the very sure band and last knot of loue Matrimonial; by the which the parents can neuer be clearly seperated a sunder; Inasmuch as that which is of hem both cannot be deuided, seeing both haue parte in euery one. And children are their parents cheefe ioy, comfort, and felicitie next vnto God; their stay and staffe and vpholders of their age; and in their children do the Parents liue (in a manner) after their death. For they dye not all togethers, that leaue collops of their owne flesh aliue behinde them; and by their children (if they be vertuously and godly brought vp) then is God honoured, and the common wealth aduanced, so that the parents and all men fare the better by them.[5]

The thread exalted by Coverdale is here made inviolable. Children verify their parents' initial existence and affirm their consequent union on this earth, emerging a source of maintenance, preservation, and strength. They are the stay and staff and upholders, firm assurances of a life spent in the service of God. As symbols of stability, children serve their parents, reflecting their origins, anticipating and guaranteeing their destiny.

The sense of continuity is personalized. "They die not all togethers that leaue collops of their owne flesh aliue behind them."[6] Viewed in this light, children are their parents made small. They have no separate identity; the connection through duplication predetermines their existence. Flesh of their parents' flesh, they are also part of a sustaining process that connects for Rogers not only to the promulgation of a dynasty but to the advancement of the commonwealth. Children extend the family thread forward into history even as they propagate its influence contemporaneously throughout the state.

The stretching in both directions tends to diminish the importance of the individual child. What matters is the affirmation of the parents' existence in the abiding presence of the continued generations. Shakespeare reflects the eternalizing impulse in the early sonnets where the child evokes not only the future but the past, recalling the green land of his parents' beginnings:

> Look in thy glass, and tell the face thou viewest
> Now is the time that face should form another,
> Whose fresh repair if now thou not renewest,
> Thou dost beguile the world, unbless some mother.
> For where is she so fair whose uneared womb
> Disdains the tillage of thy husbandry?
> Or who is he so fond will be the tomb
> Of his self-love to stop posterity?
> Thou art thy mother's glass, and she in thee
> Calls back the lovely April of her prime;
> So thou through windows of thine age shalt see,
> Despite of wrinkles, this thy golden time.
> But if thou live remember'd not to be,
> Die single and thine image dies with thee.[7]

Rogers's glass of heavenly love becomes the ideal of earthly perpetuation. The temporal qualities of a remembered spring acquire the spatial dimensions of a happy place eternally recapturable through the perpetuation of a moment of good. The child is both innocence itself and a symbol of his parents' initial glory. He embodies hope, representing "prime" as first in chronological order and best in qualitative degree. Holding up a regressing and progressing image, the speaker opens up a "window" that faces always on a preserved initiation. The mirroring child calls back a lovely spring repairing, with a golden time, a fading present. The biblical injunction repeated by Shakespeare and espoused in the marriage manuals is, Increase and multiply. As his mother's glass, the child reflects the April of his family's beginnings, while (as window) he brings in the freshness of all beginnings. Through the opacity of the mirror and the opening of the casement, the child is the ultimate hope and first light of the race. He returns to, absorbs, and then perpetuates that primal image.

The foundling story provides a means of reopening the window (so idealized in the sonnet) without following through on the tedious per diem task of maintaining its radiance. In the revitalizing return of the concluding recognition and in the imitative kindness of the adoptive interlude, the theme posits the instinctual, primal goodness of a green April and a golden time. But it goes one step beyond the sonnet, confirming, via the cruelty of its initial exposure, the reality of an inherited, biologically transmitted, sin. Thus it takes into account conflicting philosophical premises, reflected in the religious teaching and political reform of the age. By manipulating the plot's varying stages the writer can probe several strands of the Elizabethan social dialogue simultaneously. With the concluding recognition, he can assent to sermons (such as those of Thomas Becon) proclaiming the superiority of God's creation over man's contrivance. Considering the converse—man's enterprise—the poet can subscribe, through the adoptive experience, to the growing interest (evidenced by the writing of Roger Ascham) in education. Finally, affirming the significance of an individual life, the poet can, by heightening the pathos of the opening sequences, encourage a social responsibility reflecting the twin gospels of political reform (as in "The Ypres Scheme for Poor Relief") and religious charity (as in the sermons of Gervaise Babington).

Denying the good of art, Thomas Becon argued:

God's word is lively, and giveth life. So long as we believe this word, and continue in the same we live; but when we believe it not nor remain in it, we can none otherwise but perish, die and be damned. For this cause it is called the word of life. Man's invention is dead, and bringeth death. For it cometh of the affection and wisdom of the flesh, which is death. By this means did Adam with all his posterity fall into death because he, following his own invention and mind, did eat of the forbidden fruit, contrary to the word of the Lord.[8]

To worship human creativity is to counter the Lord's commandment. Becon maintains that, if there are two answers to mutability (one God-given, the other man-made), good Christians side with nature (which stems from life) over art (which responds to death). Sin is an invention, a product of the mind: a contrivance. While the logical conclusion of Becon's argument is to accept whatever happens as God's will, earthly political answers were nevertheless sought by Tudor society to problems that, in previous ages, had been left to fester until the moment of divine mediation. Clinging to a system of wardship for the aristocracy and initiating a program of welfare for the poor, Elizabethans affirmed their belief in man's power to change his life.

The upper classes revived the policy of feudal wardship as a source of revenue. The system originally arose out of the need for military troops. The tenant got land from the great barons with the promise that he would serve his lord for forty days in the field. Joel Hurstfield explains the war time invention of what was to become a peacetime institution:

> In an age of war and plague and sudden death, it frequently happened that the tenant died leaving as heir a child who was manifestly unable to render the appropriate military service. What was the lord to do but to take back the land temporarily and use it, if he wished to obtain military service from someone else? That was what was meant by the expression that the land had passed into wardship. And with the land went the child. The lord could reasonably claim that he should control the upbringing of the minor in order to insure efficient and loyal service when he came of age. In the language of the time, the lord obtained the wardship of the body. If the heir were female, the lord went further and claimed the right of consent to her choice of husband.[9]

Early death created a need for alternative families. Further, even if the parents were alive, the offspring of one household were often reared as servants by another, slightly more aristocratic, one in order to prepare them for employment or marriage afterward.[10] In the early Renaissance the scheme of substitute parenting known as wardship became a form of institutionalized adoption. How easy then to dream with Malory, Spenser, and Shakespeare that foster families, even temporary ones, offered a better life. Still later in the Renaissance the adoptive sanctuary would become a school to which the child was sent, partly to rid the parent of the necessity of parenting, partly to train the child for a career that would benefit the family later on.

Quoting Lady Jane Grey, Roger Ascham urges, in *The Schoolmaster,* that the schoolhouse might become, like the adoptive interlude in foundling stories, a refuge from cruel parents:

> One of the greatest benefits that ever God gave me is that he sent me so sharp and severe parents and so gentle a schoolmaster. For when I am in presence either of father or mother, whether I speak, keep silence, sit, stand, or go, eat, drink, be merry or sad, . . . I must do it, as it were, in such weight, measure and number, even so perfectly as God made the world, or else I am so sharply taunted, so cruelly threatened, yea, presently sometimes with pinches, nips and bobs, and other ways which I will not name for the honor I bear them, so without measure

misordered, that I think myself in hell till time come that I must go to
Mr. Aylmer, who teacheth me so gently, so pleasantly, with such fair
allurements to learning, that I think all the time nothing whilst I am
with him. And when I am called from him, I fall on weeping because
whatsoever I do else but learning is full of grief, trouble, fear, and
whole misliking unto me.[11]

Countering the harsh taunting of her parents with his fair allurements,
Mr. Aylmer entices Lady Jane into learning. The act of scholarship leads
her into a place of renewal that, by its very capacity for growth, dwarfs all
other pleasures. The world of her biological parents is associated with a
devastating belittlement. Unmade by her makers and remade by her
teacher, Lady Jane therefore counts it as her greatest benefit to have "such
. . . severe parents and so gentle a schoolmaster."[12] The kindly schoolmaster was for Lady Jane Grey the real-life equivalent of the good shepherds
in foundling stories. Her comments reflect her desire to become an analogous foundling, to rid herself of harsh parents.

The need for such a haven is apparent from another exigency of the
Reformation, one that Lady Jane's parents, disappointed by her imper-
fections, make clear in their cruelty. The prospect of the more children
the merrier was dampened by the reality of a conflicting belief: that of
inherent, inherited, sinfulness. If Shakespeare's procreative sonnets assume an age of innocence recaptured by the child, doctrinaire Puritanism
premises instead a line of destruction conveyed through the parent. Lawrence Stone maintains that for the Calvinist

the child was both the hope of the future—the embodiment of parental
ambitions to create a generation of virtue and godliness that would
presage the Second Coming—and at the same time the negation of all
such aspirations, the incarnation of Original Sin, the victim from birth
of the manifold and endless temptations of the Devil.[13]

When Jane's parents despair that her acts were not in "measure and
number . . . so perfect . . . as God made the world,"[14] they betray a fear
that, as their double, she reflects their sin. The easiest way to cope with
the malignancy the child represents is to pretend, by casting him out to
others, that he does not exist. If the upper classes were pawning off their
children, so, too, were the underlings. Like wardship, apprenticeship
proved a means of transferring the task of raising the child from one
family to another. Work laws passed the burden from a particular group
to the whole spectrum of society, rendering the state the ultimate substitute parent. If the Tudor period saw a declining belief in the philosophical
possibilities of the good, it witnessed a rising trust in the political organi-

zations designed nevertheless to achieve it. Of particular concern was the
need for legislation to govern the succorless—the abandoned, the orphaned—poor child.

"The Ypres Scheme of Poor Relief," a Continental welfare program
cited as a model in England, maintained:

> For if it be reason that a gentellemans chylde shulde haue a tutour or
> creanser appoynted to loke to him, yea and if brute bestes haue kepers
> as the shepe a shepherde the Neat a neteherd and so of other. Why I
> praye you do these nedy folkes (that ar men as well as we) alone of all
> other wander vp and downe without tutoure or keper? . . . we ought
> nat onely to ease of their calamitie but also to preserue that they shulde
> fele no grefe, for though that pouerty be accompanyed with many
> incommodyties yet a great parte of them is taken away by subuentyon
> whan one helpeth or comforteth another. And bycause that no man
> alone hath so great wytte nor so great substance that he is able to do
> thys thynge: therfore it was nedefull to haue manye mennes helpe
> whiche lyke comen tutours shall ordre and rule the comen benefyte of
> the cytie by the hole voyces and comen agrement of the same.[15]

The logic institutionalizing the ward is extended here to the lower classes.
If rich men and beasts can have substitute parents (tutors and shepherds)
why should not the poor? The underlying assumption of such policies is
that subvention, support by subsidy, will take away the incommodity of
birth, freeing everyone from a puritanically rigid determinism. Poor relief
proposes that, through art, the defects of nature can be overcome; envi-
ronment displaces heredity:

> Truly it is a greater thing and a better to be well taught than to be well
> borne. Moreouer these vntaught olde felowes worne and spent in
> noughtynes which haue spent their youth vngracyously in erroures and
> blyndnesse must be holpen and counselled to come to the right path of
> vertue. And yonge folkes that are corrupted through euyll felowship
> company that haunte and vse noughtye places losynge bothe their
> money and and soules: the prefects must so handle that they shall haue
> no lust after to kepe company with vnthriftes.[16]

A good prefect will lure the untaught old and corrupted young from evil.
Such a belief in the possibilities for transformation was undermined,
however, by the cancerous conditions that demanded it. Philosophical
assent to mutual support did not in itself guarantee the eradication of
poverty or the elimination of cruelty. But wishing, through a literary
structure, appeased the desire to reorganize the world. The need for a

fictional escape was so great because it was hard to avoid a destitution that fostered such endless social concern.

Gervaise Babington dramatizes the proximity of mythologized abandonment when he sermonizes about Abraham's pain:

> Let us observe the degrees or amplification of this cross of Abraham, by some circumstances that are layde downe, as first that Abraham must take him and sacrifice him his owne selfe and with his owne handes, a great matter and far more then if he had given him over to another. Secondly of the person to be taken, who was he, thy sonne sayth the Texte, and not thy servant. Thirdly, thy sonne, and not thy wyves sonne alone, as some sonnes be. Fourthly, unicum, thy only sonne Isaac, fifthlye, whom thou lovest, all circumstances of great moment, and greatly to be noted of us, that wee may knowe in what sorte God will be bold with us his creatures, and workemanship when it pleaseth him. We must not thinke it strange to be exercised even in those things that are deere unto us. But whatsoever they are, this to remember, that he which loveth any thing more than God, is not worthie of him. Sixtlye, that he must goe with him three days journey ere he offred him. For the old saying is . . . bitter is the delay when punishment must followe, and it is a kinde mercy to kill quickly who appointed once is to be killed. Certainely the griping thoughts and twitching passions, that Abraham felt in his minde during these three days, made this tryall of his far grater than it had been if presently he should have smit that blowe. Lastlye, that hee must offer him for a burnte offering. O depth of tryall, able to have swallowed us up, a thousand of us: bothe to laye his handes upon his deere sonne, and then to burne him to ashes, when hee had doone his owne selfe making and tending the fire till all was one and putting peece after peece into the flame, when any was without, and with his owne eyes to see all this and to looke upon it. Heere is a tryall, to tell us what God may do if it please him. [17]

Babington's explications resemble the actual eye slicing in Buñuel's *The Andalusian Dog.* The Biblical version outlines the journey up the mountain so that—like the cloud passing the moon in the Buñuel film—it is easy to read it as a symbolic eclipse on the full scale of Abraham's history. In Babington's version the audience is forced (as the audience in the Buñuel film is subsequently forced) to picture the excruciating details of the sacrifice. Through his seven-pointed argument, Babington underlines Abraham's step-by-step complicity in Isaac's fate. It is his own child who must be offered, and Abraham must do it himself: tending the fire and throwing into the flames piece by piece of what the congregant (viewing the child as a collops of the parent) understood to be himself. The sermon

119, 407

LIBRARY
College of St. Francis
JOLIET, ILLINOIS

dramatizes the moment of exposure initiating the foundling convention. It details what the literary versions gloss over: the distress—in intensifying levels—of the loss. But it also helps to explain the popularity of the fictions. In a society attuned to the cruelty of child abandonment (either literally in the number of deserted infants or figuratively through wardship, the school, or apprenticeship), aware of the exigency of dynastic perpetuation (the manuals of Coverdale and Rogers), and awakening to the need for social reform (the schemes for poor relief), the foundling plot provided a perfect wish fulfillment. In these fictions, the forlorn are immediately rescued—confirming the desirability of public and social intervention—and ultimately returned—verifying the importance of private and familial continuity. For Elizabethans, the rituals of such plots gratify humanitarian (through the art of the adoptive interlude), and then satisfy (through the nature of the concluding recognition) dynastic, impulses.

3

Finders Keepers: Preservation and the Legendary Foundling

Seeking their identity, foundlings ask, Who am I? by demanding, Who are my parents? Once the second question is answered, the first one seems, miraculously, to fall into place. The recognition annuls both the initial devastation and the ensuing uncertainty, assuring the final comfort of a known beginning. In the intensity of loss and the pleasure of recovery, all foundlings are the same. But, though they share a common experience of suffering and redemption, the plots describing this mutual thread are often woven in different patterns. The stories vary in their initiating events, adoptive sequences, and concluding discoveries. The literary foundlings of the Renaissance have their antecedents in biblical and classical sources. As the sermons of Gervaise Babington corroborate, Renaissance writers assumed their audience's familiarity with the legends and appropriated from them not only directly in allusions to mythical characters but indirectly in variations that parallel the variations in the myths.

There are four types of mythological exposure: first, that of a life-denying sacrifice (Christ and Isaac); second, that of a life-saving alternative (Moses); third, that of parental fear of supersession (Aphrodite and Cronos); and fourth, that of a child-induced separation (Persephone and Phaëthon) whetted by the appeal (as evidenced in the pastoral interlude of Greek romances) of the adoptive experience. Finally, in its obligatory recognition, the theme presents two alternatives: divine and legendary. In god stories, the child dies to find his Heavenly Father, as do the analogous foundlings Christ and Phaëthon; in legends, the child lives and returns to his earthly family, as do Moses and the heroes in such Greek romances as *Daphnis and Chloe* and *An Aethiopian History*. Formulaic foundlings are saved not through death but despite it, here and now, instead of in the New Jerusalem.

Christ completes the Old Testament "test" of faith, losing himself in

order to discover the realm that in that one moment on the scaffold he
himself begins to doubt:

> And about the ninth hour, Jesus cried with a loud voice, saying E'li,
> E'li, la' ma sa-bach' tha-ni'? that is to say, My God, my God, why hast
> thou forsaken me? (Matthew 27:46)

His question is logical—Why is the innocent child abandoned? Why does
the father demand the death? He points in his desperation to the cruel
center of the lost-child theme. The moment of loss, that ninth hour, lends
his story a requisite credibility. It has to be felt to be real. Even God must
experience the loneliness of being "forsaken," without parent or friend.
Christ is Isaac and Abraham combined, the sacrificer and the sacrificed,
the "seeker" for man and, in his final act, the abandoned child as well. In
returning to his Father he saves mankind, phrasing the experience of the
Hebrews in formulaic terms, presenting the new world through the
metaphor of the foundling. His experience casts a retrospective light on
the Old Testament.

There, the heroes were, like Christ in that one moment on the Cross,
continually forsaken. The only answer they had for a universe essentially
hostile was to make connections—to find themselves and their earthly
fathers. Once Adam was expelled from Eden and left in an imperfect and
alien realm, his successors huddled together, protected themselves by
praying for generational sustenance and by forming links in what they
projected to be the great human chain. The Old Testament reads like a
succession of "begats" where the greatest punishment is not to be able to
have children and the greatest joy is to bless, and be blessed by, them.

Within the context of a search for continuity and dynasty is the incredible
sacrifice demanded of Abraham. Despite the fact that God promises
him the very futurity he so much wants, Abraham is asked to believe in
God's promise about multiplication and to cut off the only means to
secure that future. Ascending the mountain, Abraham and Isaac went
"both of them together" (Genesis 22:8), father and son alike condemned.
And, in abandoning Isaac, Abraham has also been abandoned, made the
lost child of God. When God restores him to his fatherhood by providing
"himself a lamb" (Genesis 22:8), he speaks in the identical images of
proliferation with which he originally (in Genesis 15:4–5) endowed
Abraham's dynasty:

> That in blessing I will bless thee, and in multiplying I will multiply thy
> seed as the stars of the heaven, and as the sand which is upon the sea
> shore; and thy seed shall possess the gate of his enemies.

And in thy seed shall all the nations of the earth be blessed; because thou hast obeyed my voice. (Genesis 22:17–18)

Though Abraham wields the knife to his son, it is clear that both have been sentenced by their Creator. Alone on the mountain both have become the scorned children of the same implacable Father. When Isaac is restored, Abraham is redeemed. By "obeying" God, Abraham repossesses his fatherhood and is blessed. Human creativity equals sexual productivity. Through it, the world opens up infinitely. Denied the power of paternity, man becomes impotent and, knife in hand, self-destructive.

For the Hebrews the truth of God's presence is manifest in the human power of self-perpetuation. Without that gift, rendered throughout the Old Testament as God-given, there can be no miracle in the miracle story. When Rebekah is chosen (Genesis 24) to be Isaac's wife, the promise of unlimited fecundity is repeated in her marriage ceremony:

And they blessed Rebekah and said unto her, Thou art our sister; be thou the mother of thousands of millions, and let thy seed possess the gate of those which hate them. (Genesis 24:60)

Similarly, when Jacob dreams of his ladder ascending to heaven, his vision is one of algebraic bounty:

And thy seed shall be as the dust of the earth; and thou shalt spread abroad to the west, and to the east, and to the north, and to the south: and in thee and in thy seed shall all the families of the earth be blessed. (Genesis 28:14)

Earthly perpetuation opens the way to the skies, the protraction in time leading to an extension in space. God predicts Jacob's seed shall be, like sand or dust, endless; but the promise of man's power is couched, as is the Abraham-Isaac story, in the language of God's paternity. For, while man's seed is to emerge as copious as the dust of the earth, that same dust reverts to man's beginnings in God. Man's fertility ("seed") is linked to his mortality ("dust"). Dust is barren yet manifold. Seeds yield fruit yet seem scarce. The paradox reiterates the second creation, referring through its images of plentitude back to the passage in Genesis where man was made out of nothing—not in God's image but at his mercy: "And the Lord God formed man of the dust of the ground" (Genesis 2:7). The second creation makes man completely dependent on the divine source to which he aspires. That dependency is repeated throughout the Old Testament where the Hebrews learn they must constantly construct a passage to the originating power; a failure to appreciate God leads to impotence and sterility. But an acknowledgment builds a ladder extending at once heavenward and abroad over the earth. In the Old Testament, to reproduce is to affirm God and to forge a future.

With the most famous of the biblical lost children, however, the plot revolves around a return rather than a potential. Moses finds his sonhood, acknowledging his ancestors, and thereby establishing the aristocratic connection to God that eventually frees his nation from bondage. Bereft of the familial enclave, Moses is preserved by the very world believed to be antagonistic. Pharaoh's daughter finds and adopts him:

> And the daughter of Pharaoh came down to wash herself at the river; and her maidens walked along by the river's side: and when she saw the ark among the flags, she sent her maid to fetch it.
>   And when she had opened it, she saw the child and behold, the babe wept. And she had compassion on him, and said this is one of the Hebrew's children. (Exodus 2:5–6)

Primary in the scene is the baby's crying; secondary is the fact that he is a Hebrew. In his helplessness, the baby transcends his cultural place and converts the supposed enemy, making himself the princess's "son" and granting her a moment of compassion she might not have experienced without him.

When God revealed himself to Abraham, he spoke of the future. But to Moses, he presents himself not in a predicted embryo but in a recollected ancestry:

> I am the God of thy father, the God of Abraham, the God of Isaac and the God of Jacob. (Exodus 3:6)

The arguments throughout Exodus between a reluctant hero and a confident God reflect Moses' hesitation to acknowledge the tribe of Israel as his brethren and forefathers. Yet, in freeing them from bondage, he renders them, like himself, as little children, fearful of, and believing in, the parent who bribes them into submission. In Exodus, the abandoned progeny of Israel are treated like truants needing a combination of laws to guide them and miracles to persuade them. But through their suffering, and as a sign of their release, the Hebrews acquire the childhood from which their sojourn in Egypt kept them:

> The LORD is my strength and song, and he is become my salvation: he is my God, and I will prepare him an habitation; my father's God, and I will exalt him. (Exodus 15:2)

In the triumphal hymn, Moses celebrated not only his faith but his race. He is the son of Abraham and Isaac, the seed to whom the Promised Land was prophesied. Once the race of Moses is established, the Bible turns from the rhetoric of the past to the promise of the future. The quest in the books of Exodus through Joshua is to recapture the potential of Genesis. Within the context of revived futurity, it is logical that Moses should get to see the Promised Land but not dwell in it:

> And the LORD said unto him, This is the land which I sware unto Abraham, unto Isaac and unto Jacob, saying, I will give it unto thy seed: I have caused thee to see it with thine eyes, but thou shalt not go over thither. (Deuteronomy 34:4)

Toward the end of his life, Moses becomes, like his ancestors before him, the seed bearer. With the vision on Mount Moab he emerges, like Abraham on Mount Moriah, the progenitor of salvation rather than the embodiment of it. His reward lies in the potential of the blessing he will confer on Joshua just before he dies:

> And Joshua the son of Nun was full of the spirit of wisdom; for Moses had laid his hands upon him: and the children of Israel harkened unto him and did as the LORD commanded Moses. (Deuteronomy 34:9)

The blessing is part of the ritual of foundling stories, which includes the passing of wisdom from one generation to the next and the sanctifying of the future in light of a redeemed past. The Moses story establishes a connective pattern. First the child is abandoned and found; then the grown man extends his discovery to the future that his earthly salvation ensures, reasserting the Old Testament formula for the foundling theme. What is important to pass on there is not the knowledge "face to face" (Deuteronomy 34:10) of divine truth but the "spirit of wisdom" (Deuteronomy 34:9) borne in the seed extended throughout human time. In the New Testament, while continual reference is made to the prophecies of the Old, the emphasis is on the "face to face" aspect of the relationship between God and man. The promises made to Abraham are converted into premises upon which a further dynasty can be built:

> For the promise, that he should be the heir of the world was not to Abraham, or to his seed, through the law but through the righteousness of faith. (Romans 4:13)

For Jews, faith guarantees an earthly destiny; for Christians, it foreshadows the New Jerusalem. The quest in the Old Testament is to find historical and communal parentage—to return; in the New Testament it is to become "like the son of God"—to progress. The period between birth and death, paramount in the Old Testament, emerges irrelevant in the New. Earthly isolation is valued as an end in itself:

> Without father, without mother, without descent, having neither beginning of days nor end of life; but made like unto the Son of God; abideth a priest continually. (Hebrews 7:3)

The passage describes the priest as an Isaac without an Abraham; he can never return to his earthly father. In the New Testament the temporary void of foundling stories becomes a permanent or "abiding" state. Earthly redempion is replaced by the regenerative event. Christ's return to his Father signifies that mere survival has its limitations. Orphanhood—the state without biological father or mother—is revered as an end in itself because spiritual parenthood supersedes physical kinship. A formula for earthly salvation in the Old Testament, the foundling theme becomes, in the New, a means toward a better end. Divine presence is to be discovered only in a state of mortal absence. To be made like the Son of God is better than to be returned as the son of man.

Christ's willed isolation is often paralleled in classical mythology. Whereas the Hebrew substitute for the personal eternity of Eden was an insulating earthly dynasty, the Greek and Roman replacement for immortality was a protective earth. The classical legends emphasize a benign nature rather than what the Hebrews might call a benevolent family. Further, while the Hebrews stress the importance of male continuity, the Greeks emphasize the female principle.

The Hebrew child was welcomed by his parents as a sign of their longevity and good name. The Greek hero (god or goddess) was, contrastingly, often shunned or abandoned by his elders because he posed a threat to continuity or an embarrassment to an established reputation. The Homeric hymn "To Aphrodite," while presumably dedicated to the power of the goddess of love, sings of her vulnerability to the passion that "subdues the tribes of mortal men and birds that fly in air and all the many creatures that the dry land rears, and all that the sea."[1] The Aphrodite of the hymn is caught by the trap she so often set for others. At the moment of Aeneas's conception, even before he is born, Aphrodite plans to abandon him because he represents "great shame among the deathless gods" (p. 423) to her. Simply by "being," Aeneas proves that his mother is no better than the other gods whom she subjected to the trap of human sexuality. He is a reminder that she, too, is part of the cycle of endless desire and madness from which she originally deemed herself, by virtue of her asexual beginning and inspirational function, apart. Her sex with Anchises is an aberration, a source of great misery. Aeneas will always be a sign of her weakness. As her son, he will be "a scion to delight the eyes" (p. 425). But his father is warned never to acknowledge his child; he is to claim that the boy is the offspring of one of the "flower-like Nymphs who inhabit this forest-clad hill" (p. 425). Through Aphrodite's intervention, the natural world becomes hospitable. The mountain nymphs will rear the boy. Ranking neither with mortals nor immortals they bear the gift of nature that appears to be a maternal protection. As parent Aphrodite abandons her child, but as god she warrants that the earth will become gentle and the mountains a second womb.

While Aeneas suggests the sullied reputation of his mother, Aphrodite herself emerges from an even darker antecedent. Her life embodies her father's death. Hesiod describes the patricide and its motives in *The Theogeny*. When Heaven cast out the sons whom he "hated from the first," Earth plots his destruction. Cronos kills his father at her instigation, literally causing a coitus interruptus:

> And Heaven came, bringing on night and longing for love, and he lay about Earth spreading himself full upon her. Then the son from his ambush stretched forth his left hand and in his right took the great long sickle with jagged teeth, and lopped off his own father's members and cast them away to fall behind him.[2]

Dismembering his father, Cronos fosters a child who in turn becomes the source of a generative cycle from which she is by birth exempt. While the mountains become a substitute parent for Aeneas, the sea functions here as Aphrodite's mother; nature preserves a self-destructive race of gods whose history depicts a cycle of exposure and revenge. Unlike the Hebrew patriarchs who, acknowledging their mortality, found in their children a chance to perpetuate their name and faith, the Greek gods, already guaranteed immortality, saw the younger generation as a threat to their influence and strength. In *The Theogeny*, the struggle for power is internal, children usurping their fathers. As an infant, the heavenly child is helpless but, as divine, he carries within him a potential that threatens the parent who should be nurturing him. The sexual needs of the father are therefore divorced from his procreative function. Cronos's swallowing of his offspring represents his effort both to retain the power released in the sexual act and to regain the strength that the children sap. Aphrodite, whose life signifies the death Cronos caused, embodies the reproductive process that Cronos subsequently tries to quell. While Aphrodite instigates the inevitable cycle of sexual generation, her literal generator

(Cronos) conversely attempts to halt the endless renewal that his children epitomize. Infanticide out of fear of supersession is an aspect of the foundling theme central to the Greek myths.

Nature perpetuates a cycle that Cronos seeks to avoid. The replacement ritual of the seasons—the usurpation of the old by the new—threatens his desire to reign forever. As the "bringer of seasons,"[3] Demeter represents the loss and return Cronos attempted to transcend. She is his opposite—a nurturer, not an eater—of her offspring. Her story has two sides: the first is that of the mother who seeks the stolen child; the second, that of the child who is returned from the lower depths by the intercession of the mother. Primarily, the myth stresses the uniqueness of the lost object. Demeter's function as a seasonal goddess depends on constant replacement and substitution—but her feelings as a wronged parent demand only the single reparation of her stolen child. Throughout the Homeric hymn Demeter's mood seems doubly wrathful; she feels what she imagines her daughter felt—the pain of violation. Some versions even suggest that she herself was literally raped.[4] She appears variously "distressed in her dear heart" (p. 301), as filled "with grief . . . terrible and savage" (p. 295) and as "wrath in her heart" (p. 313). Although Persephone is ultimately returned, the myth suggests that the recovery cannot dispel the vision of darkness experienced with the loss. The Eleusinian rituals are, according to the Homeric poet, "awful mysteries which no one may in any way transgress or pry into or utter, for deep awe of the gods checks the voice" (p. 323). In speculating what the miracle of the ceremony is, C. Kerenyi argues that it is an experiential one involving not merely a knowledge of death but a being in it:

> It is one thing to know about the seed and the sprout and quite another to have recognized in them the past and the future as one's own being and its continuation. Or, as Professor Jung puts it: to experience the return, the *apocatastasis*, of one's ancestors in such a way that these can prolong themselves via the bridge of the momentary individual into the generations of the future. A knowledge with the content, with the experience of being in death, is not to be despised.[5]

The link between the generations extends beyond this life, both before and after the present incarnation. The initiated carry with them the inescapable burden of an always-to-be-repeated loss. The wrath, experienced through her participation in the rape, returns annually to Demeter.

While it shatters the mother, the experience of the rape is different for Persephone. She finds in the demonic world an identity that suggests why the return Demeter covets is not so vital to her. Her independence is evident in the Homeric hymn by her failure to revise history as she recounts the rape to her mother:

> All we were playing in a lovely meadow, Leucippe and Phaeno and Electra and Ianthe, . . . we were playing and gathering sweet flowers in our hands, soft crocuses, mingled with irises and hyacinths and rose-blooms and lilies, marvellous to see, and the narcissus which the wide earth caused to grow yellow as a crocus. That I plucked in my joy. (P. 319)

Her description of the moments before the rape parallels that of the Homeric poet in the opening lines of the hymn:

> Apart from Demeter, lady of the golden sword and glorious fruits, she was playing with the deep-bosomed daughters of Oceanus and gathering flowers over a soft meadow, roses and crocuses and beautiful violets, irises also and hyacinths and the narcissus, which Earth made to grow at the will of Zeus and to please the Host of Many, to be a snare for the bloom-like girl—a marvellous, radiant flower. It was a thing of awe whether for deathless gods or mortal men to see: from its root grew a hundred blooms and it smelled most sweetly, so that all wide heaven above and the whole earth and the sea's salt swell laughed for joy. (P. 289)

For both poet and girl, the sense of original pleasure is not lessened by the subsequent happenings. Hades does not extend its darkness to the upper world nor does it taint Persephone's description with a premonition of what her mother sees as an always-to-be-expected gloom. The Prince of the Underworld can neither erase the beauty of the flowers nor destroy Persephone's pleasure in them. For Demeter, the blooming flowers will always contain the seeds of evil, destroying innocence because they robbed her of her daughter. The reconciliation of foundling stories usually portends not only marriage for the younger generation but a restoration of the child to the parent, a return as well as a thrusting forward in sexual union. The dynasty is preserved when the marriage is blessed; the rape in the myth preempts the blessing. Demeter has lost her parental control. Persephone now gets her psychic and physical sustenance from another source, and that source, symbolized by the pomegranate, establishes her identity as separate from her mother. Her initial fall—and subsequent return to the Underworld—is self-willed. The Persephone myth indicates the limitations of motherhood, the sense in which the parental role must inevitably end. If the cycle of life is to continue, the parent must come to recognize the short time span of her usefulness.

The Ovidian story of Phaëthon suggests another dark reunion, this time one that the parent tries to avoid. Here the child seeks the father in order to experience the truth of his noble descent. The ordeal Phaëthon undergoes is an expression of his desire not only to return to his source but to recover the male principle: the origin of power and light. Mere parental concern does not suffice as proof of birth. In the Ovidian version, the sun god's pleas for Phaëthon's life fall upon deaf ears:

> Because thou woulde be knowne to bee my childe thou seemst to
> crave
> A certaine signe: what surer signe I pray thee canst thou have
> Than this my feare so fatherly the which I have of thee
> Which proveth me most certainly thy father for to bee?
> Beholde and marke my countenaunce. O would to God thy sight
> Could pierce within my wofull brest, to see the heavie plight,
> And heapes of cares within my heart.[6]

For Phaëthon, the proof of his divine origins lies in his ability to do what his father does—drive the sun's chariot for a day. With his failure, the earth becomes scorched. In the Demeter-Persephone myth the land is barren because of the separation between parent and child. Here, the connection brings destruction with it. The child, sent falling, like Icarus, to the earth, is lost far from his native land, in a distant part of the world after having, if only briefly, experienced his origins.

If Persephone and Phaëthon introduce a temporary death wish, other figures in Greek mythology appear also to follow the tragic, rather than the comic, pattern of the foundling theme. The search for the Golden Fleece begins with an Isaac-like infant sacrifice (the Golden Fleece was Hermes' substitution for the child who later had to flee) and ends, though the child is saved, in ultimate destruction. Medea herself escapes from her father only to kill her children. The legend of the royal house of Thebes culminates in Oedipus's patricide; that of Athens ends with Phaedra's "murder" of Hippolytus, that of Atreus with Orestes' revenge on Clytemestra.

Generally speaking, happy endings occur where the gods themselves are involved. The legends of Dionysus, Perseus, and Hercules conclude in triumph. Equipped with a greater than human strength, they are able to overcome all enemies, natural and supernatural. The ordinary kings manage only to destroy themselves or to "inherit" an unavoidable sin from which the only escape is a death they seem to relish, judging from the enormity of their acts. While the mythological gods are greater than men and can, therefore, almost literally twist the world for their ends, in the later Greek romances nature is mythologized so that it might cure mankind of its humanly derived sin. The romances capitalize on the newness of the abandoned children, commonly inaugurating their plots, by wresting them from corrupt cradles.

In this regard, Greek and Roman literature and myth portray the Good Earth in contrast to what the Hebrews might have called the Good Family. Romulus and Remus, in the Roman parallel story to Exodus, are nursed by beasts. The myth suggests "the superiority of animals to men"[7] and nature's instinctive maternity. In escaping civilization, the lost child finds at once his true origin (nature as generator)[8] and his ultimate destiny (nature as what Aristotle calls "the good towards which one tends").[9] Central to the theme's formula in classical literature is, in Ernst Robert Curtius's phrase, the *locus amoenus* or "pleasance"[10] through which the child recaptures a golden innocence relinquished by the corrupt society abandoning him.

Through his exposure, the lost child uncovers a superior realm. When he is returned to his parents, he brings with him the light of the golden world that has been his solace. The reconciliation of foundling stories ensures that the redeemed child will purify civilization with the healing balm of his primitive experience. In *Daphnis and Chloe* nature is so sweetened that even its dismal aspects are bathed in a golden light:

> When I was hunting in Lesbos, I saw, in a wood sacred to the Nymphs, the most beautiful thing that I have ever seen—a painting that told a love story. The wood itself was beautiful enough, full of trees and flowers, and watered by a single spring which nourished both the flowers and the trees . . . there were women having babies and other women wrapping them in swaddling clothes, babies being exposed, sheep and goats suckling them, shepherds picking them up, young people plighting their troth, pirates making a raid, enemies starting an invasion.
>
> After gazing admiringly at many other scenes, all of a romantic nature, I was seized by a longing to write a verbal equivalent to the painting.[11]

Longus describes both the painting and its setting as "the most beautiful thing that I have ever seen." But the picture itself, at least as much as he relates here, describes human desperation, not joy: babies being born, exposed, pirates making a raid, enemies starting an invasion. What renders it beautiful is precisely the idealized nature Longus cites, the guarantee that all will turn out well. Nature appears soft and the romance assured of a happy ending. The exposure emerges as necessary for the ritual, as do the pirate raids and enemy invasions—all components of the

obligatory (but temporary) pain leading to an expected release. Transforming the painting to a "verbal equivalent," Longus absorbs its art into
the artifice of his stylized plot.

The lost-child romances have in common a benign nature and heroes
who are so chaste that they manage within the course of their own love to
make up for the excesses of their parents. In *An Aethiopian History*,
Theagenes and Cariclia pass through fire unscathed because of their pu-
rity. The royal heroes are abandoned carelessly, but the fact that they care
so much for each other allows them, once found, to give their parents the
continuity they so much crave. Sexuality is saved for a future in which the
young pair will eventually found and serve a renewed kingdom.

The happiness of the central family spreads throughout the realm. At
the end of *An Aethiopian History*, when it is discovered that Cariclia and
Theagenes are indeed royal, Heliodorus describes the effect of the
stratagem he has provided:

> The people in another place rejoyced, and almost daunced for joy, and
> with one consent were all gladde of that which was donne, marry all
> they understoode not, but gathered the most part of Cariclia. Per-
> happes also they were styrred to understand the trueth by inspiration
> of the Gods, whose will it was that this should fall out woonderfully, as
> in a Comedie. Surely they made very contraye things agree, and joyned
> sorrow with mirth, teares and laughter together, and turned fearefull,
> and terrible things into a joyfull banquette, in the end, many that weapt
> beganne to laugh, and such as were sorrowfull to rejoyce, when they
> founde that they sought not for, and lost that they hoped to finde, and
> to be shorte, the cruell slaughters which were looked for every
> momente, were turned into holy sacrifice. [12]

In these romances, things turn out "woonderfully" despite all the previous weeping; here the necessary sorrow appears in a ceremonial light, the
brutality of slaughter redeemed by the holiness of sacrifice.

The found child in all the stories signifies that "terrible things" can be
transformed into "joyfull banquettes." Behind all the variations in the
plot is the desire for a happy ending. The Christian faith in an afterlife
glosses the myth so that Christ and his followers might discover their
Heavenly Father. The Hebrew idea rests on the haven of dynasty, the
Greek romances on the hermitage of nature. The legends connected to
such gods as Aphrodite and Cronos explore the possibility that continuity might be worse than death and that the endless cycle of nature is
itself monstrous. This demonic underside is apparent as well in the initial
cruelty of abandonment. The foundling theme toys with death, but refuses ultimately to give into it, providing always a recovery for loss.

Emphasizing the importance of an individual life, the stories insist that the particular child is irreplaceable; no substitute will console the desolated losers. The legends of Persephone, Isaac, and Moses assert that the existing person—as he is, as he always was—matters. Such an affirmation withstands the devastation of an indifferent world and the wrath of an avenging god, heightening the regenerative possibility of individuating touch and the restorative potential of identifying speech. The right word of the returned child is his own.

The foundling myths upon which Renaissance writers drew either for characters (as in Spenser's appropriation of Venus who literally appears in his work) or metaphors (as in Shakespeare's allusions to Demeter in *Pericles* and *The Winter's Tale*) variously present the good of nature and the good of art. Glorifying the adoptive realm, Malory's *Le Morte d'Arthur* resembles in its happy moments the golden interlude of the Greek romances. In its dark episodes (the desertion of Mordred) it echoes those Old Testament passages (Genesis 22, Exodus 2) where a child was exposed for a greater good. In its ambiguous recognition, it parallels the myth of Phaëthon where the world falls apart as a son demands the divine right of his origin.

4

Finding and Losing "Beaulté and Noblesse": Adoption in Malory's *Works*

Many of Malory's stories—those of Arthur, Launcelot, Gareth, Tor, Tristram, Galahad, and Mordred—involve foundlings whose recovery is predicted at their birth or, in the case of Arthur, even prior to their conception. But, though the heroes of *Le Morte d'Arthur* generally find their parents, the period of loss is more gratifying than the time of reconciliation. The exalted artistic principles, crucial to the adoptive sections of foundling plots, preempt (in the joy they provide) the restored hereditary lines generally defining happy endings in such stories. This change in emphasis occurs because the Arthurian code suggests that the individual dynasty is less important than the preserved kingdom; the sustaining fellowship of the court replaces the protective enclave of the family. Merlin's adoption of Arthur promulgates a belief that this is the best of all possible worlds. Conversely, because it reenacts the Christ story, the Grail quest teaches the knights that, as Arthur laments at the end, there is on earth "no truste for to truste in."[1] After the quest the kingdom loses its cohesion and the Round Table falls apart.[2] Galahad's departure for a better realm, his rejection of Launcelot in favor of his Heavenly Father, counters the adoptive principle, implying that real happiness lies only in a divine end.

The values of adoption are advanced by Merlin, who raises and protects Arthur. In terms of the foundling formula, *Le Morte d'Arthur* explores, perhaps more than any other work, the possibilities of fostering—the ways in which the artificially created enclave can substitute for the natural one. This grand design is orchestrated by Merlin who sees its possibilities and attempts to manipulate them fully. He also knows its limitations and struggles to work around them. Merlin establishes Arthur's security in the first book when he substantiates Arthur's credibility

40

despite what he (even then) knows to be the end precipitated by the Grail quest. He is both virtuoso manipulating through magic a plan of his own invention and prophet predicting through intuition the dictates of divine creation. He attempts to promulgate and perpetuate the good of art even though he recognizes that ultimately all must submit to the demands of nature.

Already in the first book, he plays a dual role. As magician, he attempts to outwit destiny, or at least bend it for a while. In the guise of strategist, Merlin adopts Arthur and fosters his career. He engineers Arthur's ascendance to power and helps him establish control over the knights who challenge him. The opening of "The Book of Arthur" recounts Merlin's role in the king's upbringing and in the early stages of his reign. At each juncture Merlin reveals himself to court and king, letting them know their successes are the result of his capacity to tilt events in Arthur's favor. But as the book progresses, and even as Arthur rises to power, Merlin, recognizing the limits of his own maneuvers, predicts the king's future demise. In his second role, as prophet, Merlin acknowledges a power greater than his own; above and beyond his own design he sees an unrelenting destiny that rules that the natural line of familial moral virtue outweighs the created circle of his expansionist designs. "The Book of Arthur" records the conflict between Merlin the magician and Merlin the prophet.[3] That conflict (between the desire to change and the need to accept the existent situation) reflects the art/nature controversy. In the last episode of the first section, Merlin contradicts his own fateful vision by attempting to kill Mordred, much as Pharaoh interfered with divine will by commanding the child murder in Exodus. But if Merlin fools himself, he manages even more successfully to beguile the court into believing that it can, by its own powers, create an order that will outwit destiny. In the middle books, the knights feel assured of the invincible society they create, partially because Merlin the magician disobeys the warnings of Merlin the prophet.

Le Morte d'Arthur describes the adoptive security that arises out of Merlin's making Arthur's aspirations his own and, subsequently, out of Arthur's appropriating his knight's burdens as he incorporates them in the fellowship of the yearly Pentecostal pledge. The opening books—in the stories of Arthur's rise to power, Pellinor's marred quest, Nyneve's rescue of Pelleas, and Gareth's association with Launcelot—emphasize an element essential to the adoptive stage of foundling plots: the idea of interchangeable parts. By taking on one another's causes, the knights demonstrate that what matters is not the safety of the individual but the survival of the mainstream. In the concluding books, the ascendancy of familial values suggests that the whole cannot substitute for the parts. The knights abandoned at the outset (Galahad and Mordred) seek the recognition denied them in the central section of their foundling plots.

As the purveyor of the good of art, particularly of his own art, Merlin the magician seems completely in control. The plot he designs is logically unnecessary—the disguise of Uther, the casting out of Arthur—complications of a storyteller who enjoys the design he weaves. When Igraine refuses Uther's advances, Merlin is called to aid the ailing king achieve his desire for the queen. The magician agrees to help, striking a hard bargain on his own behalf:

"Syr," said Merlyn, "I knowe al your hert every dele. So ye wil be sworn unto me, as ye be a true kynge enoynted, to fulfille my desyre, ye shal have your desyre." (P. 8)

Taking advantage of Uther's extreme state, Merlin forces him into a corner, fulfilling his creative enterprise by satisfying the king's sexual longing. Replacing the king, Merlin becomes the substitute parent—an intervening godfather who assumes responsibility for Arthur's destiny in the foundling plot he structures. It is Merlin who devises the strategy for the sword pulling and who recruits Ban and Bors to help establish Arthur's supremacy in battle. Thus, through the mysticism of the sword ritual and the militarism of the knightly conquest, Merlin ensures that there are no challengers to Arthur's throne.

As the first section closes, the prophet sounds the note of doom, presenting himself in various disguises and unveiling gradually to Arthur the truth the magician sought to evade. The sequence of events is puzzling. After Arthur begets Mordred in precisely the same manner as he was begotten—Uther "desyred to have lyen by" (p. 7) the wife of the duke of Cornwall; Arthur "desired to ly by" (p. 41) Lott's wife—he has a dream about the destruction of his kingdom by monsters and serpents. The dream troubles him but he attempts to put it out of his thoughts by hunting, whereupon he meets the Questing Beast. Pellinor tells Arthur that the king is destined not to follow it. Twice troubled now (first by his dream, subsequently by his failure to be allowed the quest), Arthur meets Merlin who, disguised as a child and then as an old man, reminds him of his sin:

"Yes," seyde the olde man, "the chylde tolde you trouthe, and more he wolde a tolde you and [y]e wolde a suffirde hym, but ye have done a thynge late that God ys displesed with you, for ye have lyene by youre syster and on hir ye have gotyn a childe that shall destroy you and all the knyghtes of youre realme."

"What ar ye," seyde Arthure, "that telle me thys tydyngis?" "Sir, I am Merlion, and I was he in the chyldis lycknes."

"A," seyde the kynge, "ye ar a mervaylous man! But I mervayle muche of thy wordis that I mou dye in batayle." (P. 44)

Arthur is made aware of his future and his past simultaneously. The dream of serpents and griffins is actualized by the presence of a beast he is not even permitted to chase. Wrestling with the limitations imposed on his ability to act and with marvels beyond his scope, Arthur is apprised of the human condition. He sees a monster linked to the generative cycle. The connections between the fostering of the dream and the fathering of his child seem umbilical. But the related occurrences (Arthur's conception and Mordred's begetting; Arthur's dream and the Questing Beast; the child and the old man) underline the essential ambiguity of the dilemma the court faces and for a time overcomes. In Arthur's dream he slays the dragons; in Merlin's prophecy he is slain. In Arthur's birth the adultery is not questioned; in Mordred's, it becomes the reason for God's wrath. In the child's message, Arthur's beginnings are told; in the old man's his ends. With his conception, Arthur became the foundling nurtured by Merlin. With his manhood, Arthur creates still another foundling who emerges the monster portended in his dream. The hunter becomes the hunted; what worked once no longer seems viable. There appear to be conflicting messages even in the auguries.

Because of these conflicts, Merlin the magician refuses to take seriously the lesson Merlin the prophet has just given. The acknowledgment of Arthur by Igraine, following so quickly thereafter, diminishes the impact of the king's dream. To counter Ulphius's accusations that, because she remained quiet about Arthur's origins, she is "the falsyst lady of the worlde and the most traytoures unto the kynges person" (p. 45), Igraine claims that she did all at Merlin's command. Ulphius then turns to Merlin, blaming the magician for the kingdom's storms. It is Merlin's confession that reconciles Arthur to his mother, prompting the customary avowal, verification, kissing, and crying of all such moments in the foundling convention. With the false modesty of his "forsothe, sir, yee" (p. 46), Merlin acknowledges not only that he was the instigator of the original trouble but also that he is the perpetrator of the present joy. Without his creating the conditions for loss, there never would have been the happiness of the recovery ritualistically enacted.

The feast engendered by Merlin's admission of responsibility subsumes, almost negates, the gloom fostered by his prediction of disaster. Merlin confirms here that he made it possible for Arthur to avoid the face of the serpent unleashed in his nightmare. Once having seen the parameters of its existence, the court lives as if it had not learned them, partly because, immediately following the moment of revealed doom, it finds an instance of disclosed salvation. Arthur learns of his abandonment and rescue simultaneously. Despite what he apprehends about his past vulnerability, Arthur believes in his present invincibility because, at each critical juncture, he was protected. If, now, Arthur discovers how close he (as helpless child) came to death and how often he (as growing youth) was shielded from it, why should he cease to believe in the probabilities of manipulation that might still be left (as reigning king) to prolong his realm? What Arthur assimilates about his distant origins, together with what he knows about his immediate past, fortifies him against what he hears about his imminent and ultimate future. Just as Merlin helped Arthur win the battles to establish his throne so, antecedently, did Merlin prepare Arthur to achieve that throne, guaranteeing, in the recognition scene, that his design for the tale was appreciated. The triumphant tone of the magician's "forsothe, sir, yee" suggests more than a confession of guilt. It demonstrates a pleasure in creation that defies the admonition to be "heavy." Thus Merlin ignores his own prophecy, rejoicing as artist in the recognition he engineered.

In the final episode of the first section, Merlin acts against his own advice, attempting to manipulate Arthur's future in much the same way as he had arranged his birth:

> Merlyon tolde kynge Arthure that he that sholde destroy hym and all the londe sholde be borne on May-day. Wherefore he sente for hem all in payne of dethe, and so there were founde many lordis sonnys and many knyghtes sonnes, and all were sente unto the kynge. And so was Mordred sente by kynge Lottis wyff. And all were putte in a shyppe to the se; and som were four wekis olde and som lesse. And so by fortune the shyppe drove unto a castelle, and was all to-ryven and destroyed the moste party, save that Mordred was cast up, and a good man founde hym, and fostird hym tylle he was fourtene yere of age, and than brought hym to the courte, as hit rehersith aftirward and towarde the end of the Morte Arthure.
>
> So, many lordys and barownes of thys realme were displeased for his children were so loste; and many putte the wyght on Merlion more than o[n] Arthure. So what for drede and for love, they held their pece.
> (Pp. 55–56)

Using the prophet's knowledge, the magician seeks the means to avoid its truth. Like his father, Mordred is cast out at Merlin's command, in an attempt to recapitulate the initiating events and so ward off the predicted disaster. But the narrator relates that "fortune" intervenes, referring not only to the end previously written in the *Mort Artu* but to the destiny already forecast by the magician himself. As Ulphius blamed Merlin for Arthur's abandonment, so the court here, too, puts the "wyght" on Merlin. Because they anticipate a future based on Merlin's successes in the past, the lords, who might otherwise have rebelled, succumb to their anxieties about Merlin's power. The parents who had to relinquish their children remained quiet just as Igraine did out of fear and love, a formula that allowed Merlin to fulfill his desires in Arthur; the present reenactment duplicates the process by which Arthur achieved his success. Only here the exposure is particularly cruel. Rather than acting as savior, Merlin behaves as executioner. Mordred is left to the elements which, for him at least, turn out (as they do in the legends of Romulus and Remus) to be gentle. Through the May-day expulsion, the ending of the first section indicates that, behind the facade of forgiveness upon which the Round Table is founded, lies a murderous impulse. Through the enactment of the child-exposure plot, it demonstrates that Merlin ignores his own advice by attempting to supplant fortune. Nevertheless, Merlin's plan lends confidence to Arthur. The stability based on established success, rather than on prophesied certainty, allows the court to function, despite the diminishing protection of the magician, as though it belonged permanently to the world it presently leaves behind. That security enables Arthur to premise his fellowship on a code already violated in Merlin's expulsion of Mordred.

On the quest following the feast celebrating Arthur's marriage, Sir Pellinor behaves less than honorably. When he returns to the court, Merlin warns him that his refusal to succor a lady will not go unnoticed:

> "Truly ye ought sore to repente hit," seyde Merlion, for that lady was youre owne doughtir, begotyn of the lady of the Rule, . . . And because ye wolde nat abyde and helpe hir, ye shall se youre beste frende fayle you whan ye be in the grettist distresse that ever ye were othir shall be. And that penaunce God hath ordayned for you that dede, that he that ye sholde truste moste on of ony man on lyve, he shall leve you there ye shall be slayne." (Pp. 119–20)

As Merlin describes it, the pattern of God's revenge is one of clear cause and effect: "because ye wolde nat abyde and helpe hir, ye shall se youre beste frende fayle you whan ye be in the grettist distresse that ever ye were othir shall be." It duplicates the structure of God's punishment for Arthur's lust in the begetting of Mordred "for hit ys Goddis wylle that youre body sholde be punysshed for your fowle dedis" (p. 44). But in the

same way that Merlin (on behalf of Arthur) believed that he could avoid
fate by altering Mordred's circumstances, so Pellinor (living in this cli-
mate of bolstered confidence) believes that the death awaiting him might
be averted:

> "Me forthynkith hit," seyde kynge Pellynor, "that thus shall me be-
> tyde, but God may well fordo desteny." (P. 120)

Showing with the "forthynkith" a compunction for his sin, Pellinor implies that, by repenting, he can eliminate the cause of God's anger. In
turn, he hopes that God might "fordo" his punishment by intercepting a
destiny predicted to be unalterable. Pellinor's assurance frees him to function within the confines of fate and allows him to believe that he might, as
Arthur seems to have done, enjoy his own immutability.

As if to confirm that belief, Arthur announces the code under which
the Round Table will function:

> Thus whan the queste was done . . . than the kynge stablysshed all the
> knyghtes and gaff them rychesse and londys; and charged them never
> to do outerage nothir morthir, and allwayes to fle treson, and to gyff
> mercy unto hym that askith mercy, uppon payne of forfiture [of their]
> worship and lordship of kynge Arthure for evirmore; and allwayes to
> do ladyes, damesels and jantilwomen and wydoes [socour:] strengthe
> hem in hir ryghtes, and never to enforce them, uppon payne of dethe.
> Also, that no man take no batayles in a wrongfull quarrell for no love
> ne for no worldis goodis. So unto thys were all knyghtis sworne of the
> Table Rounde, both olde and younge, and every yere so were the[y]
> sworne at the hyghe feste of Pentecoste. (P. 120)

At the end of the first section Arthur (through Merlin) attempted to start
off with a clean slate, protecting his dominion by eliminating Mordred,
who stood as a sign of his sin. At the end of the feast celebrating the
Pentecost, Arthur (through his own decree) once more begins afresh,
accepting the slightly stained knights into the fold and compelling them
to obey rules they had not followed in the course of their quests.
Eradicating in the future any signs of previous failure, the knights hope to
destroy the destiny resulting from their tarnished past. The prefix *for-* in
Pellinor's "forthynketh" and "fordo," as well as in Arthur's "forfeiture,"
suggests a simultaneous annulment and anticipation. Repenting for the
past, Pellinor and Arthur seek to preempt destiny. Similarly, by promising mercy in the future, the knights attempt to overcome their failure to
give it in the past. Arthur sets himself up as the kind of god he would like
to see operating on his own behalf. The knights will lose (forfeit) the

esteem they hold as part of the fellowship if, from now on, they do not forgive others. They are expected to offer mercy (pardon for the past) so that they will themselves be forgiven (saved in the future) and included in the protected ring of the court. The anticipated reformation brings the court back to a secure world and forward into a safe one. Antecedent pardon ensures subsequent protection.[4] The axis of security, essential to the adoptive interlude, moves from Merlin to Arthur to the knights of the court as they gather to be sworn—to affirm their faith (and to have it confirmed)—in the probability of their own duration. Through the art of the pledge, the knights lend each other a refuge that would only be given by a loving and forgiving natural parent. The fellowship prolongs childhood innocence by encouraging the belief that merely being sorry and promising to be good guarantees safety "for evirmore." With the "for evirmore," Arthur renders the moment of the pledge and the solidity of the fellowship perennial.[5] The repetition each year convinces the knights that they might continue to function in a world made safe through the auspices of Merlin's grace. In the middle books the belief in the protective custody of adoption, originally held by Merlin, and affirmed by Arthur in the pledge, is passed on to the knights in the story of Pelleas and Nyneve, which proposes that the course of love can easily be deflected, and then in the legend of Gareth, which demonstrates for a while that the path of heredity might be averted.

Because the knights feel confident that they can work around the destiny that decrees their end, they return annually to the table convinced that their world will not effectively change and that they can, by their own actions, protect one another. That stability exists because, even when Merlin is gone, there are other (still lesser) gods ready to help. One of these protectors, appearing in a digression, is Nyneve who saves Pelleas from the hopeless love of Dame Ettard. Betrayed by Gawain, Pelleas finds Arthur's knight in a pavilion with his lady, tries twice to kill them both but suspends his murdereous impulses because Gawain belongs to the high order of knighthood. Pelleas vows instead to take to his bed and never rise again, bidding his knights bear his body to Ettard to tell her that he saw her with Gawain. Miraculously, he is saved by a goddess who promises that she shall "warraunte"—save by guaranteeing—his life. By making the disdainful Ettard feel what Pelleas felt, she turns a victimizer into a victim. Interposing on Pelleas's behalf, she frees him to go on living. When she promises him a cure for his madness—love for love—he in turn falls prostrate and thanks God for this grace. She counters: "Thanke me therefore" (p. 172). The Damosell of the Lake demands Pelleas's gratitude. Though she might command it as goddess, she gets it as a woman who (like any other seductress) has won her man from the clutches of a rival. Pelleas should be obliged to her, for she is, after all, magical; her victory is wrought through her own powers. Her "thanke me," like Merlin's bow at Arthur's recognition scene, is spoken in the tone of a comic epilogue where the hero comes forth in triumph to garner applause for the happy ending he has secured. Pelleas does not have, as he believes, God's blessing. Instead he has been granted earthly mercy, a giving and a taking of love. In winning for herself the most "lykely knight," Nyneve allows the fellowship to go on believing in grace, "sente" not to some remote Jerusalem but here, now, to this earth. Nyneve rescues Pelleas by substituting herself for Ettard. She loves him, as Merlin had adopted Arthur, and therewith "warraunts" his life.[6]

Such guarantees allow the fellowship a carefree existence in a world favored by the proven concerns of the gods for it and the reliable sanctions of the knights on behalf of one another. Gareth and Sir Brunoir le Noir can hide their origins and toy with the prospect of proving their worth because time does not stymie them. Their world expands from a fixed center (the annual feast of the Pentecost) to which they can always return. The court now trusts such "fair unknowns"[7] because they have been preceded by other strangers who proved noble. Sir Lamerok expresses about La Cote Male Tayle what could as well be said of Beaumains:

> "Sir," seyde sir Lamerok and sir Gaheris, "hit were well done to make hym knyght, for hym besemyth well of persone and of countenaunce that he shall preve a good knyght and a myghty. For, sir, and ye be remembird, evyn suche one was sir Launcelot whan he cam fyrst into this courte, and full fewe of us knew from whens he cam. And now is he preved the man of moste worshyp in the worlde, and all your courte and Rounde Table is by sir Launcelot worshypped and amended, more than by ony knyght lyvynge." (Pp. 459–60)

Because Launcelot emerged from obscurity well worshiped, the other knights are emboldened to expand their circle. Their sense of security stems from the fact that men of good birth have established their worth (as did Arthur when he came a stranger to the court and defended it so well) chronologically prior to their having been recognized as rightful inheritors of an aristocratic name.

Gareth becomes an analogical foundling because he chooses to be one. Without altering the fundamental nature of his being, he wears disguise after disguise and transforms himself with the ring given him by Dame Lyonesse. The court trifles with metamorphosis, feeling none of its Ovidian complications, because it unveils each time only another layer of what remains certain.[8] That stability is maintained because the knights convening at the Round Table are so determined to stand by one another. As Nyneve guarantees for Pelleas so Launcelot endorses ("warrauntes," p. 299) Gareth's value and thereby enables him to become what he is destined to be: a knight of great worth. When Gareth is finally recognized at the end, Launcelot also takes pleasure in the victory; he reacts as if the knight he adopted[9] were his own son:

> Lorde, the grete chere that sir Launcelot made of sir Gareth and he of hym! For there was no knyght that sir Gareth loved so well as he dud sir Launcelot; and ever for the moste party he wolde ever be in sir Launcelottis company. (P. 360)

Launcelot's unrestrained joy is that of a man whose instinctive generosity has been tested and proven correct. Gareth's accomplished nobility confirms and returns Launcelot's faith in him. In vowing to stay "for ever" in the company of Launcelot, Gareth extends the confidence of their first union.

But the adoptive principle upon which the kingdom establishes its trust is challenged on the quest for the Grail. The pivotal lost child in this case is Galahad who, in finding his Heavenly Father, initiates a process of legitimization that Mordred will ultimately complete in his revenge. At the beginning of the quest, Launcelot has a vision explained to him in terms of a genealogy emerging as his own. The family line begins with Joseph of Arimathea and ends with Galahad, the son of Launcelot begat on King Pelles' daughter. Learning that Galahad, "the good knight," is his heir, Launcelot uses the same reasoning as Pellinor and Arthur before him to argue that Galahad should intercede on his behalf before the High Father:

> "Well," seyde sir Launcelot, "meseymyth that good knyght shold pray for me unto the Hyghe Fadir, that I falle nat to synne agayne." (P. 930)

The hermit warns Launcelot that his belief is futile, rendering the trust, which in the earlier books represented a proven virtue, as the false hope of superstition:

> "Truste thou well," seyde the good man, "thou fayrest much the better for hys prayer, for the sonne shall not beare the wyckednesse of the fader, nor the fader shall nat beare the wyckednesse of the sonne, but every man shall beare hys owne burden. And therefore beseke thou only God, and he woll help the in all thy nedes." (P. 931)

Launcelot hears a message reiterated throughout the Grail section: "Every man shall beare hys owne burden." Because they ruptured the bonds of kinship, the knights have lost the possibility for genealogical advocacy.

The story of the Round Table's original formation is repeated as the knights begin the quest. But the revisionist interpretation of the Queen of the Waste Lands, for example, stresses that the fellowship was formed at the expense of the parents whose sons joined it:

> And ye have sene that they have loste hir fadirs and hir modirs and all hir kynne, and hir wyves, and hir chyldren for to be of youre felyship. (P. 906)

Forsaking their homes, the knights sacrificed the familial for the communal. The narrator himself comments (though much less strongly so than in the French text)[10] that in "tho dayes the sonne spared nat the fadir no more than a straunger" (p. 913). At court, private loyalty was replaced by group responsibility. Merlin cared for Arthur, Arthur for his knights, Launcelot for Gareth.

The quest for the Grail emphasizes the ultimate isolation of the individual who surrendered his family for the Round Table. Here, there is no Merlin to espouse his cause, no Damosell of the Lake to wreak his vengeance. The imperative that "every man shall beare hys owne burden" frees the knights of an inherited fate. Whereas formerly Merlin attempted to disencumber Arthur of Mordred, and whereas earlier Arthur sought to protect Pellinor from his weakness, now each knight looks out for himself. Within the fellowship, release came from a conscious effort to bypass individual destiny by a protective nurturing. On the quest, personal salvation reigns supreme. If the son does not "beare," in the sense of inherit, the sins of the father, he need not "beare," in the sense of sustain, them in his parents' stead. What is lacking in this freedom is the mutuality of burden constituting the point of the Round Table. Like Arthur and Pellinor before him, Launcelot fails to see the limitations of earthly grace. He operates still on the assumption that his son will naturally, as Launcelot would for any other knight, intercede on his behalf.

The reunion between Launcelot and Galahad leads only to an inevitable separation. When Galahad is called away he senses that he shall never return:

> "Fayre swete fadir, I wote nat whan I shall se you more tyll I se the body of Jesu Cryste."
> "Now, for Goddis love," seyde sir Launcelot, "pray to the Fadir that He holde me stylle in Hys servyse."

> And so he toke hys horse, and there they hard a voyce that seyde,
> "Every of you thynke for to do welle, for nevermore shall one se
> another off you before the dredefull day of doome." (P. 1013)

In order to meet the High Father, Galahad must leave his "fayre swete
fadir." Having found him, the son abandons Launcelot, bringing to a
dark climax all the earthly recognition scenes in the *Works*. The voice
calling Galahad portends an irrevocable loss, not only the end of the
present but the end of the future: "the dredefull day of doome." Reunion
will be impossible because there will be no world. The separation between father and son suggests the enormous chasm between the earthly
and heavenly spheres, the spatial distance expressed as a temporal span.
Nevertheless, Galahad's last words before his ascent are to his father:
"My fayre lorde, salew me unto my lorde sir Launcelot, my fadir, and as
sone as ye se hym bydde him remembir of this worlde unstable"
(p. 1035).

Going to a permanent realm, Galahad accentuates the instability of this
one, warning Launcelot that nothing earthly remains. The quest for the
Grail breaks the circle of knightly dependence by affirming that the trust
at its base is hollow. Returning to his Heavenly Father, Galahad repairs a
broken chain of consanguinity with links to Joseph of Arimathea. And,
by reestablishing the supremacy of the inherited line, he sets a pattern
that will be followed in the concluding books when Mordred seeks recognition in the form of revenge.

Learning of Gareth's death, Arthur concludes that Gawain's familial
ties will outweigh his courtly concerns:

> "Well," seyde Arthure, "the dethe of them woll cause the grettist mor-
> tall warre that ever was, for I am sure that whan sir Gawayn knowyth
> hereoff that sir Gareth ys slayne, I shall never have reste of hym tyll I
> have destroyed sir Launcelottys kynne and hymselff bothe, othir ellis
> he to destroy me. And therefore," seyde the kynge, "wyte you well,
> my harte was never so hevy as hit ys now. And much more I am soryar
> for my good knyghtes losse than for the losse of my fayre quene; for
> quenys I myght have inow, but such a felyship of good knyghtes shall
> never be togydirs in no company. And now I dare sey," seyde kynge
> Arthur, "there was never Crystyn kynge that ever hylde such a fely-
> shyp togydrs. And alas, that ever sir Launcelot and I shulde be at
> debate! A Aggravayne, Aggravayne!" seyde the kynge, "Jesu forgyff
> hit thy soule, for thyne evyll wyll that thou haddist and sir Mordred,
> thy brother, unto sir Launcelot, hath caused all this sorow." (Pp. 1183–
> 84)

The now-ascendant familial unit insists that every link matters. Mourning
the future, Arthur thinks in terms of the collective past here obscured. By

nurturing one another, the knights saved themselves, creating an artificial family rather than raising their own children. When it fails in the Grail, the court discovers that the order of blood relations reigns supreme. Galahad returns to his Father in heaven, restoring his natural lineage. Gawain must avenge the death of his brother. In the same way Mordred demands the inheritance severed by Arthur's rejection of him. The asp that starts the battle is the serpent of Arthur's early dream, the generational monster rising up to express a dynastic right.

That resurgence recalls the path of doom that the knights had, in their circle of mutual support, ignored. Merlin's prediction of disaster is fulfilled. Launcelot recognizes the nature of the loss:

> "Truly," sayd syr Launcelot, "I trust I do not dysplese God, for He knoweth myn entente: for my sorrow was not, nor is not, for ony rejoysyng of synne, but my sorow may never have ende. For whan I remembre of hir beaulté and of hir noblesse, that was bothe wyth hyr kyng and wyth hyr, so whan I saw his corps and hir corps so lye togyders, truly myn herte wold not serve to susteyne my careful body." (P. 1256)

Launcelot weeps for a future without hope, recalling thereby a time when this world was a happy place. The concept of grace, passed from Merlin through Arthur to the knights, presupposed that "beaulte and noblesse," traditionally thought of as qualities inherited through familial legacy, were properties shared in courtly fellowship. The "with" in Launcelot's lamentation suggests that gentility transpired simultaneously to Arthur and Guinevere's temporal and spatial presence. To be "with" the king and queen was to be living when and where it might be possible, by proximity, to imbibe heroic lineaments. Launcelot evokes both the "supporting power" of magic and the preserving strength of friendship signified by Merlin's espousal of Arthur, Arthur of his knights, and his knights of one another. But on the quest for the Grail, the knights learn that the trust they placed in the system of extended earthly adoption can no longer be countenanced. Now tragically isolated, Launcelot grieves for a time—that lost adoptive sequence—when "beaulté and noblesse" were embodied in a fellowship subsuming familial loyalty. The kingdom planned by Merlin and presided over by Arthur created a larger family, one where the good of art actualized the potential good in man. When nature surfaces at the end—in Mordred's dynastic, the knights' vengeful, and the commoners' mercenary feelings—it leaves the created good of the adoptive interlude as a memory that stimulates in Launcelot a "sorrow [that] may never have ende." When Malory concludes about the controversy over whether Arthur shall come again that "here in thys world he chaunged hys lyff" (p. 1242), he speaks of change as inexorable. Since Arthur's reign was based on *inter*change (the replacement of family dynasty by courtly enclave), this last change is a retraction—like the taking back of Excalibur—that signals no return. The substitution so exalted in Malory's version of the foundling plot will no longer support the kingdom.

5

Transformation in Sidney's *Old Arcadia*

In *Le Morte d'Arthur*, the good of the adoptive interlude does not extend itself into the recognition. In *The Old Arcadia*, it does. Despite the fact that they seem to work against the order of nature, the transformations wrought by the art of the pastoral sequence facilitate the happy endings. *The Old Arcadia* is about transformation—about the ways in which the artificial abets the natural. The work contains two sets of counterpointed foundlings—one in the main story, the other in the eclogues: first, Pyrocles and Musidorus are reflected in Strephon and Klaius;[1] then the poet is paralleled by Philisides.[2] The heroes and the poet are linked because they seek related fulfillments—they of love, he of their plot. Though the poet is not a character in the work, his presence is felt at the opening when he intrudes often to remind his audience (the "dear ladies" he keeps addressing) that the narrative is fiction. It is felt even more strongly (though less intrusively) when, in certain key passages at the end (pp. 265, 385) and in the preface (p. 3), he allies himself to the heroes. By then he esteems his work, as they have viewed their love all along, worthy of earnest pursuit.

In their efforts to achieve that love, the heroes imitate the styles of the women they love. Thus they break from their princely pasts by playing a woman and a shepherd, respectively. They transform themselves to become like what they love. And they succeed by taking the best aspects of their transformations and using them as the source of their revitalizations. The poet succeeds when he stops thinking of his characters as amusing sillies meant for the entertainment of the "dear ladies"[3] of his audience, when he acknowledges, in book 4, that he is involved with them in what he calls "the wormish condition" of mankind. His climax as a writer coincides with the heroes' fulfillment as lovers. The heroes change when they recognize the value of the life they want; the poet changes when he recognizes the heroes' values—when he begins to take their lives seriously. As they imitate the women they love, he imitates the heroes he admires, acknowledging his kinship to them.[4]

But Strephon and Klaius change more devastatingly. Not only do they, like the heroes, deny their past; they destroy it utterly. Philisides—the poet's alter ego—follows another extreme; he gives up trying and so annihilates the future. Strephon, Klaius, and Philisides are examples of the wrong kinds of transformation; their changes are impossible to reverse. The shepherds cannot return; Philisides cannot progress. The heroes and the poet strike a balance between the self-destruction of Strephon and Klaius and the nihilism of Philisides. Pyrocles and Musidorus dissolve their connections to the past and yet unwittingly find ways to return to it. The narrator, feeling the same sympathy for them that they feel for those they love, invents reasons—via a deus ex machina—for them to have a future. Together, then, they fulfill the foundling formula, as the princes reconnect to their royal origins and are ensured of their dynastic destiny. In the double sestina and Philisides' poetic history, the destructive phase of each set of stories is revealed. Strephon and Klaius raze the pastoral place, and Philisides revokes the fostering parent, of the adoptive interlude. The heroes' response to love is healthy. Experiencing the same feelings, their counterparts go mad.

The double sestina records the effort of Strephon and Klaius to eradicate their pasts. It details the conversion of a point in space by a series of events in time. It speaks to the problems of *The Old Arcadia* because it plays on the connection between memory and hope. By nullifying in its process the scene of love, the poem raises questions about its initial occurrence. Did the memory exist or only the hope? The foundling theme depends on the substitution of physical support for psychological comfort. Thus pastoral realms and foster parents replace paternal protection and maternal nurturing. In the double sestina the material world is rescinded, and the shepherds are left with nothing outside themselves. They live inside their heads. At its simplest level the poem describes mental change in terms of physical loss. The poets are crazed because they have no bearings, as if they were alone in a disappearing forest without a compass. But they are also plagued with guilt (haunted by their own haunting song) because they have willed their loss deliberately. The double sestina explores the dimensions of child-induced separation. It describes both the process by which place can be mutilated and the feelings of the destroyers after the destruction occurs. The haunting rhythm achieved through the repeated evocation of place words ("mountains," "valleys," and "forests") reminds the speakers constantly of what they lose even as it renders those places (like church bells ringing from nowhere discernible) as mirages. Strephon and Klaius are foundlings who lose the world. Foundlings are different from others because they are bereft of the security of parental custody. Strephon and Klaius are still more insecure because they destroy the one thing the heroes retain—the setting, the place, of love. They are foundlings without an adoptive interlude because the place where it ought to occur disappears in the process of the poem. Having eliminated the physical world, the poets are left to feel only their metaphysical isolation.

The sestina opens onto a conventional pastoral. The shepherd's world begins like that of the heroes but ends by being no world at all:

> Ye goat-herd gods, that love the grassy mountains,
> Ye nymphs, which haunt the springs in pleasant valleys,
> Ye satyrs, joyed with free and quiet forests,
> Vouchsafe your silent ears to plaining music
> Which to my woes gives still an early morning,
> And draws the dolour on till weary evening.[5]

The realm of the satyrs and nymphs is at first predictable—grassy, pleasant, and quiet—essentially unfettered. Their domain appears eternally Arcadian until the shepherds request that the gods listen to the song, voicing at once the grievous content (plaint) and the leveling process (planing) of their psyches. If the first three end words encompass space ("mountains," "valleys," "forests"), the last include time ("music," "morning," "evening"). In the course of the poem that structure will be shattered as the temporal events destroy the stable realms. In the first two stanzas the shepherds connect the Arcadian landscape to the invulnerable gods guaranteeing its permanence. They range from the depths of the valleys through the heights of the mountains to the spheres of the stars, encircling within the zodiac of their prayers the full spectrum of possible help.

But when they ask, each of them repeating what the other says, these gods to "vouchsafe [their] silent ears to plaining music," they already anticipate the fact that there can be no rescue. If the gods listen to the complaint then they might become planed, leveled by a failure they cannot understand. The satyrs and nymphs who guarantee the landscape by their eternal presence are requested to commit an act that might constitute their imminent transmutation. In their prayers, Strephon and Klaius already seem bent upon transforming the scene of love into a witness for death.

Undermining the gods they invoke, the poets also desolate the selves they remember. While they advance from day to evening, they infect their world so that the pleasant valleys of the first stanzas become the woeful and (finally) the afflicted depressions of the second and third. Formerly, the poets were at home in the external landscape; now they are exiled, transplanted to the internal realm, the monstrous mountains of huge despair. But the banishment is self-imposed. Klaius is "heart-broken," suffering both from a devastating grief of the heart and so sensitized to pain by that heart that the rest of his body responds in a domino reaction, crushing mountains into molehills of space, and then building, as David Kalstone puts it, "mountains out of molehills" of pain.[6] In the first half of the poem, the poets are conveyed to a psychological netherworld.

In the second half, however, they reenter the physical realm, their transformed selves distorting the landscape so that nothing certain remains. Not only is the present bleak and the future dark but the past is effaced because the place in which it occurred is wiped out. There is no pastoral in which an adoptive interlude can evolve. The landscape swims away in the current of appearances. First the poets saw their inward passions destroying their outward semblances, the poisonous movement extending even to the landscape. But in the end the ravaged world is taken as the source of pain. Almost by reflex, the poets act as if the now-filthy exterior were encroaching on their still-pristine interiors. They divert a realm of negative occurrences into a state of murderous desire, Strephon admitting that his stature is "more base than are the basest valleys." He is less than the little left of the world. From this diminished and unstable position, the speakers recall what held the world together. It was a joy anticipated in the possibility of Urania:

> For she, whose parts maintained a perfect music,
> Whose beauties shined more than the blushing morning,
> Who much did pass in state the stately mountains,
> In straightness passed the cedars of the forests,
> Hath cast me, wretch, into eternal evening,
> By taking her two suns from these dark valleys.
>
> (P. 330)

Like some giant puppeteer, Urania kept things in balance, exceeding nature even as she maintained its stability. Thus, though she remains, for both of them, a coveted destiny, she was, for each of them, a secure origin. Her disappearance plunges the shepherds into eternal darkness.[7] Since the sun derives its light from her eyes, Urania leaves the world desolated by her absence. It is she who "hath cast" Strephon the "wretch, into eternal evening," plunging him into the sea of darkness that drowns his hopes. As wretch he is designated (cast) to play the role of nonentity he constructs throughout the poem. From the position of inward emptiness, the shepherds proceed to make the outward world a reflection of their hollow selves. If Urania wounds the lovers, they destroy themselves and the world, extending (casting) their lot on the realm. Strephon and

Klaius view Urania's departure from them as an abandonment. She is the caster-out. They are the castaways. They turn their destiny (as lovers) into an origin (as mother)—and then proceed to pose as deserted children.

The contraction of the six central end words in the three last lines of the poem stresses the suffocating process of the sestina form. By the repeated use of indicatives, the poets reduce the once-evolving macrocosm to the now-dissolving microcosm:

> These mountains witness shall, so shall these valleys,
> These forests eke, made wretched by our music,
> Our morning hymn this is, and song at evening.
>
> (P. 330)

The question the poem raises by pointing to *these* mountains, *these* valleys and *these* forests is answered in the now-assumed causality of *this* hymn and song. Ordinary space and ordinary time have been displaced by the poetically induced landscape. There remains no certain scene in which to establish the roots of possibility. The mountains witness, in the same sense as the dreadful cries substantiate, a consummation wrought by the shepherds themselves. The denatured landscape coldly oversees their death even as it dispassionately testifies (bears witness) to the dehumanized territory of the shepherds' diminished selves. Since the mountains, forests, and valleys do not exist objectively, no memory sustains once-held beliefs. The singers are left without a *that* to contrast with a *this*, without a *then* by which to measure the *now*. Everything merges into an extended darkness, rendering mountains, valleys, and forests into wretched (weak) reflections of the poets' vanished past. Strephon and Klaius respond to love's blows by using the pent-up frustrations of denied passion to blow up the world.

Philisides, on the other hand, is left in a passive state. Strephon and Klaius eradicate the adoptive place. Philisides eliminates an adoptive person. He banishes himself from Mira, retreating from the scene:

> And banished do I live, nor now will seek a recov'ry,
> Since so she will, whose will is to me more than a law.
> If then a man in most ill case may give you a farewell;
> Farewell, long farewell, all my woe, all my delight.
>
> (P. 344)

Like Strephon and Klaius, Philisides is miserable, but while the shepherds contrive to make it look like there remains no objective delight to seek, Philisides subjectively excludes himself from its possibility. In revealing his history, Philisides begins chronologically, describing first his biological parents, then his philosophical origins, and finally, his amorous initiation. As the saga progresses, he wipes out each set of progenitors, until he—like Strephon and Klaius—is left without the adoptive protection that might exist as a base from which to establish a future. Like the heroes, he forsakes the biological parents he evokes in the childhood story. Then he denies the philosophical origins he seeks in the initial solace of his sleep.[8] Finally, he defines himself as the spawn of Mira even as he ultimately rejects her:

> In such, or suchlike, sort in a dream was offered unto me the sight of her in whose respect all things afterwards seemed but blind darkness unto me. For so it fell out that her I saw, I say that sweet and incomparable Mira (so like her which in that rather vision than dream of mine I had seen), that I began to persuade myself in my nativity I was allotted unto her. (P. 340)

Mira emerges both a sight in a dream transpiring in the past and a force in a vision inspiring the future. His true ties are with Mira. In his "nativity [he] was allotted to her." She is now mother to his desire, father to his fate. If Strephon and Klaius mourn the absence of Urania, Philisides laments the presence of Mira: "And Mira I admired; her shape sank in my breast." To "admire" Mira is to add her (add Mira) to the self, which is precisely what Philisides does as he describes his absorption of her. When she sinks into his breast, he shrinks from himself, banished in the ashes of Diana's curse, burning in the fire of Venus's threat. The object of his aspiration (like Stella in the first of the sonnet series) is so planted in his being, yet so unreachable as other, that Philisides has no self left to save, no goal possible to achieve. He is annulled by admiration. By absorbing Mira he has eliminated her otherness, sucking her into himself just as Strephon and Klaius internalized the landscape. They have no objective memories; he has no objective future. They have all swallowed the outside sources of comfort. To stop the chase, as Philisides vows here, is to cease to exist:

> But having spent some part of my youth in following of her, sometimes with some measure of favour, sometimes with unkind interpretations of my most kind thoughts, in the end having attempted all means to establish my blissful estate, and having been not only refused all comfort but new quarrels picked against me, I did resolve by perpetual absence to choke mine own ill fortunes. (P. 341)

Urania departs leaving Strephon and Klaius in darkness. Philisides leaves, having exhausted what he believes to be all his means.

Because he cannot establish the "blissful estate" he craves, he chooses to erase the vision that propels him forward. But in choking his own "ill fortunes" he actually obstructs what he just called his origin, making himself (by his own resolve) the abandoned child, the outcast victim, of circumstances. Refusing to pursue, he stifles his life and remains, through this perpetual absence, in a permanent state of limbo. Philisides left his biological parents when he fell asleep, his philosophical heritage when he started to dream, and finally, his spiritual source when he refused to act. The vision is blocked, the drive stymied in the despair that dominates his being. Having removed himself from his inspiration, he also prevents himself from attaining it. Philisides makes the future impossible just as Strephon and Klaius render the past unreachable. The shepherds are exposed by Urania's departure and they proceed to destroy the world. Philisides exposes himself, leaving Mira's presence and defining himself by his "perpetual absence." Thus he forfeits the protective nurturing of what he defines as his substitute parent.

While Strephon and Klaius cause the landscape to wash away, and while Philisides swims to a distant shore, Pyrocles and Musidorus remain rooted in the Arcadia where they sighted love. Though they have "disannulled"—as Euarchus maintains (p. 412)—their biological birthright, they remain certain about their beginnings and positive about their directions in love. Further, while Strephon and Klaius destroy their initiation (the landscape of memory) and while Philisides withdraws from his inspiration (the object of desire), the heroes retain both the purpose and place of love. In short, having sacrificed (like Strephon, Klaius, and Philisides) the old certainties, they embrace (unlike the characters in the eclogues) the new values—those of the adoptive interlude. Challenged by the skeptical Musidorus, Pyrocles defends his version of love:

> "It is counted without measure, . . . because the workings of it are without measure; but otherwise in nature it hath measure, since it hath an end allotted unto it."
> "The beginning being so excellent, I would gladly know the end."
> "Enjoying," answered Pyrocles, with a deep sigh.
> "O," said Musidorus, "now you set forth the baseness of it since, if it end in enjoying, it shows all the rest was nothing."
> "You mistake me," answered Pyrocles, "I spake of the end to which it is directed; which end ends not no sooner than the life."
> "Alas! Let your own brain disenchant you," said Musidorus.
> "My heart is too far possessed," said Pyrocles.
> "But the head gives you direction."
> "And the heart gives me life," answered Pyrocles. (P. 23)

When Pyrocles turns from theory to practice, he also returns from rhetoric to action, speaking of an origination conceived in terms of the satisfaction expected through a continuous present: enjoying. Love is at once something to possess as object and to relish as process, its end (the fulfillment of desire) a constant source of renewal. Thus Pyrocles remains faithful to the transformational ethos of the adoptive interlude.

Seeing that Pyrocles is bound onto the spiral of passion, Musidorus tries to unwind his friend by reminding him of reason. "Let your own brain disenchant you," he argues. But when Pyrocles answers both that his heart is too far possessed and that it gives him life, he ties his new end to his former beginning. If Strephon and Klaius evoke an irretrievable past, Pyrocles speaks of an achievable future by calling it a place previously inhabited. If he is "too far possessed" then he already exists on that line, is moving toward that time, where enjoyment is possible. Propelled by the heart initiating life, he is possessed by the prospect prolonging it. The vision of a movable enjoyment is central to *The Old Arcadia*. Just as a child is not an end in itself but an extension of a dynasty, so is love a dynamic rather than a static emotion. Its perpetuation restores an initial intensity.

In order to realize the ideally renewable end, Pyrocles and Musidorus return to the initially painful beginning of their love. While Strephon and Klaius wipe away the remembrance of a starting point, while Philisides questions its occurrence, Pyrocles and Musidorus find solace in the place and time of their awakening. Cleophila returns to the site of her first "sighting":

> The only recreation she could find in all her anguish was to visit sometimes that place where first she was so happy as to see the cause of her unhap. There would she kiss the ground, and thank the trees; bless the air, and do dutiful reverence to everything that she thought did accompany her at the first meeting. But as love, though it be a passion, hath in itself a very active manner of working, so had she in her brain all sorts of invention by which she might come to some satisfaction of it. (P. 113)

She pays homage to the scene of her "unhap." "Unhap" means misfortune, but its juxtaposition here suggests *re*fortune, the substitution of a new identity for an old one. Here Pyrocles withdraws to the place where he developed the self he hoped would win his love, thanking the trees, kissing the ground, honoring the scene of the unmaking that precipitated his rebirth. To go back to the source of inspiration—"everything that did . . . accompany . . . the first meeting" is to reactivate the brain for the invention leading to satisfaction. Unlike Strephon and Klaius (who destroy the forests of their initiation) and Philisides (who is not even certain about where it occurred), Pyrocles remembers the site of his awakening so that its reality will make possible the consummating union of his desire. He pulls back to the inauguration of his love and finds, in that return, "the invention by which [he] might come to some satisfaction."

The process of return is repeated when both heroes retreat, together, to their starting point:

> Cleophila (to whom the not-enjoying her dear friend Dorus had been one of her burdenous griefs) took hold of this opportunity, and calling her beloved cousin with her, went to the same place where first she had revealed unto him her enclosed passion and was by him (as you may remember) with a friendly sharpness reprehended. There, sitting down among the sweet flowers (whereof that country was very plentiful) under the pleasant shade of a broad-leaved sycamore, they recounted one to another their strange pilgrimage of passions, omitting nothing which the open-hearted friendship is wont to lay forth, where there is cause to communicate both joys and sorrows—for, indeed, there is no sweeter taste of friendship than the coupling of their souls in this mutuality either of condoling or comforting, where the oppressed mind finds itself not altogether miserable, since it is sure of one which is feelingly sorry for his misery; and the joyful spends not his joy either alone or there where it may be envied, but may freely send it to such a well-grounded object, from whence he shall be sure to receive a sweet reflection of the same joy, and (as in a clear mirror of sincere goodwill) see a lively picture of his own gladness. (P. 168)

By returning to the same place where they first revealed their "enclosed passion," Pyrocles and Musidorus relive their first impression, making it at once (in the recapitulation) verifiable and (in the rejoining) reflective. Because they both felt the same thing in the same place then, so are they now able to move forward in what the narrator calls the "coupling" and the "mutuality" of shared experience. The "sweet flowers" and the "pleasant shade" provide the scene for the sweeter taste of friendship; in its permanence the landscape warrants the constancy of their emotion. The movement backward in the setting yields a movement forward in the telling that renders the new birth in love identifiable. Their sympathy for each other provides "a well-grounded object . . . a sweet reflection . . . a clear mirror." The "lively picture" joining their aspirations makes mutual the individualized, and concrete the ambiguous, emotion. While Strephon and Klaius leave themselves nothing to remember, Pyrocles and Musidorus confirm their desire in the revived certainty of its initiation— pulling back to a familiar territory before they leap forward to a living image. The "lively picture" of their past renders possible the lovely prospect of their future.

That "lively picture" culminates in book 3 as the lovers almost achieve satisfaction. The reference backward to setting and the suggestion forward to desire can be seen at the moment when Musidorus is at last alone with Pamela:

> The sweet Pamela was brought into a sweet sleep with this song, which gave Musidorus opportunity at leisure to behold her excellent beauties. He thought her fair forehead was a field where all his fancies fought, and every hair of her head seemed a strong chain that tied him. Her fair lids (then hiding her fairer eyes) seemed unto him sweet boxes of mother of pearl, rich in themselves, but containing in them far richer jewels. Her cheeks, with their colour most delicately mixed, would have entertained his eyes somewhile, but that the roses of her lips (whose separating was wont to be accompanied with most wise speeches) now by force drew his sight to mark how prettily they lay one over the other, uniting their divided beauties, and through them the eye of his fancy delivered to his memory the lying (as in ambush) under her lips of those armed ranks, all armed in most pure white, and keeping the most precise order of military discipline. And lest this beauty might seem the picture of some excellent artificer, forth there stale a soft breath, carrying good testimony of her inward sweetness; and so stealingly it came out as it seemed loath to leave his contentful mansion, but that it hoped to be drawn in again to that well closed paradise, that did so tyrannize over Musidorus's affects that he was compelled to put his face as low to hers as he could, sucking the breath with such joy that he did determine in himself there had been no life to a chameleon's, if he might be suffered to enjoy that food. (P. 201)

Contemplating the present Pamela and comparing her to conventionally pastoralized nature (roses, fields, pearls), Musidorus wanders over her body, moving from rich gem to richer life. But as he searches from the top of her face to the bottom, Musidorus retreats beyond the pastoral world that governed his love so far and into the military past that determined his life before that. His "fancy" delivered to his memory images of his heroic life, returning him now that he is about (he thinks) to reach his desire to the princely bearings he thought long ago lost. As he advances toward satisfaction, Musidorus emerges the hero in attack. The apostrophes ("fighting . . . chains . . . assaults . . . forces . . . ranks . . . armed discipline") are militaristic. But while Musidorus pictures Pamela as a prize to be won in battle, he also sees her as the source of his identity. She presents not a "picture of some excellent artificer" but a breathing testimony of her "inward sweetness." Pamela is "the contentful mansion . . . [the] well closed paradise," where Musidorus longs to dwell. Though she rouses him to reconvene his former military prowess, she also compels him to accept his present physical dependence. She emerges both the anticipated object of his desire and the antecedent spring of his life. In her presence he becomes a helpless infant, "sucking" her breath with a submissive joy. The triumph of his conquest lies in the pleasure of his surrender. If to be nourished by Pamela involves remaking his being, then there is no other joy but "enjoying that food." Musidorus achieves the living goal, the breathing picture, of continuing support in love. What starts off in shame ends up in triumph, the lover capturing a prize that renders him both the active hero he was and the nurtured child he becomes. He changes to remain himself. For a moment in book 3 the lovers experience the triumph of their methodology: the exaltation of transformation. While Strephon and Klaius destroy the pastoral harbor, and while Philisides denies himself the adoptive mother, Musidorus accepts Pamela as both place and nurturer. He sucks, like an infant, Pamela's food, even as he calls her the "well closed paradise," the *locus amoenus*, of his love. In the rebirth that proclaims his indebtedness to the place and the foster parent of the adoptive interlude, he recaptures the military strength of his original birthright. Though he has achieved nothing in fact, in thought he has once again found his heroic self.

Books 4 and 5 demonstrate the limits of imagination. It is at this point that the narrator reveals his involvement with the heroes, his identification with their plight:

> The everlasting justice (using ourselves to be the punishers of our faults, and making our own actions the beginning of our chastisement, that our shame may be the more manifest, and our repentance follow the sooner) took Dametas at this present (by whose folly the others' wisdom might receive the greater overthrow) to be the instrument of revealing the secretest cunning. (P. 265)

No longer isolated instances of absurdity, the princes' flaws represent all men's sins: "our faults." In the same way, when the narrator explains that Euarchus, the very man whom the princes hoped to protect in his innocence, is the one who will learn the exact details of their corruption, he speaks with a shared irony:

> Wherein the chief man they considered was Euarchus, whom the strange and secret working of justice had brought to be the judge over them—in such a shadow or rather pit of darkness the wormish mankind lives that neither they know how to foresee nor what to fear, and are but like tennis balls tossed by the racket of the higher powers. (Pp. 385–86)

If there is a continuous state of present joy toward which the heroes and narrator struggle, so too is there a continuous pit or unavoidable shadow toward which all mankind, including narrator and heroes, essentially tends. The arbitrary working of justice hinders the aspiring will of man.

In this context the deus ex machina can be understood. When Sidney sides with his heroes, doing for them what they could not quite do for themselves, he expresses his belief in man's capacity to control his life, despite Adam's Fall (or the heroes' decline) from original perfection. By moving forward, Pyrocles and Musidorus regain the past. Losing themselves in love, the heroes ultimately find themselves as men, just as Sidney reconstitutes the images of his imagination through the book he writes. The irrepressible impulse to create becomes the living image that preserves the initially inspiring vision.

The pattern of Pyrocles' early metamorphosis is actually repeated by the sequence of his final emergence:

> Transformed in show, but more transformed in mind,
> I cease to strive, with double conquest foiled;
> For (woe is me) my powers all I find
> With outward force and inward treason spoiled.
>
> For from without came to mine eyes the blow,
> Whereto mine inward thoughts did faintly yield;
> Both these conspired poor reason's overthrow;
> False in myself, thus have I lost the field.
>
> And thus mine eyes are placed still in one sight,
> And thus my thoughts can think but one thing still;
> Thus reason to his servants gives his right;
> Thus is my power transformed to your will.
> What marvel, then, I take a woman's hue,
> Since what I see, think, know, is all but you?
>
> (Pp. 28–29)

In his transformation, Pyrocles loses the disinterested quality that characterized his heroic exploits (as they were recalled in the eclogues). Because his eyes are "still," so are his "thoughts." But the play on moving and stillness embodies the dynamic of Arcadia. Though Pyrocles breaks with his past, he cements his future, establishing a faithfulness ("still in one sight") that is continual ("my thoughts can think but one thing still"). Movement toward a perpetuating arrest underlines the heroic impulse.

To become the pursued object (Pyrocles experiencing a woman's role, Sidney sharing his characters' fate) is to seek an imaginative change whose

motive is sympathetic. Finally, to work toward achieving the end of
enjoying, despite the fallen posture of mankind, is to exercise an ultimately preserving strategy. In his apologies to the "fair . . . worthy . . .
ladies" of his audience (pp. 27, 29, 49, 54, 55), Sidney admits that the
work is insignificant and his heroes' machinations ridiculous. In the
course of the romance, he depicts the self-destructive potential of
Strephon and Klaius (who kill off the past) and the self-denying hibernation of Philisides (who undermines the future). Yet he also presents the
self-transforming exploits of the heroes, who risk the certain to win the
possible. Granting them their wishes, Sidney smiles approvingly on their
struggle. The kingdom is saved once everyone is recognized and power
restored. The future is guaranteed in the solemnities of the marriage and,
"lastly," the celebration honoring both the son of Pyrocles and "Melid-
ora," the "faire daughter," of Musidorus. That *lastly* becomes the *firstly*
of a better future. The impetus toward improvement in the *ameliorating*
child carries out the scheme of the romance.

Despite the uncertainty of loss, perhaps because of it, the heroes have
found their own way to change and "still" to return. They realize, in the
concluding lines, the generational future of the foundling plot—just as
the narrator, in his preface, speaks of its initial exposure. There Sidney
uses the theme as a metaphor for the romance, comparing himself to the
"cruel fathers among the Greeks" (p. 3). Casting the work as a would-be
foundling, he declares himself ready to "cast" it out. But even as he
denigrates the pages that follow, Sidney speculates about what might have
happened had they not (still another procreative image) been "delivered."
He changes from cruel father to passive mother:

> In sum, a young head not so well stayed as I would it were (and shall be
> when God will) having many many fancies begotten in it, if it had not
> been in some way delivered, would have grown a monster, and more
> sorry might I be that they came in than that they gat out. (P. 3)

Sidney surfaces as a receptive vessel for the muse, impregnated with
fancies. Assuming a female guise, he responds to the barrage of fancy by
giving birth to the work dedicated to the countess of Pembroke. Against
the onslaught of teeming possibility (pictured as numerous as sperm) the
poet could either let himself swell and be permanently disfigured, like
Strephon, Klaius, and Philisides, or let himself open and release his transformations, like Pyrocles and Musidorus. Unable to prevent the fancies'
attack, the writer (as violated woman) labors to let them out, preserving
what he made so that his lost child might find sanctuary.

In setting himself up as victim, the narrator likens himself to his heroes.

Thus all come round to the goodness of nature by recognizing—and in fact submitting to—the goodness of art. For the heroes the external inspiration is love, for the poet it is fancy. In his metaphor, Sidney becomes, like Pyrocles in his disguise, a woman. But through that transformation both emerge better men. By accepting the best aspects of the adoptive interlude, they realize the best aspects of their nature, the poet leaving behind a romance for his sister to read, the heroes preserving a dynasty for their children to inherit.

Spenserian Hesitation: Finding without Keeping

For he comes, the human child,
To the waters and the wild
With a faery, hand in hand,
From a world more full of weeping than he can understand.
W. B. Yeats, "The Stolen Child"

In *The Old Arcadia*, the resolution occurs shortly after the narrator acknowledges his affinities to his characters. They, like him, are plunged in the pit of darkness, a shadow from which they can be released only by divine grace or poetic trick. But though they are limited in their resources for self-extrication, they win because they are winning. The poet likes, and likens himself to, his heroes and so intervenes on their behalf. In *The Faerie Queene*, this supportive connection is not there, partly because Spenser frees himself from the demands of the foundling formula upon which his characters' consummation depends. Una and Pastorella find their parents, Britomart a vision of her progeny. But their expected weddings never take place. In book 1, the poet weaves two foundling plots involving irreconcilable conclusions: Saint George's hagiography demanding a renunciation of earthly entanglements; Una's love story requiring the nuptial ceremony the saint story negates. The middle books are structured around three heroines—Florimell, Amoret, and Britomart. Only Florimell marries. In the sixth book, the poet reveals why he denies the social commitment of the plot he ostensibly follows when he exalts the Petrarchan inspiration he privately seeks. As Colin Clout, he pipes a totally different song, one glorifying the loss Una, Britomart, and Pastorella have struggled to overcome. Though *The Faerie Queene* remains incomplete, the poet has, by the end of book 6, realized himself in the Mount Acidale vision. There, the art/nature controversy of the book, ostensibly settled in the natural reunion of the foundling plot, is resolved finally in the artistic glorification of poetic emergence. Pastorella, whose very name identifies her as an archetypal foundling, is deprived, like Una and Britomart, of the dynastic future constituting her fulfillment. Spenser's appropriation and dismissal of the formula in *The Faerie Queene* reveals as much about his poetics as does Shakespeare's full use of it in the four last plays. But even the partially realized foundling plots allow him to escape the ordinary mechanics of the "weeping world" and to explore—via the prolonged sojourn of the lost interlude—the denial essential to his poetic emergence.

6

Two Irreconcilable Foundlings: The Love Story and the Saint Story in Book 1 of *The Faerie Queene*

Book 1 contains two intertwining foundling plots—the saint story of the formulaic Red Cross Knight and the love story of the analogous Una. Since her happy ending depends on remaining with Red Cross and since his depends on remaining with God, the would-be couple (like Marvell's lovers) find themselves "on parallel lines that can never meet." Their stories are mutually exclusive. The Red Cross Knight cannot both marry Una as the father of her children and become Saint George as the destined child of God. The foundling motif is the subject not only of the primary plot lines; it figures in several digressions as well. In the early cantos there are four children desecrated by their elders (Lucifera, Duessa, Phaëthon, and Hippolytus) who are the inverse of four parents cherished by their charges in canto 10 (Charissa, the goodly matron, the Almner, and God). Additionally, the pastoral assumptions of the adoptive interlude betray the Red Cross Knight at four critical times in the book: once in Error's forest; once in Archimago's hermitage; once in Pride's castle; and, finally, in Orgoglio's trap. At each of these junctures, he reveals his innocence about the exploitative nature of the universe, letting down the knightly guard that he ought to maintain. The characters are, then, doubly hopeful. They anticipate both the formulaic completion of their foundling plots and the pastoral goodness of the adoptive sections. They are beguiled on both counts by their own expectations. This naiveté on the part of the Red Cross Knight connects to his failure—in the opening cantos—to maintain the heroic code. Ironically, it is Una who restores the knight to himself. He *does* free her kingdom of its monster; he *does* return her to her parents but, because of what she enables him to discover about himself, he can never become part of her love story.

The exploitative pattern is revealed in the very first canto with the description of Una's parents and echoed five stanzas later in the description of Error. The narrator describes Una as an analogous foundling:

> So pure an innocent, as that same lambe,
> She was in life and euery vertuous lore,
> And by descent from Royall lynage came
> Of ancient Kings and Queenes, that had of yore
> Their scepters stretcht from East to Westerne shore,
> And all the world in their subiection held;
> Till that infernall feend with foule vprore
> Forwasted all their land, and them expeld:
> Whom to auenge, she had this Knight from far compeld.[1]

Una's parents were, as C. S. Lewis writes,[2] expelled from Eden where they experienced complete dominion. Like the lamb she carries, Una is pure but, like the lamb, she is a sacrificial victim of the royal lineage from which she descends, its image, and—as exposed child who compels the knight from afar—its only hope for salvation. The two words in the stanza indicating her trap are "subiection" and "compeld." It is by imposing their will over all the world (subjection) that Una's parents reigned and it is through the submission of the Red Cross Knight to their daughter's plight (compulsion) that they hope to be mended. In order to recoup their power, they send Una off to enlist the knight to perform for them.[3] Una and the Red Cross Knight inherit (the one through birth and the other through conscription) the parents' problem. As they are deprived of their position by the monster, she is cast out into the world. There is a shift of power expressed as an internal as well as external loss:

> Till that infernall feend with foule vprore
> Forwasted all their land, and them expeld.

The chaos wrought by the fiend involves both the physical destruction of the country and the metaphysical annihilation of its inhabitants. The "vprore" did to their minds what it did to their lands—"forwasted," exhausted, them. The monsters appear then not so much as opposites of the heroes as potential replacements of them. Suggested in the emptiness of "forwasted" is the idea that one form of energy (presumed evil) simply fills in the vacuum created by the absence of another (presumed good). The monster exists as an ambiguous representation of the characters' weakness. With the expulsion so contiguous to the exhaustion, the connection between the lost-child plot and the heroic code emerges. That code demands, as the Beowulf poet suggests, that the hero be wide-awake, ready for the enemy at every moment. In a Christian-heroic

poem, to be unready is to be both vulnerable and culpable. Una's parents
are "expeld" and replaced by the monster because they were "forwasted,"
lulled, like Hrothgar, into believing they were secure. The Red Cross
Knight, hoping to save them, is "compeld" by the same vulnerability. His
naiveté leads him to expect a safe world; his zealousness leaves him a
victim of an exhaustion that has already defeated the parents he is bound
to save.

The knight's belief that he can escape the tormenting monster for a
while is challenged in the first refuge he seeks, Error's forest. Hoping to
find a place free from Satan, the Red Cross Knight and Una are "forwasted" by their own faith:

> Led with delight, they thus beguile the way
> Vntill the blustring storme is ouerblowne;
> When weening to returne, whence they did stray,
> They cannot find that path, which first was showne,
> But wander too and fro in wayes vnknowne,
> Furthest from end then, when they neerest weene,
> That makes them doubt, their wits be not their owne:
> So many pathes, so many turnings seene,
> That which of them to take, in diuerse doubt they been.
>
> (1.1.10)

Like Strephon and Klaius, the lost children lose themselves, experiencing
their mental displacement in terms of a spatial disorientation. The syntax
of the opening line is deliberately unclear; logically it should read "led
with delight they were beguiled of the way." But Spenser uses the verb
"beguile" in a transitive sense; the characters are personally responsible,
have made the forest into a wandering wood by forgetting their purposes.
As they forsake their physical bearings, they forfeit their psychological
equilibrium. Thus their minds influence the landscape, which in turn
governs their sense of balance. They now have doubts about the source of
"their wits." Emptied through self-delusion, they feel as if they have been
filled by powers not "their own."

Compelled by the originating monster, Una and the Red Cross Knight
find in their search for solace the very enemy they hoped to escape. The
first five stanzas of the opening canto describe Una's parents and their
monsters, while stanzas 11 and 12 introduce another monster, as mother,
feeding and eating off her children. The only interval between them is the
deception of the wandering wood. In seeking the pastoral refuge of the
adoptive interlude, the Red Cross Knight encounters no protective harbor, no alternative parent, only yet another version of Una's presumptu-

ous forebears. Lost in the forest, he confronts more of what he was escaping. He believes the world will foster him. It is this very optimism that first gets him lost and then thrusts him into the mouth of the monster. The Error is his. She represents his mistaken confidence, using her children as he was used by Una's parents:

> And as she lay vpon the durtie ground,
> Her huge long taile her den all ouerspred,
> Yet was in knots and many boughtes vpwound,
> Pointed with mortall sting. Of her there bred
> A thousand yong ones, which she dayly fed,
> Sucking vpon her poisonous dugs, eachone
> Of sundry shapes, yet all ill fauored:
> Soone as that vncouth light vpon them shone,
> Into her mouth they crept, and suddain all were gone.
>
> (1.1.15)

Like the Nile annually flooding the land with water monsters, Error is infinitely capable of replicating herself. The children are shielded by her from all "vncouth" (dangerous and different) light. But for the thousand young ones sucking on her poisonous dugs and protected by her here, the refuge is only a seeming one. They are "mothered" merely to be used by her later on as she spews them forth to attack her enemy in a "floud of poyson horrible and blacke" (1.1.20). The cycle of mutual plunder is further extended at her death when the initially consumed offspring "flocked all about her bleeding wound, / And sucked vp their dying mothers blood, / Making her death their life and eke her hurt their good" (1.1.25). Devouring their dam, the imps are in turn eaten and killed as their bellies burst with her poison. Una and the Red Cross Knight are faced in that forest with a reflection of their own situation. Instead of providing an anticipated comfort, their encounter presents a lesson they have still to absorb: the earth affords no protection.

Even after the waking loss or "daymare" of the Error episode, the Red Cross Knight is not prepared for the world compelling him. What awaits him now is an actual nightmare. He falls prey to Archimago because he is so willing to let go, despite the debacle in the forest. Disappointed by the woods, the heroes are all the more in need of rest. They seek it in the next best thing: a hermitage. "Rest is their feast" (1.1.35) and they long to be "all drownd in deadly sleep" (1.1.36). Having seen too much waking, they are anxious to be immersed in the forgetfulness of night. "Void of euill thought" (1.1.46), the sleeping knight is open for the visions Archimago intends to stuff into him:

Thus well instructed, to their worke they hast,
And comming where the knight in slomber lay,
The one vpon his hardy head him plast,
And made him dreame of loues and lustfull play,
That nigh his manly hart did melt away,
Bathed in wanton blis and wicked ioy:
Then seemed him his Lady by him lay.

(1.1.47)

Archimago inspires a wet dream connecting love and death. "Bathed in wanton blis," the knight loses his faith in Una through a combination of the magician's sexual arousal and his own puritanical strictures. The dream, over which he seemingly triumphs, leaves him melted of his "manly hart." Though he abandons Una, he is ready for Duessa. Having once more let down his guard, he frees Archimago to determine the subsequent course of events.

The first book constantly returns to the theme propelling it into being—that of parental dominion and abandonment. Forsaking Una and "still flying from his thoughts" (1.2.12), the Red Cross Knight ironically meets Duessa, whose history parallels that of the woman whom he betrays:

Melting in teares, then gan she thus lament;
The wretched woman, whom vnhappy howre
Hath now made thrall to your commandement,
Before that angry heauens list to lowre,
And fortune false betraide me to your powre,
Was, (O what now auaileth that I was!)
Borne the sole daughter of an Emperour,
He that the wide West vnder his rule has,
And high hath set his throne, where Tiberis doth pas.

(1.2.22)

As Una's parents rule the East, Duessa's rule the West. Between the two outcasts there remain no worldly islands unchallenged by would-be usurpers. Impressed, both by the plight of her fall and the condition of sexual excitement into which Archimago has cast him, the Red Cross Knight repeats first the experience of the pleasance, where the wood in the form of Fradubio (1.2.31–45) parallels his already determined metamorphosis into a creature totally controlled, and second, the experience of the hermitage where the prisoners in the House of Pride again reflect his essential lack of freedom.

If the parents of Duessa and Una split the world between them, Lucifera lays unique claim on the whole sphere. Not content to rule in hell, which she inherits, she temporarily manages the earth. But her aim is to become the child of God. She wants to unseat Jove himself. Except for the battle with Sansfoy and the view of Lucifera's prison, which directly affect the knight, the events of cantos 4 and 5 are meant to edify the audience.[4] The mythological and invented foundlings in the sequence bear the scars of dynastic injuries. The children described ought to inherit the dominion of their parents but, either by a self-imposed rejection or an externally impressed force, they fail to become what they were destined to be. The stories seem to spin off each other as they progress from the earthbound Lucifera through Phaëthon up to heaven and through Prosperina to hell, back to the skies with Duessa and her confrontation with Night, through hell again with Aesculapius and back to a shattered earth with Hippolytus. The four negative parent-child relationships of these cantos form thematic parallels to the four positive ones that will appear in canto 10. First, the narrator relates the myth of Phaëthon, which he interprets not the way Ovid tells it (as the story of a son trying to verify his lineage), but as the tale of a child attempting to usurp his father—a child "proud of such glory and aduancement vaine" (1.4.9). Next, Lucifera is described as similarly ambitious. Daughter of "griesly" Pluto and "sad Prosperina" (1.4.11), she thought "her pearelesse worth to pas / that parentage" (1.4.11). Prosperina, herself a lost child, produced a daughter who longs to be one as well. Rejecting her inheritance, Lucifera aims for heaven. When Duessa attempts to save Sansfoy, she invokes her "griesly" (1.5.20) ancestor. By identically describing Pluto and Night, the narrator links heaven and hell. Duessa appeals to Night to save her lover, claiming that they are related. The recognition scene that follows seems a parody of all the formulaic foundling recoveries, including that of Una and her parents, in the book. If the heroes seek a return to some sort of primitive order—a world in which they can be sheltered as they were in the womb—the antiheroes demand a place where they, too, can find comfort. Duessa appropriately addresses Night:

> O thou most auncient Grandmother of all,
> More old than Ioue, whom thou at first didst breede,
> Or that great house of Gods caelestiall,
> Which wast begot in Daemogorgons hall,
> And sawst the secrets of the world vnmade,
> Why sufffredst thou thy Nephewes deare to fall
> With Elfin sword, most shamefully betrade?

(1.5.22)

What are the secrets of the world unmade? Are they truths of that nether-world existing before creation or divinations of the chaos after the dragons will have destroyed it? Finding her ancestor, Duessa demon-strates that the monsters, like the heroes, long to return to the protective enclave of a first source. They seek the same beginnings. Duessa thinks hers occurred even before the world existed. Since she is an "unmaker"— a destroyer—she links beginnings and endings.

The fourth myth in the context of foundlings brings the unmaking into the context of the family and thereby relates the chaotic force to the sexual drive. Having convinced Night to act on her behalf in rescuing Sansfoy, Duessa is led to Aesculapius's cave where she is told the story of Hippolytus, whose plight becomes the reason for the magician's impris-onment:

> Hippolytus a iolly huntsman was,
> That wont in charet chace the foming Bore;
> He all his Peeres in beautie did surpas,
> But Ladies loue as losse of time forebore:
> His wanton stepdame loued him the more,
> But when she saw her offred sweets refused
> Her loue she turned to hate, and him before
> His father fierce of treason false accused,
> And with her gealous termes his open eares abused.
>
> (1.5.37)

Hippolytus represents an extension of the Error story, another sign of the fragile child-parent relationship. Loved by his wanton stepdam, Hip-polytus turned from "iolly" to "cursed" as he refused her advances. Here the mother becomes the sexual aggressor, the father the jealous husband and the son the victim of his subsequent rage. The monster of parental fury tears the child apart, spewing him—like Error's children—piecemeal into the world.

Through the legends of Hippolytus, Prosperina, and Phaëthon, cantos 4 and 5 indicate that the satanic element has an inbred familial structure; through the encounter of Duessa and Night they emphasize that the monsters, like the heroes, struggle toward a future somehow connected to a remembered and idealized time of safety. With the Darkness episode, Spenser delves into yet another aspect of the foundling motif, recoursing to the time antedating creation, imagining the world before God said, "Let there be light." The ambiguity of "unmade" (1.5.22) connects a future doom to a past void.

The proximity of Darkness impinges (though he sleeps unaware) on the security of the Red Cross Knight. When he awakens, he discovers in the

House of Pride the same endless prison that exists in hell. Back on earth, the narrator describes the dungeon restraining Lucifera's prisoners:

> Besides the endlesse routs of wretched thralles,
> Which thither were assembled day by day,
> From all the world after their wofull falles,
> Through wicked pride, and wasted wealthes decay.
> But most of all, which in that Dongeon lay
> Fell from high Princes courts, or Ladies bowres,
> Where they in idle pompe, or wanton play,
> Consumed had their goods, and thriftlesse howres,
> And lastly throwne themselues into these heauy stowres.
>
> (1.5.51)

The lovers are at once victims and victimizers, condemned by each other to the fall from "high Princes or Ladies bowres." They are still other versions of the exploiters impelling the central characters. Their pride lies in "idle pompe" and "wanton play," the consumption of material goods and the wasting of time; their devils—like those of the mythological characters just examined—are self-imposed and their imprisonment self-proscribed. They "throwne themselues" into the torment that becomes their continuous present. The Red Cross Knight flees from a dungeon only to find himself trapped by the very traits that would have caught him initially. Following his earlier pattern, he moves from hermitage to harbor. Believing once more in the possibility of earthly sanctuary, he reunites with Duessa, finds yet another forest and:

> Vnkindnesse past . . . gan of solace treat,
> And bathe in pleasaunce of the ioyous shade.
>
> (1.7.4)

The "pleasaunce" of the pastoral retreat becomes an adverb, a description of their submergence in the shade and a foreshadowing of the mythologically ordained drowning that will sap the Knight's strength. The predisposition to an earthly harbor leads the Red Cross Knight to a consolation in the form of precisely the kind of sexual inundation that made him vulnerable to Duessa in the first place. The "*vn*kindness" (anger) between Duessa and him is "past." The kindness (likeness) to his naive self remains. The "pleasaunce" of the bower leads the knight back to the beguilement of the wandering forest. Overcome by the waters of the well he is

> Disarmd, disgrast, and inwardly dismayde,
> And eke so faint in euery ioynt and vaine,

Through that fraile fountaine, which him feeble made,
That scarsely could he weeld his bootlesse single blade.

                                                    (1.7.11)

The knight is "dismayde," both externally deprived of the courage to
fight and inwardly dismantled of the resistance to evil. Thus enfeebled, he
is in the physical and psychological position that the forces of Darkness
(Duessa and her whole satanic ancestry) intended to place him. Emptied
of self, he is imprisoned by his own desires in a dungeon controlled by
the offspring of the wind whose breath symbolizes the power of chaos
and whose name (Orgoglio) demonstrates that good and evil are inter-
changeably inflatable. The knight is once more "forwasted," exhausted
and hence devastated.

The volatility and contiguity of the satanic and heavenly elements
reach into the happier sections of the book, as the Red Cross Knight is
imprisoned by Darkness and released by light. The light assumes a pla-
tonic order, moving from Una through Fidelia, Speranza, and Charissa
up to Contemplation and the New Jerusalem. As truth, Una never bends,
remaining faithful in her love for the knight and in her desire to save him
so that he might release her. The narrator describes her "as rock of dia-
mond steadfast evermore," shining inwardly and reflecting all that sun-
shine offers, unshakable in her faith.[5] From the foundling Satyrane (the
knight who rescues her from savages) to the changeling Arthur (the
knight who releases her lover), Una discovers the lost children and allows
them to find their most noble selves by saving her. She will now restore
the Red Cross Knight to himself, reviving his body and spirit so that he
can free himself of his demons and her kingdom of its monsters. It is Una
who brings him to the house of Caelia where he learns about forgiveness
and solicitude. These lessons contrast to what the knight discovered
about exploitation in the earlier cantos.

Redemption is manifest through four images of familial love, preparing
for the knight's discovery of his true parents. For the false mothers of the
opening, canto 10 presents exalted ones. First Charissa is described:

A multitude of babes about her hong,
Playing their sports, that ioyd her to behold,
Whom still she fed, whiles they were weake and young,
But thrust them forth still, as they wexed old.

                                                    (1.10.31)

Unlike the foundlings who structure the plot, Charissa's brood is protected in its weakness and prepared for manhood, achieving both love and
freedom.

The second image of motherhood is depicted in Mercy, who leads the knight up the mountain toward his ultimate vision. The episode between the knight and matron forms a bridge between earthly and heavenly grace:

> The godly Matrone by the hand him beares
> Forth from her presence, by a narrow way,
> Scattred with bushy thornes, and ragged breares,
> Which still before him she remou'd away,
> That nothing might his ready passage stay:
> And euer when his feet encombred were,
> Or gan to shrinke, or from the right to stray.
> She held him fast, and firmely did vpbeare,
> As carefull Nourse her child from falling oft does reare.
>
> (1.10.35)

After having been reduced to nothing through the teaching of Fidelia and Speranza, the knight is then raised by Mercy, as mother, gently by the hand to his destiny. At the moment the Red Cross Knight finds himself as a man, he is made a child once more and led up that hill to a future in which he sees himself as a redeemer.

The third image of generosity is that of the Almner, whose function is to give but whose capacity for the job is explained in terms of a hereditary endowment that enables him to be securely selfless:

> The second was as Almner of the place,
> His office was, the hungry for to feed,
> And thirsty giue to drinke, a worke of grace:
> He feard not once him selfe to be in need,
> Ne car'd to hoord for those, whom he did breede:
> The grace of God he layd vp still in store,
> Which as a stocke he left vnto his seede;
> He had enough, what need him care for more?
> And had he lesse, yet some he would giue to the pore.
>
> (1.10.38)

The play on "stocke" as the source of a line of descent and as the accumulation of goods indicates the proper passing of character and grace from generation to generation. The Almner reserves the godliness he has in trust for his seed, keeping only "enough" for himself and enabling those he bred, both by birth and through care, to thrive on the gift he shares.

The fourth image of familial love comes in the ultimate place, at the end as well as the beginning of the knight's ascent: in the New Jerusalem. Contemplation explains God's feeling for the knight:

Faire knight (quoth he) Hierusalem that is,
The new Hierusalem, that God has built
For those to dwell in, that are chosen his,
His chosen people purg'd from sinfull guilt,
With pretious bloud, which cruelly was spilt
On cursed tree, of that vnspotted lam,
That for the sinnes of all the world was kilt:
Now are they Saints all in that Citie sam,
More deare vnto their God, then younglings to their dam.
                                                              (1.10.57)

The chosen people in the New Jerusalem are now "more deare vnto their God, then younglings to their dam." The Father emerges maternal in his solicitude, the Lord, like the Venus in book 4, the hermaphroditic Creator of his brood. Once the relationship between Charissa and her children is established as wholesome and good, so too can the relationship between Mercy and the Red Cross Knight, and God and his children, become clear. Understanding what it means to be helped, the knight learns that he, hitherto only a receiver of grace, will one day not only find it but give it. Triumphant himself he will grant victory to his nation.

But the final image is the most complex one, for at the end of his journey, the Red Cross Knight discovers what he sought at the beginning: a mother's affection, seen here as the natural love of a creature for its offspring—not something won or earned but something given—a birthright. In reaching the New Jerusalem he is reborn as child, gaining a past and a future he never knew existed. He discovers that he springs "from ancient race of Saxon kings" (1.10.65), was stolen as a baby, and will end up inheriting a kingdom, as England's patron, and a heaven, as God's saint. But the knight must wait to participate in the hagiography. He must return to Una. Before descending, he thanks Contemplation:

O holy sire (quoth he) how shall I quight
The many fauours I with thee haue found,
That hast my name and nation red aright,
And taught the way that does to heauen bound?
This said, adowne he looked to the ground,
To haue returnd, but dazed were his eyne,
Through passing brightnesse, which did quite confound
His feeble sence, and too exceeding shyne.
So darke are earthly things compard to things diuine.
   At last whenas himselfe he gan to find,
To Vna back he cast him to retire.
                                                              (1.10.67–68)

His heavenly purpose found, the knight comes back to earth confused, "so darke are earthly things compard to things diuine." That brightness now confounds his "feeble sence" since it "too exceeding" shines. Heaven overwhelms the knight with its light in the same way as the hell of the giant's dungeon and Despair's arguments outdid him, leaving him uncertain about who he is. What "self" does George find? Is he a faerie knight or an English saint? Is he to be Una's husband or the pure and heavenly soul he saw in the New Jerusalem? Canto 10 begins in certain darkness fostered by the experience with Despair and ends in the darkness of uncertainty, this time judged as relative to the eternally shining lights of the New Jerusalem for which the knight is ultimately destined. Despite the turn of events in the house of Caelia, the Red Cross Knight continues as if by atrophy on the old quests. Expelled temporarily by Contemplation from the "other world," he tries once more to redeem himself in this one. "To Vna back he cast him to retire." His return to Una is a temporary retreat from his destined role. Whatever he does now diverts him both from his real self and the saint story in which he will one day participate.

But the narrator continues with the love story as if the interlude on the mountain had not occurred. Remembering how much time has passed, Una spurs the knight on in his battle to restore her kingdom. Canto 11 parallels the earlier ones. Once more the knight fights with a monster who, like Grendel, embodies the fatal flaw, the overweening pride, of the kingdom he terrifies. In canto 7, with the water of an enchanted well, the knight loses his power and is overcome by drowning. In this canto, another enchanted well allows him to regain his faculties and revive his strength. The well of life, like the tree of life that is to follow, rejuvenates the knight and returns the spirit lost wallowing in the earlier sequences. The descriptions of the knight's rising approach the mythical, the knight appearing as Titan, the victorious hero born in, rather than swallowed (as he was previously) by, the sea.

The twelfth canto concludes nothing but that Una and the Red Cross Knight have the intention of marrying. Their future together is uncertain. The king, ready to adopt the orphan through marriage, calls him "sonne" (1.12.17). In canto 12, the knight is offered an earthly father and a home, in canto 10 his Heavenly Father and the New Jerusalem. The two possibilities appear parallel in perfection. Una is so "faire and fresh as freshest flowre in May" (1.12.22), and her lights seem as dazzling as those heavenly ones in canto 10:

> The blazing brightnesse of her beauties beame,
> The glorious light of her sunshyny face

To tell, were as to striue against the streame.
My ragged rimes are all too rude and bace.

(1.12.23)

Not only is Una the best of all possible earthlings; she emerges in this description "heavenly" and celestial, her beauty, like that of the New Jerusalem (1.10.57), too exalted for the narrator's "ragged" rhymes. Apologizing for his inability to describe Una's compelling power here, the narrator is also unable to weave her story to an end. Una is left, despite her capacity to "possess" (1.12.40) the knight (as she earlier compelled him) and to cause him to "melt" (1.12.40) in love (as he earlier was weakened by Morpheus), exactly as she began in canto 1: "to mourne" (1.12.41).[6]

Preferring, as Yeats put it, the "journey more than the end,"[7] Spenser finishes neither the love story nor the saint story. The Red Cross Knight returns to Cleopolis, and Spenser is ready for another voyage:

Now strike your sailes ye iolly Mariners,
For we be come vnto a quiet rode,
Where we must land some of our passengers,
And light this wearie vessell of her lode.
Here she a while may make her safe abode,
Till she repaired haue her tackles spent,
And wants supplide. And then againe abroad
On the long voyage whereto she is bent:
Well may she speede and fairely finish her intent.

(1.12.42)

The directive is positive; he will unload the ship of its burden, let it rest a while in Eden and then reset it again—"abroad"—at large and free. The earthly future of the heroes remains at worst mournful and at best uncertain, the heavenly destiny at once predicted but at last untold. Spenser's manipulation of the foundling plot leaves his characters aware of their past but with a future that he refuses to grant them. In launching rather than resting his poem, Spenser expresses his reservations about what constitutes a happy ending, promoting the poet's long voyage (1.12.42) over his characters' desired end. At first, the Red Cross Knight is duped by his belief in the goodness of the world (in the pastoral refuge of the adoptive interlude); later, Una is betrayed by her belief in happy endings (in the marriage usually accompanying the recognition). Thus, while Sidney uses the best aspects of the adoptive interlude to expedite the completion of the formula, in book 1 Spenser emphasizes the worst side of the interlude and then fails to flesh out the conclusion he initially augured. Similarly, in the middle books of *The Faerie Queene*, he raises his characters' hopes even as he dashes them. But there he comes closer to revealing why he distrusts the familial continuity upon which their happiness depends.

7

Two Creations: Succession and Generation in Books 3 through 5 of *The Faerie Queene*

The main stories in books 3 through 5 involve foundlings who never reach fulfillment. Amoret is adopted by Venus but does not find—fails even to search for—her biological mother. Artegall, who will (according to Merlin) learn his true background through Britomart, leaves her at the end of book 5. Like Una, Amoret and Britomart never marry. The only marriage to take place is that of Marinell and Florimell who are shown, not only through their names but through the metaphor describing their union, to be part of the dehumanized nature Spenser praises.

Spenser's reservations about marriage are revealed in two contradictory definitions of reproduction: what he calls vegetative "succession" in 3.6; and what he calls animal "generation" in 4.10. Succession is associated with the mimesis of art—the making of exact replicas. Generation is associated with the differentiation of sexuality—the making of individualized entities. Succession involves substitution. In the garden of book 3, one Adonis fills the place of the other just as the leaves of spring replenish the leaves of fall. As depicted in book 4, generation involves forfeiture and implies that nothing can replace the lost self. The reproduction of succession retains the maker's inspiration; the reproduction of generation demands the loss associated with sexuality and child rearing. Those in the middle books who succeed (Chrysogone, Venus, Isis, Artegall) give without sacrificing what they contain. Those left to languish (Britomart and Amoret) seek fulfillment in a lineage that presupposes a lifelong commitment first to the beloved and then to the child. If Spenser is, as W. B. C. Watkins calls him, "the first great poet of married love,"[1] he does not acquire this reputation from *The Faerie Queene*. He writes about love, but his stories lead, in book 4, to Venus or, in book 5, to Isis, both androgynous representatives of a self-contained creative mystery. Spenser links the central characters through his varying use of a reproductive metaphor—the image of the sun fertilizing the flower. When he applies it to Marinell and Florimell, its appearance signals their deliverance to each other. Contrarily, when he places Amoret in the flowering garden, that experience does not enable her to flower in love. Finally, when he uses the flower to describe Britomart, it signals both her awakening in book 3 and her rejection in book 5.

Marinell starts out as a victim of the gods, but ends up achieving the fulfillment others in the middle books never realize. Yielding to her son's desire for Florimell, Cymodoce allows him to become part of the natural cycle, which repeats, in the diurnal ebb and flow of the sea and the seasonal rise and fall of the plants, a permanent ritual of revitalization. Cymodoce's felt pain translates into persuasive argument. She mourns, but then fights for the release of her son, using her connections with the gods to promote her progeny. The poet describes Marinell's revival:

> Who soone as he beheld that angels face,
> Adorn'd with all diuine perfection,
> His cheared heart eftsoones away gan chace
> Sad death, reuiued with her sweet inspection,
> And feeble spirit inly felt refection;
> As withered weed through cruell winters tine,
> That feels the warmth of sunny beames reflection,
> Liftes vp his head, that did before decline
> And gins to spread his leafe before the faire sunshine.
>
> (4.12.34)

Awakening to Florimell, Marinell erases the "sad death" of winter and acquires a boundlessness denied humanity. When Spenser uses the sun and flower here, he switches the metaphor's sexual roles. Because of her association with the sun's beams, Florimell becomes the male force imbuing Marinell with a life desire. As a weed, Marinell becomes Florimell, the revived female flower. Since the sun is a star, Florimell represents the properties of multiplicity Spenser associates with the sea and Marinell. She emerges, in the androgynous confusion, parent to his rebirth, providing him with the inspiration to flower. Marinell wins by losing himself to Florimell, and by accepting his place as a pawn, albeit a fortunate one, of the gods. Both are part of the multiplying universe signified by the engendering sun and receptive flower.

Amoret begins where Marinell ends, as the child of floral conception. But she winds up tragically abandoned and then tortured by the gods who at first seemed to have chosen her. The elements so responsible for Marinell's resurrection combine to produce Amoret and Belphoebe. Their birth is made possible by a fusion of water, sun, and "celestiall grace." Relying on old texts, the poet tells how Chrysogone conceives:

The sunne-beames bright vpon her body playd,
Being through former bathing mollifide,
And pierst into her wombe, where they embayd
With so sweet sence and secret power vnspide,
That in her pregnant flesh they shortly fructifide.
   Miraculous may seeme to him, that reades
So straunge ensample of conception;
But reason teacheth that the fruitfull seades
Of all things liuing, through impression
Of the sunbeames in moyst complexion,
Do life conceiue and quickned are by kynd:
So after Nilus invndation,
Infinite shapes of creatures men do fynd,
Informed in the mud, on which the Sunne hath shynd.

                                          (3.6.7–8)

Spenser provides historical and natural proof for the existence of Amoret and Belphoebe. Explaining clinically how such children might be formed, he turns to the example of the flooding Nile, ironically recalling the description of Error's babes vomited forth in book 1. However logical the process, the gods do play a role here, for Chrysogone is destined to conceive. Her flesh, as the poet says, is pregnant, already expecting. Like Marinell's beginnings in love, Amoret's birth in life is described in terms of an artless energy, the child absorbed as pollen through the mother's receptive body. Chrysogone becomes the metaphor central to Spenser's vision: Pierced by the sun, she flowers.

   Canto 6 is about reproduction, the wondrous riches, the "infinite shapes" of the earth. Amoret and Belphoebe embody the possibilities exemplified by their fecund but somehow dehumanized mother.[2] They are products of a world always ready to produce them. But they are also actual children found by the most sexual of second mothers. And though Belphoebe is to be brought up in "perfect Maydenhed," Amoret is more interesting to the poet. She does experience the humanity from which her mother, in a swoon at her conception and unaware of her birth, is exempt. For Venus, she is simply a substitute for a malingering Cupid:

But Venus hers thence farre away conuayd,
To be vpbrought in goodly womanhed,
And in her litle loues stead, which was strayd,
Her Amoretta cald, to comfort her dismayd.

                                          (3.6.28)

Once having acquired her, the goddess drops her off in the Garden of Adonis and commits her to be fostered there (trained and tendered) by a mother (Psyche) now three times removed. If the story of Marinell and Cymodoce is sparked by maternal passion, that of Amoret is spoiled by maternal impassivity. She blooms as a paragon and then is left to her enemies, to live what the poet calls her "rueful history" (3.6.53).

The garden to which Amoret is brought before Scudamor takes her into that sad story is an island of safety surrounded by a sea of time. The enclave is based on constant renewal and survives by a process denying the personal. In the midst of that paradise is the mountain where Adonis remains "eterne in mutability" (3.6.47). Surrounded by the flowers signifying love's transformational cruelty and surfacing above the boar that killed him once, Adonis is by "succession made perpetual." The flowers—hyacinth, narcissus, amaranth—suggest an Ovidian comfort for loss, the garden emerging an eternal source of replacement. This motion toward renewal represents both (what James Nohrnberg calls) "the charity of the pagan gods"[3] and their ultimate indifference toward individuation. Like the knights of Arthur's court, Amoret is an interchangeable part in a larger process. Venus substitutes the child for Cupid, herself for Chrysogone, and Psyche for herself, tossing Amoret into safety but away from love. The engendering through floral sweetness accompanying Amoret's conception evolves into the perpetual revival of the gods, heightening her ultimate denial by them. The Garden of Adonis typifies the coolness of succession, an apathy based on the aspect of flowers that is the source of the poet's inspiration: their mutability. One blossom replaces another as the gods enjoy constant fruition. The poet describes the bower:

> And all about grew euery sort of flowre,
> To which sad louers were transformd of yore;
> Fresh Hyacinthus, Phoebus paramoure,
> And dearest loue,
> Foolish Narcisse, that likes the watry shore,
> Sad Amaranthus, made a flowre but late,
> Sad Amaranthus, in whose purple gore
> Me seemes I see Amintas wretched fate,
> To whom sweet Poets verse hath giuen endlesse date.
>
> (3.6.45)

Writing of continuing life, "eternity in mutability," Spenser interlaces his story with a tradition, supported by "sweet poets," of love's end. Adonis seems to have survived the wild boar of stanza 48. That survival is rooted (through rhyme) to the gore of stanza 45. If Adonis represents the positive side of metamorphosis ("by succession made perpetual"), the flowers signify all that is demeaning ("foolish and sad") in the transformation wrought by love. Yet the genus survives through the process of replacement called succession. The flowers enter and reenter the garden, eternally duplicated.

Scudamor views another model of that duplication in book 4 as he describes Venus:

> But it in shape and beautie did excell
> All other Idoles, which the heathen adore,
> Farre passing that, which by surpassing skill
> Phidias did make in Paphos Isle of yore,
> With which that wretched Greeke, that life forlore,
> Did fall in loue; yet this much fairer shined,
> But couered with a slender veile afore;
> And both her feete and legs together twyned
> Were with a snake, whose head and tail were fast combyned.
>   The cause why she was couered with a vele,
> Was hard to know, for that her Priests the same
> From peoples knowledge labour'd to concele.
> But sooth it was not sure for womanish shame,
> Nor any blemish, which the worke mote blame;
> But for, they say, she hath both kinds in one,
> Both male and female, both vnder one name:
> She syre and mother is her selfe alone,
> Begets and eke conceiues, ne needeth other none.
>
> (4.10.40–41)

Symbolized by the snake whose head and tail were "fast combyned," Venus is at once the beginning and end of life, its inspiration and culmination. As "syre and mother" herself alone, she represents creativity, the emblem of the altar on which she stands and for which she is worshiped. Like Chrysogone, Venus miraculously connects water and sun but she contains their energy within herself. And it is as goddess of generation, as daily replacer of the earth's riches, that she is seen by her admirers and victims:

> Then doe the saluage beasts begin to play
> Their pleasant friskes, and loath their wonted food;
> The Lyons rore, the Tygres loudly bray,
> The raging Buls rebellow through the wood,
> And breaking forth, dare tempt the deepest flood,
> To come where thou doest draw them with desire:
> So all things else, that nourish vitall blood,
> Soone as with fury thou doest them inspire,
> In generation seeke to quench their inward fire.
>
> (4.10.46)

Venus encourages the "saluage beasts" and "all things . . . that nourish
vitall blood," propelling them, as she did in the Homeric hymns, by fury.
The only way for them to "quench [the] inward fire" kindled by her is in
the generation for which she—distantly cool—is self-sufficient.

Here Spenser subtly inserts the distinction between the replication he
exalts and the generation he questions. Plants reproduce by keeping
within themselves the fire of the sun. "Lyons," "Tygres," "raging Buls"
(and presumably those humans similarly crazed) can only reproduce by
putting out or quenching their inward fire. When Scudamor seeks to
quench his desire with Amoret, he subjects her to the fiery torture of
Busyrane; were he to succeed in love, and put out the fire like the bulls
and tigers, then both would become victims of the generational cycle.
Venus seems to anticipate the double trap in the scene describing her
presumed acquiescence to Scudamor's passion:

> And euermore vpon the Goddesse face
> Mine eye was fixt, for feare of her offence,
> Whom when I saw with amiable grace
> To laugh at me, and fauour my pretence,
> I was emboldned with more confidence,
> And nought for nicenesse nor for enuy sparing,
> In presence of them all forth led her thence,
> All looking on, and like astonisht staring,
> Yet to lay hand on her, not one of all them daring.
>
> (4.10.56)

The "amiable grace," the aloof amusement, of Venus's politesse, undermines the seriousness of Scudamor's quest and makes the horror of what
ensues in Busyrane's castle all the more devastating. While in book 3
Venus seemed to care for Amoret, in book 4 she hardly notices the face of
the child she adopted. Mother of all, Venus abides perennially in the
garden, removed from the cycle she initiates, laughing at human endeavors ("pretence") with the knowledge that they lead ultimately to the
death she transcends. As sire and dame in one, she is the source of a
generative cycle in which she does not need to participate, inspiring love
without loving. Her unique power explains her insensitivity to the mere
mortals at her feet. She achieves alone and inwardly the preservation that
they seek in a continuing posterity. Amoret and Scudamor, believing that
they have been blessed with a future, learn instead that Venus's smile has
nothing to do with them. Their story is dropped, the lovers tragic victims
of the gods' intense concern for, and then sudden denial of, their lives. In
writing of Amoret, Spenser seems at first, as Venus was in adopting her,
vitally interested in her fate. But she disappears from the book, left

wandering after her rescue—unfulfilled in love, incomplete as a woman.

Similarly, Britomart, the heroine of the middle books, begins with high expectations. Mothered by Glauce, fostered by Merlin and later Isis, she seems to have wit and good fortune on her side. But while Amoret is passively bounced from god to god and then rescued by character after character, Britomart actively instigates and pursues her own fate. When Merlin first prophesied the dynasty she was to bear, Britomart's reaction includes the floral metaphor, her awakening pictured as a self-generative response:

> The doubtfull Mayd, seeing her selfe descryde,
> Was all abasht, and her pure yuory
> Into a cleare Carnation suddeine dyde;
> As faire Aurora rising hastily,
> Doth by her blushing tell, that she did lye
> All night in old Tithonus frosen bed,
> Whereof she seemes ashamed inwardly.
> But her old Nourse was nought dishartened,
> But vauntage made of that, which Merlin had ared.
>
> (3.3.20)

Rising, like the carnation, to the warmth of confession, Britomart turns from wan to red, inflamed by the heat of the heaven and instilled by the excitement of the earth. Through the poet's analogy, she has already arrived in her wishes at the place (Titon's bed) that will gratify her passion. She is the dawning flower embraced by the sun.

Predicting Britomart's progeny, Merlin sees beyond the emblematic moment of passion, promising not only a bower of love, but a childbed of rebirth:

> The man whom heauens haue ordayned to bee
> The spouse of Britomart, is Arthegall:
> He wonneth in the land of Fayeree,
> Yet is no Fary borne, ne sib at all
> To Elfes, but sprong of seed terrestriall.
> And whilome by false Faries stolne away,
> Whiles yet in infant cradle he did crall;
> Ne other to himself is knowne this day,
> But that he by an Elfe was gotten of a Fay.
>
> (3.3.26)

When Britomart marries Arthegall, she will reveal his ancestry even as she helps forge his destiny in his native country; she will make him a formulaic foundling. The dual convenant of sexual fulfillment and love perpetuation renders Britomart heroic and dynamic. She is Artegall's hope and origin, figured as the wife of a British king and the instrument of his recognition. She will be mother to his restoration. Such promises leave Britomart impassioned (3.3.43) and perplexed. It is Glauce who questions how she might fulfill the prophecy:

> But read (said Glauce) thou Magitian
> What meanes shall she out seeke, or what wayes take?
> How shall she know, how shall she find the man?
> Or what needs her to toyle, sith fates can make
> Way for themselues, their purpose to partake?
>
> (3.3.25)

By considering means, Glauce acknowledges that human "toyle" might be necessary to achieve a fated end; she therefore urges Britomart to be a man in pursuit so that she might emerge a woman in love. In book 3, casting herself as witty slave and Britomart as Rosalind or Viola, Glauce invents the machinations of a comic plot. But despite a brief meeting with Artegall in book 4, Britomart winds up, in book 5, where she began, her bright prospect appearing, through the connection between Venus and Isis, similar to Amoret's false hopes.[4]

If the Venus of book 4 is clothed in splendor and enveloped by a snake "whose head and tail were fast combyned," the Isis of book 5, likewise fringed in silver and gold, has "at her feet a crocodile, that with her wreathed taile her middle did enfold" (5.7.6).[5] Surrounded by Osiris, she also contains him. As Venus is "sire and mother . . . herselfe alone" (4.10.41), Isis—with Osiris so close—shares the qualities that equally define her love's power.

When the goddesses react to the characters they inspire, their attitudes are identical:

> To which the Idoll as it were inclining,
> Her wand did moue with amiable looke,
> By outward shew her inward sence desining.
> Who well perceiuing, how her wand she shooke,
> It as a token of good fortune tooke.
>
> (5.7.8)

As Venus's "amiable glance" encourages Scudamor (4.10.56), Isis "inclines" toward Britomart. And, as Venus prods Scudamor with her laugh, Isis, too, looks "amiable." The repetition of the word itself, considered in the contexts of the passion the goddesses instill, is distancing. They grant, with "amiability," a measure of hope to their worshipers, though they fail, through indifference, to act on their behalf. This "inclination" is at most that—a nodding in the direction, not a guarantee, of end.

With the Eleusinian mystery of her dream, Britomart becomes Isis. She mothers the lion and is fathered by the crocodile, freed by him to create her dynasty as, in Merlin's prophecy, she liberates Artegall to find his origin.[6] In the dream she achieves what the goddess already possesses: the state of sire and mother in one. But in her reality, she is less secure, meeting up with Artegall only to be dropped by him. Britomart is beguiled into experience without having it. She is pulled into the shrine, lulled by the "amiable" glance of the goddess into thinking she has achieved her end. Isis's "outward show" has little to do with her inward willingness to carry out a presumably ordained design. Britomart believes in the destiny shown before her. When the priests interpret her dream, they speak of Isis's power to see behind her disguise:

> Magnificke Virgin, that in queint disguise
> Of British armes doest maske thy royall blood,
> So to pursue a perillous emprize,
> How couldst thou weene, through that disguized hood,
> To hide thy state from being vnderstood?
> Can from th' imortall Gods ought hidden bee?
> They doe thy linage, and thy Lordly brood;
> They doe thy sire, lamenting sore for thee;
> They doe thy loue, forlorne in womens thralldome see.
>
> (5.7.21)

As Merlin smiled (3.3.17) when he foresaw Britomart's future, detecting Glauce's guile, so here Isis catches Britomart, penetrating, in the connection of rhyme, past ("blood") and future ("brood"). Britomart twice discovers her fate—the "long event" (5.7.22) coming after the short adventures here unfolding. But in belittling, with their laughter, Britomart's comic enterprise, and in foiling the devices of her witty slave, the gods deprive the princess of the means to achieve her end, disparaging, with their promises, her energetic prowess. Eased in her "troublous thought" (5.7.24), Britomart pursues the promised future, trusting in the haven she heard.

When she finally frees Artegall from Radigund, she is again abandoned by him. Once released, Artegall seeks only his immediate quest for Gloriane. In canto 8, the poet changes his tone toward Britomart, turning the story away from her:

> Nought vnder heauen so strongly doth allure
> The sence of man, and all his mind possesse,

As beauties louely baite, that doth procure
Great warriours oft their rigour to represse,
And mighty hands forget their manlinesse;
Drawne with the powre of an heart-robbing eye,
And wrapt in fetters of a golden tresse,
That can with melting pleasaunce mollifye
Their hardned hearts, enur'd to blood and cruelty.
   So whylome learnd that might Iewish swaine,
Each of whose lockes did match a man in might,
To lay his spoiles before his lemans traine:
So also did that great Oetean Knight
For his loues sake his Lions skin vndight:
And so did warlike Antony neglect
The Worlds whole rule for Cleopatras sight.
Such wondrous powre hath wemens faire aspect,
To captiue men, and make them all the world reiect.

                           (5.8.1–2)

Comparing Britomart to stereotypical temptresses (Omphale, Delilah, and Cleopatra), the poet implies that any dalliance with her would be the source of Artegall's unmanning. Britomart emerges as the snare, wrapping Artegall in fetters, enticing him into precisely the same pleasance that repeatedly trapped the Red Cross Knight in book 1. The snakelike intertwining signifying Isis's power in canto 7 becomes—one canto later in the reversal of awakening—the bait of possessive womanhood. Though Merlin sees Britomart as mother of Artegall's self-knowledge, and though Isis predicts that he is father to her recognition, the poet depicts their union as "heart-robbing" (5.8.1) and debasing. To be himself in canto 8, Artegall must once again leave Britomart in languor and unrest (5.8.3). She is unable to act because of grief, unwilling to move because of disbelief. Having been buoyed by Isis, she is left dangling by her love, deprived of the energy to continue by Artegall's denial and robbed of the will to live by the gods' betrayal.[7]

When Merlin outlined Britomart's destiny, her reaction in expectancy was compared to a flower and the sun (3.3.20). But the promise signified by that early dawning never blossoms in the later episodes. Instead the actual rebirth is given by Artegall to another woman, as the prince, pursuing his quest, inspires Irene to realize herself:

Like as a tender Rose in open plaine,
That with vntimely drought nigh withered was,
And hung the head, soone as few drops of raine
Thereon distill, and deaw her daintie face,

Gins to looke vp, and with fresh wonted grace
Dispreds the glorie of her leaues gay;
Such was Irenas countenance, such her case,
When Artegall she saw in that array,
There wayting for the Tyrant, till it was farre day.

(5.12.13)

Artegall frees Irene to reveal the full glory of her inward rose. The fruition that should have been granted to Britomart is bestowed, as sun and
liquid, instead on a stranger, given without passion by Artegall whose
mission does not end with the restored princess. He continues as if the
flowering kingdom here were merely a place where he chose for a moment to deposit his evaporating strength. The metaphor of the blooming
flower is depersonalized, removed from Artegall, as the gods are dis-
tanced from the mortals whose ends they predict.

For the prince to remain with Britomart is for him to lose the potency
he here so easily manifests. The lack of involvement is precisely what
enables him to withstand the sting of the Blatant Beast, the poison of
envy and detraction. "Yet he past on and seem'd of them to take no
keepe" (5.12.42). The simultaneous removal from love and hate "preserves" Artegall on his adventures even while it leaves Britomart languishing in desire. The distance propels the knight, as it governs Venus
and Isis, "keeps" him, like them, self-contained. The procreative complex
involving the loss of self that Britomart revealed in the metaphor of her
floral embarrassment at Merlin's discovery is forsaken in favor of the
creative energy "distilling" at Irene's awakening (as it does in Marvell's
"On a Drop of Dew") for a moment of perfection that appears both a
concentration of everything and a dissolving into nothingness. That burst
of energy reveals Artegall's propensity to appear—like the gods—
amiable, without remaining—like the parent—loyal. The fifth book is
clearly Artegall's, but the fact that Britomart is left so cruelly alone as a
symbol not of her lover's completion in union but of his depletion in
dalliance indicates the poet's doubts regarding the marriage his characters
expect. Artegall, still in quest, reserves for himself the potential Britomart
longs to absorb. With his central character in perpetual motion, still
"holding" (5.12.43) on his way, the poet, predicting further adventures
somewhere else, deprives his audience of the satisfaction his narrative
promised. Thus, the two formulaic foundlings, Amoret and Artegall,
participate in plots never completed. Britomart, who acknowledges the
goodness of generation, is compared (in book 5) to archetypal temptresses and left (at the end) alone. Granting to Irene the floral fulfillment he
earlier predicted for Britomart and calling Artegall's time with her a

dalliance, the poet changes his attitude toward the heroine to whom he gave such a bright dawn. Success is only associated with the process of succession symbolized by the absorption of Marinell and Florimell in their metaphorical roles. Their androgynous union is a duplication similar to the artistic creation of Venus and Isis or the floral replacement in the Garden of Adonis. With the generation so crucial to the happy ending of foundling plots, Spenser associates the failed stories of Britomart and Amoret.

8

Two Recreations: Pastorella's Return and the Poet's Emergence in Book 6 of *The Faerie Queene*

In book 6 Spenser surfaces as the sole creator of his world, independent of muse and mate, retreating through the vision on Mount Acidale into the recreation—the duplicating succession—of his own art. This self-containment contradicts the communal ritual around which the foundling plots in the stories of Tristram, Aladine, Calepine's babe, the saluage man, and Pastorella revolve. Spenser's handling of the theme is the same as it is throughout *The Faerie Queene.* In book 6, however, the number of foundlings is so great that Spenser's dismissal of the generational process negates, more strongly than in any other book, the procreative norm that process would ensure. The noble origin of the children is affirmed, either obliquely by the narrator or overtly by the plot, but the promised marriage for all of them never takes place. Most conspiciously, Pastorella returns to the womb but does not herself become a mother. Like Artegall, Calidore continues on his original quest, forfeiting the comfort of Pastorella's beauty for the challenge of the Blatant Beast. Despite the community of pastoral (defended by Meliboe) and the community of court (revitalized by Pastorella's return), book 6 is Spenser's sharpest rejection of the social process. The book defends instead the poet's personal resources. By short-circuiting all his foundling plots, Spenser reiterates his doubts about the value of sexual generation defined in 4.10. The real story of the sixth book lies not with Calidore and Pastorella but with Colin Clout and the poetic succession defined first in 3.6.

If book 1 has two stories so does book 6. The first story is the conventional narrative of the heroes, culminating in Pastorella's return; the second, detailing the poet's emergence, reaches its pinnacle with Colin Clout's vision on Mount Acidale. The two stories conflict because the lost-child plot feeds into marriage and progeny; Colin Clout's story thrives on the death of love. Spenser approaches the sixth book "wearily" and warily, convinced of the doom connected with the contemporaneous presence of the Blatant Beast but willing to try once more—as he had so often before—to become involved in the plot that might take him to strange ways and new paths. He begins as a tired old man, waiting to be reinspired by the imps of the proem (6.2). There, he asks the poetic children on Mount Parnassus to "guide" his weary steps, much as found children might revitalize their parents. The steady progression, beginning in the proem, from one foundling to another—the imps of Parnassus, to Tristram, to Aladine, to Calepine's babe, to the salvage man, to Pastorella—marks Spenser's intensifying resistance to the optimistic formula of their stories. The belief in the saving power of children is transferred from the voice of the poet in the proem (6.2), to that of a character in the middle sections (6.4.36), to the audience in the concluding canto (6.12.21). Finally, in canto 12, the poet cannot even summon up the energy to describe Claribell's joy in Pastorella's recovery. His silence reflects his disinterest in the original pursuit.[1]

Book 6 begins expectantly, echoing in the story of Tristram the rejuvenation of the Mount Parnassus sequence. Calidore's pleasure in Tristram's youth is related with sympathetic joy:

> All which when well Sir Calidore had heard,
> Him much more now, then earst he gan admire,
> For the rare hope which in his yeares appear'd, . . .
>   Full gladd and ioyous then young Tristram grew,
> Like as a flowre, whose silken leaues small,
> Long shut vp in the bud from heauens vew,
> At length breakes forth, and brode displayes his smyling hew.
> (6.2.34–35)

The foundling suggests the "rare hope which in his yeares appear'd." Calidore, who treats Tristram paternally, is rewarded, as Humphrey Tonkin points out, by the blossoming child he initiates into formal manhood.[2] As in the middle books, the flower symbolizes an inward radiance objectified. The relationship is reciprocal, the elder nurturing a seed stored and returned by the young. At this point, Calidore resembles the poet. Having traveled much, both find in children the inspiration to continue their journeys.

But something happens in the course of the book that seems to jaundice the easy reciprocity and stymie the "rare hope" here so lovingly planted. This doubt surfaces as the poet emphasizes his remoteness from the cen-

tral narrative concern. The distancing process begins in canto 3 with the
lament of Aldus. The wayward Aladine is returned wounded and his
father is distraught. He mourns, as the poet is quick to comment, his own
loss:

> When he saw his sonne so ill bedight,
> With bleeding wounds, brought home vpon a Beare,
> By a faire Lady, and a straunger Knight,
> Was inly touched with compassion deare,
> And deare affection of so dolefull dreare,
> That he these words burst forth; Ah sory boy,
> Is this the hope that to my hoary heare
> Thou brings? aie me, is this the timely ioy,
> Which I expected long, now turnd to sad annoy?
>   Such is the weakenesse of all mortall hope;
> So tickle is the state of earthly things,
> That ere they come vnto their aymed scope,
> They fall too short of our fraile reckonings,
> And bring vs bale and bitter sorrowings,
> Instead of comfort, which we should embrace;
> This is the state of Keasars and of Kings.
> Let none therefore, that is in meaner place,
> Too greatly grieue at any his vnlucky case.
>
> (6.3.4–5)

Berating the child he should succor, Aldus complains of the loss in old age
of the "timely ioy"—the generational perpetuity—that he had expected
from his son. Though he gets him back, the father laments the "tickle . . .
state of earthly things," feeling "compassion" only for himself and
finding comfort only in the fact that he does not suffer alone.

Similarly the childless Mathilde and Sir Bruin fear that all they have
accomplished in quelling Cormorant will be undone by their failure to
consolidate the victory with heirs:

> For th' heauens enuying our prosperitie,
> Haue not vouchsaft to graunt vnto vs twaine
> The gladfull blessing of posteritie,
> Which we might see after our selues remaine
> In th' heritage of our vnhappie paine:
> So that for want of heires it to defend,
> All is in time like to returne againe
> To that foule feend, who dayly doth attend
> To leap into the same after our liues end.
>
> (6.4.31)

Without children to sit in their throne, the royal couple leave their land open to the monster who, like the one haunting Una's parents, seeks to usurp their place. Mathilde longs for a child as a buffer against the lurking powers of evil. Calepine comforts her with the baby he finds, seeing in him proof positive of the superstition that foundlings are harbingers of luck:

> And certes it hath oftentimes bene seene,
> That of the like, whose linage was vnknowne,
> More braue and noble knights haue raysed beene,
> As their victorious deedes haue often showen,
> Being with fame through many Nations blowen,
> Then those, which haue bene dandled in the lap.
> Therefore some thought that those braue imps were sowen
> Here by the Gods, and fed with heauenly sap,
> That made them grow so high t'all honorable hap.
>
> (6.4.36)

The imps dwelling on Mount Parnassus for the benefit of the poet dwindle into the imps planted on earth for the rescue of the characters. The poet's comfort in the opening becomes Calepine's resource here: lost children may be the seed of God, sown to maintain all "honorable hap," the hope guaranteed by its revitalizing conjunction with fate. Calepine's platitudes reflect the poet's growing disinterest in the foundling plot, a lassitude demonstrated with each successive version.

Canto 5 opens with another lost child: the saluage man. The poet defines his noble origins even as he withholds the denouement of his story:

> Plainely may in this wyld man be red,
> Who though he were still in this desert wood,
> Mongst saluage beasts, both rudely borne and bred,
> Ne euer saw faire guize, ne learned good,
> Yet shewd some token of his gentle blood,
> By gentle vsage of that wretched Dame.
> For certes he was borne of noble blood,
> How euer by hard hap he hether came;
> As ye may know, when time shall be to tell the same.
>
> (6.5.2)

Hinting at some far-distant recognition, the poet plays god with his characters, manipulating them like puppets as he calls attention to "sparks and tokens" he never will relume. No longer mouthing a belief in the benevolent powers of the gods, he asserts his own strength, determining both the future end ("hap") and the circumstances leading to it ("time"). As he moves from canto to canto, he intrudes in the plot, stressing his influential presence. Repeatedly, one character's story is postponed at his whim; he designs terrible straits for Serena, but then turns to another thread in the narrative. Her "discourse [he] now must delay, / Till Mirabellaes fortunes [he does] further say" (6.7.50). When he returns to her, he fails to record her marriage to Calepine, vowing that "the end whereof Ile keepe vntill another cast" (6.8.51). The "other cast" never appears.[3] All the foundling digressions foreshadow the main story, which only begins in canto 9.

Relating the saga of Pastorella's kidnapping, the poet minimizes her suffering and assumes a philosophical tone, widening still further the wedge between himself and his characters:

> The ioyes of loue, if they should euer last,
> Without affliction or disquietnesse,
> That worldly chaunces doe amongst them cast,
> Would be on earth too great a blessednesse,
> Liker to heauen, then mortall wretchednesse.
> Therefore the winged God, to let men weet,
> That here on earth is no sure happinesse,
> A thousand sowres hath tempred with one sweet,
> To make it seeme more deare and dainty, as is meet.
>
> (6.11.1)

Reducing sexual passion to physical appetite, he compares the experience of love to the preparation of a meal seasoned by "one sweet." A fortunate encounter, like a delicacy, is appreciated for its rarity. It is fitting ("meet") that his characters be made to learn (as Aldus knows; as the poet has come to see) that "here on earth is no sure happinesse." Patly rationalizing, he puts his hero and heroine through the throes of wild brigands and pirates in order to take them out of their idyll and back to the court where they belong, thereby enabling Calidore both to trap the Blatant Beast and to find a princess; further, the princess, following the conventions of the lost-child pattern, finds herself. At the end, through the proper talisman, Pastorella's past is revealed—how she was abandoned by her imprisoned mother, how she was found by Meliboe, how she had a "rosie marke" by which she could be identified, and how Lady Claribell's maid found the mark. Pastorella appears to the maid as a sign of God:

> My liefe (sayd she) ye know, that long ygo,
> Whilest ye in durance dwelt, ye to me gaue

A little mayde, the which ye chylded tho;
The same againe, if now ye list to haue,
The same is yonder Lady, whom high God did saue.

(6.12.17)

The miracle is that the child is identical to the one lost: "The same againe." The king and queen regain their past and find once more the child and childhood thought gone forever. As it was for Calidore in Tristram and for Calepine in the babe, their hope is confirmed by what they believe to be the will of God.

But the poet remains here, as throughout the book, aware that he, not God, is the one pulling the strings and that this is a world manipulated by him. The Pastorella sequence is totally conventional. It follows nearly all the rituals of the lost-child plot. Because it is so absolutely formulaic, the scene in 6.12.19–20 (depicting the mother's eager questioning, her unbelief at the truth, her wonder, and her tears) evidences the poet's distance from the plot he has staged. Addressing his audience, he claims his inability aptly to express Claribell's joy:

Who euer is the mother of one chylde,
Which hauing thought long dead, she fyndes aliue,
Let her by proofe of that, which she hath fylde
In her owne breast, this mothers ioy descriue:
For other none such passion can contriue
In perfect forme, as this good Lady felt,
When she so faire a daughter saw suruiue,
As Pastorella was, that nigh she swelt
For passing ioy, which did all into pitty melt.

(6.12.21)

If, in book 1, the poet failed to describe the New Jerusalem because it was "too high a ditty for his simple song" (1.10.55), here he refuses because it seems too low a story for his exalted powers. The very rhetoric with which he admits his failure to "contriue" her mother's passion illustrates the tokenism of his interest in Pastorella's fate. His appeal to an actual mother to take his place as describer serves only to underline the artificiality of the restitution. If Calepine's expression of the hope to be found in the lost child signifies his appropriation of the poet's initial aspirations, here the dismissal of Claribell's joy to that described by "some mother" who might feel it more demonstrates that the optimistic illusion of restoration now lies in the mind of the reader. Detaching himself from his characters, the poet alienates himself from his audience as well, finding in his isolation from everyone's fate the godlike indiffer-

ence he wishes to emulate. The indifference is manifest in the unfinished
plot lines of the first story (the chronicle of the characters in cantos 1
through 12) and explained in the poetic emergence of the second story
(the biography of Colin Clout in canto 10).

As Colin Clout, the poet is privy to information denied both character
and audience. He understands how to make a world. And that world, the
pleasance of book 6, like the Garden of Adonis of book 3, is a temporarily perennial circle where "trees of honour stately stood / And all winter
as in sommer bud" (6.10.6) But, unlike the Garden of Adonis, this is an
original retreat. In book 3 Spenser pays tribute to his classical sources,
but in book 6 the origin of the pastoral is personal. Acidale is a *locus
amoenus* of his own design and the gradually unveiled graces are his
creation.

They are viewed at first through Calidore's eyes and then explained by
the poet. Calidore sees but cannot know. A character divorced from the
poet, he is limited in his vision:

> Vnto this place when as the Elfin Knight
> Approcht, him seemed that the merry sound
> Of a shrill pipe he playing heard on hight,
> And many feete fast thumping th' hollow ground,
> That through the woods their Eccho did rebound.
> He nigher drew, to weete what mote it be;
> There he a troupe of Ladies dauncing found
> Full merrily, and making gladfull glee,
> And in the midst a Shepheard piping he did see.
>   He durst not enter into th' open greene.
> For dread of them vnwares to be descryde,
> For breaking of their daunce, if he were seene;
> But in the couert of the wood did byde,
> Beholding all, yet of them vnespyde.
> There he did see, that pleased much his sight,
> That euen he him selfe his eyes enuyde.
> An hundred naked maidens lilly white,
> All raunged in a ring, and dauncing in delight.

$$(6.10.10–11)$$

Aware that he is an intruder, Calidore first hears the music and the sound
of thumping feet and then sees the dance. He views a temporal and spatial
figuration; the dancers move in time (range) and form a circle (are arranged). In stanza 10, the central figure is not—as she materializes later—
the shepherd's love. Rather, the source of the sound attracting Calidore
and providing the rhythm for the dancing feet is the shepherd later

identified as the poet. The play in the twice used "raunge" on seemingly random movement and on ordered structure underlines the ambiguous nature of the vision's source. At first Calidore discloses the shepherd in the act (in the midst) of choreographing the apparently spontaneous dance enveloping him. The time sequence becomes important. The vision unfolds gradually before Calidore's eyes (as it does before the reader) in a pattern that seems, partly because it is circular, to have sprung full blown and completed. But Calidore actually witnesses a chronological development. The poet, in stanza 10, stands in the center and is at the origin of the dance, even though, in stanza 12, Calidore spots a damzell at the helm:

> All they without were raunged in a ring,
> And daunced round; but in the midst of them
> Three other Ladies did both daunce and sing,
> The whilest the rest them round about did hemme,
> And like a girlond did in compasse stemme:
> And in the middest of those same three was placed
> Another Damzell, as a precious gemme,
> Amidst a ring most richly well enchaced,
> That with her goodly presence all the rest much graced.
>
> (6.10.12)

The garland is both floral vision and poetic sequence in the line "And like a girlond did in compasse stemme." The three circles—"garland . . . compasse . . . and stem"—are connected, in their juxtaposition, to a control resembling one fixed by the stars on a mariner's instrument of navigation.

Though the shepherdess stands in the middle, her presence there is devised (compassed) in the garland of praise, as verse, created by the initiating poet piping at its stem. Apostrophizing himself, the poet repeats his initial triumph:

> Those were the Graces, daughters of delight,
> Handmaides of Venus, which are wont to haunt
> Vppon this hill, and daunce there day and night:
> Those three to men all gifts of grace do graunt,
> And all, that Venus in her self doth vaunt,
> Is borrowed of them. But that faire one,
> That in the midst was placed parauaunt,
> Was she to whom that shepheard pypt alone,
> That made him pipe so merrily, as neuer none.
>   She was to weete that iolly Shepheards lasse,

> Which piped there vnto that merry rout,
> That iolly shepheard, which there piped, was
> Poor Colin Clout (who knowes not Colin Clout?)
> He pypt apace, whilest they him daunst about.
> Pype iolly shepheard, pype thou now apace
> Vnto thy loue, that made thee low to lout:
> Thy loue is present there with thee in place,
> Thy loue is there aduaunst to be another Grace.
>
> (6.10.15–16)

The poetic act emerges at once lonely ("that shepheard pypt alone") and uniquely happy (the shepherd piped "so merrily as never none"), suggesting the oneness at the beginning of the world and evoking Adam's joy in Genesis as he brought forth Eve. At the center of creation stands the seductive and fecund woman waiting for the male seed: Colin Clout playing on his pipe. The deified shepherdess illustrates that, despite the divine surroundings, poetry finds its origins not in what is given but in what has been denied. The shepherd pipes because the shepherdess makes him "lout." While the poet is laid low by love, he glorifies his lady, transforming her into the goddess he worships. He gives her the ability to give without ever letting her down from the Petrarchan pedestal he has erected.

As the poet progresses from a description of the ring to a focus on the center, he identifies Clout as himself and emphasizes the centrality of the shepherd. "He pypt apace, whilest they him daunst about." Clout keeps time while the Graces follow his lead, forming a circle at his beck and call. The poet urges himself on: "Pype iolly shepheard, pype thou now apace"; in the "apace" he stresses the compulsion of the playing; in the "now" he underlines the immediacy of its quality. The music itself brings the shepherdess physically and momentarily to him. As he pipes "now apace," she is present there with him "in place." Because of his playing, the lady is drawn into the center and joins him "in the midst," which becomes the instant ("present") of the vision itself. Time and space converge as the circle closes in on itself and absorbs, through the process of "aduancement," the heavenly qualities—both the being and the giving—implied in the presentness of Grace.[4]

Curious to know why he was so "rapt with pleasaunce," Calidore disrupts the dance with his question about its source. The vision has passed, but it lives on in the memory of the shepherd-poet. As he retells it, he recreates the circle and obeys his self-given mandate to play on. Describing the shepherdess, he deifies her again:

> Another Grace she well deserues to be,
> In whom so many Graces gathered are,

Excelling much the meane of her degree;
Diuine resemblaunce, beauty soueraine rare,
Firme Chastity, that spight ne blemish dare;
All which she with such courtesie doth grace,
That all her peres cannot with her compare,
But quite are dimmed, when she is in place.
She made me often pipe and now to pipe apace.

(6.10.27)

The "souerainty" he gives will keep her firm in chastity and thus immune from the blemish of spite—the malice of the Blatant Beast who is the enemy of the book. By rendering her at once divine and impenetrable, Clout "places" her in the heavenly sphere where, like Adriadne's crown, she dims all the lesser stars of the world. The image of the shepherdess resurrected by the poet is identical to the vision Calidore originally saw. But the telling enables Clout still to pipe "now apace." She is both inspiration and song, the poet's beginning and end, calling him into being, but being because of his piping. The presence of her gift is defined in the absence of his gratification. She is and is not, as the poet commands. He appears and then withdraws as she shines "in place," dimming all earthly things with her heavenly brilliance. Exalting his love, Colin Clout submits to her and acquires in that "louting" the energy necessary for poetry. He remains piping rather than realizing his dream. In the unfolding appearances—wrought by Clout's transcription of the original vision—he keeps her, like the Adonis of book 3, "eterne." She lives not because of natural generation but because of artistic succession. In repeating the vision, Clout provides the duplication realized by Genius in 3.6. Further, like the Venus of book 4 and the Isis of book 5, he becomes for her "syre and mother" in one. In his repetition, he eternally makes her. And the remaking depends on her elusiveness—her refusal to say yes or to participate in the sexual cycle central to the characters. The shepherdess is duplicated not by the child she might one day produce but by the song the poet "pype[s] now."

Calidore, on the other hand, still hoping to experience the satisfaction of his desire, is compelled by the "enuenimed sting" (6.10.31), forcing him to retreat from the mountain. Cupid's dart is for him the call of love, waiting to be fulfilled—the serpentine attraction of Pastorella who, like the temptresses compared to Britomart in 5.8.1–2, beckons the courteous knight to her womb. But Pastorella is left without the consummation of marriage. Throughout the sixth book, the poet demonstrates his fascination with the possibilities represented by the revitalizing energy of passion. At the same time he seeks a oneness in his art that sexual increase negates. In the end, happiness emerges as a vision achieved (like the

shepherd piping merrily alone) inwardly, at the center, by the poet himself. While the foundling theme depends upon generation, making it the
source of a saving perpetuation, Spenser only halfheartedly submits to its
rituals, recognizing that his inspiration lies in the death of love. To know
this, to have experienced for a moment such an unraveling loss, is to have
found the source of poetry. The image of the poet perpetually in pursuit
suggests an ongoing passage from the formed through the formless to the
formal as Clout regales the negatively responding woman with his posi-
tively echoing song. A fecund world beckons, a Petrarchan woman denies, and the shepherd counters, piping merrily apace, with an impulse—
always achievable, always renewable—of his own.

When Spenser dismisses the foundling formula after subscribing, in
Pastorella's story, to so many of its details (her name, her sojourn with
Meliboe, her knightly rescue, her tearful reunion, her "rosie mark"), that
dismissal recalls the mournful conclusions of Una, Amoret, and
Britomart in the earlier books. When he unveils so beautifully the
goodness of art in Colin Clout's vision, his doubts about marriage and its
dynastic impetus, revealed in the conflicting stories of book 1 and in the
dangling heroines of books 3 through 5, are crystallized. Spenser's initial
use of the formula and his subsequent abuse of its concluding rituals
coincide with his tribute both to the magnificent flowering of nature and
to the necessary withdrawal of art. He can achieve that duality because he
redefines nature. The nature Spenser echoes in his art is the succession of
the vegetative kingdom; the nature he denigrates is the generation of
animal lust. Keeping alive through his piping the denying shepherdess, he
solves the art/nature controversy by imitating, in Clout's regenerative
song, the fecund Genius of the garden and the androgynous Venus of the
myth.

Shakespearean Explorations

> Into that native shield she slid,
> Mistress of an idea, child
> Of a mother with vague severed arms
> And of a father bearded in his fire.
>> Wallace Stevens, "Celle qui fût Héaulmiette"

"My dismal scene I needs must act alone," Juliet realizes when she finalizes the rupture with her parents initiated by her question "What's in a name?" In the balcony scene, Juliet is the "mistress of an idea," giving birth to a Romeo, emboldened by the confidence she plants in him, strong enough to "take [her] away." The lovers become parents to each other, forfeiting their families for love. Similarly, Richard III wills his isolation—only he aims to achieve power. He casts himself as the castaway of nature, emphasizing his inherited defects so that he can justify an aggrandizement proportionate to the deprivation he magnifies. Richard III is master of an idea of himself, based on a desolation central to the foundling experience. Though they are essentially different plays, both *Richard III* and *Romeo and Juliet* describe an art that fails to compensate for the comfort (*Romeo and Juliet* 4.3.17) sacrificed in the heroes' struggle to create their own lives.

107

9
Richard III and Genesis 4

Because the foundling theme presupposes that the child is the victim either of an unrelenting fate or of cruel parents, the lost phase presents a state of coveted innocence. Even a Cain can blame his villainy on the cruel manipulation of the God who exposes him. Richard III works the notion of inherited disability to his advantage, consciously exaggerating the size of his loss to lend himself a motive for a gain so colossal that it makes him the largest man in the world. By so doing, he launches a chain reaction leaving him no alternative but to behave precisely as Cain did in Genesis. In the bible, God sets Cain up for the fratricide; in Shakespeare's play, Richard frames himself, emphasizing what Freud calls his "congenital disadvantages"[1] so that he might appear the unhappy pawn of fate.[2] He creates a deprived self even as he bewails the conditions presumably causing his loss. Assuming the part of Cain, Richard invents his destiny, shrinking into the mold of disenfranchised victim simultaneously as he waxes into the role of grandiose avenger.[3] The Cain story dramatizes abandonment in terms of sibling rivalry. The underpraised child feels exposed by both the parent and the favored brother. Alone, he has no protector. To get back to, and perhaps at, the parent, the child must eliminate the competition.

Richard wills himself into being what God cornered Cain into becoming: the scorned child of nature.[4] After rejecting his homage, God argues against Cain's despair by promising his ascendance over his brother:

> And the LORD said unto Cain, Why art thou wroth? and why is thy countenance fallen?
> If thou doest well, shalt thou not be accepted? And if thou doest not well, sin lieth at the door: and unto thee shall be his desire, and thou shalt rule over him. (Genesis 4:6–7)

The ostensible comfort only increases Cain's pain because God predicts a dominion he seems already to have retracted. First he refuses the offering;

then he tells Cain that the rejection is immaterial, and later, in a still further reversal, he informs Cain that he will "rule" over his brother. While denying the competitive urge, God prefabricates conditions that fan its flames (his dismissal of Cain's gift), generating a situation in which Cain's appetite for rulership is intensified (his forecast of Cain's triumph over Abel). As God baits Abraham by telling him that his seed shall be plentiful (even as he demands that he sacrifice the only means toward achieving the promised fertility), so God promises Cain dominion while denying him the occasion to achieve it. In the Abraham story, God threatens to deprive the father of his anticipated fecundity. Here God negates Cain's power by scorning his efforts to "do well." Given the simultaneous granting and withholding, Cain can only get what he wants by eliminating the competitor.

When God questions Cain about Abel's whereabouts after the murder, Cain's answer—"Am I my brother's keeper?"—sums up his pain. Cain's belligerence after the act has a retrospective impact. Does God expect the belittled child to have been large enough to overcome his involuntary inferiority? Should he have become the protector of his subjugator? Is Cain the keeper now in terms of the preserver of his family? Or is Cain to be the keeper in terms of the ruler or restrainer of his brother? If he is to be the perpetuator, then he must deny God's promise that he will triumph over his brother. If he is to be the dominator, then he must ignore the dictum to be uncompetitive. Choosing to eliminate (and thereby not to keep) Abel, Cain permits himself both to become a self-measurer and to hold unchallenged rule. His fratricide, within the parameters defined and the expectations fostered by God, becomes inevitable. *Richard III* goes one step beyond Genesis 4. Cain supplants his brother; Richard attempts to obviate both the brother and God as he creates the conditions of deprivation that fuel his desire to become the sole determinant of his destiny.

In the three major soliloquies of the play (1.1.1–38; 1.2.231–67; 5.3.178–204), Richard creates, enhances, and then destroys the self that God urged Cain to become. First, he establishes for his personal use the motive God gave Cain, contracting his image into the shadow of the rejected brother. Second, he enjoys the freedom such a rejection gives him, multiplying his vision in the "glass" of the determined usurper. Finally, in the last speech, he sets the tactics of self-victimization and self-aggrandizement against one another as he attempts to deny the multiplicity of the second soliloquy and return to the solidity of the first. But the man who became a god capable of judging his own deeds discovers that he must in the end condemn his creation and convict that evil in the self whose seed he planted at the opening and over whose growth he presided in the course of the play. The first two soliloquies are built on mutually dependent rhetorical premises that Richard carefully establishes in order to raise himself into a position whereby he can become the central and cosmic arbiter of his world. The third, which alternates hysterically between the first two, illustrates that the logic of the initial structure fails—that there is a void in the artificially created helm of Richard's universe, an emptiness in the self he tried so hard to inflate.

While Cain is innocent until God corrupts him by rejecting his offering and tantalizing him with power, Richard starts out by appropriating for himself the role God thrust on to Cain:

> But I, that am not shap'd for sportive tricks,
> Nor made to court an amorous looking-glass;
> I, that am rudely stamp'd, and want love's majesty
> To strut before a wanton ambling nymph:
> I that am curtail'd of this fair proportion,
> Cheated of feature by dissembling Nature,
> Deform'd, unfinish'd, sent before my time
> Into this breathing world scarce half made up—
> And that so lamely and unfashionable
> That dogs bark at me, as I halt by them—
> Why, I, in this weak piping time of peace,
> Have no delight to pass away the time,
> Unless to spy my shadow in the sun,
> And descant on mine own deformity.
>
> (1.1.14–27)

Scorning the "amorous looking-glass" of present and future regeneration because of its expansionist image, Richard denies himself a normal past. His aim here is to diminish the size and reduce the pace of those large words—"strutting" and "ambling"—not by demonstrating how he can be doubled and quickened by love but by showing how he is deprived and slowed down by nature. He describes himself as unfinished, "sent . . . /Into this breathing world scarce half made up." While everyone else seems to have world enough and time for love, Richard calls himself incomplete; instead of a full person searching for a double, he is a half-self, striving for fulfillment. He begins hiding from ladies. He concludes "halting" before dogs. Unable to pursue as lover, he is harassed as freak. While others run, he limps, his retardation attributed to the whim of a fate causing him to be born before his time. As the pretended pawn of a nature that he calls deceptive, Richard himself dissembles, challenging the force that created him by imitating, as does Cain, its capacity to destroy. He elects to evade the role of lover (or multiplier of selves) by embracing the part of villain (or destroyer of others):

And therefore, since I cannot prove a lover
To entertain these fair well-spoken days,
I am determined to prove a villain,
And hate the idle pleasures of these days.

(1.1.28–31)

With the double-edged "determined," he expresses his ambition to succeed in terms of his compulsion to proceed as the stepchild of nature. And, with the hypothetical "since," he shapes his role in the play as a reaction to an irresistible force, initiated chronologically prior to his birth, ordaining an inherited injustice that he must subsequently—and without apparent alternative—rectify. Made small himself, he will reduce the world. At the opening of the speech, he spurns the amorous reflection of love; here he covets the diminishing shape of himself. His shadow becomes a child for him, a separate creation he designs for his own purpose. It is the source of delight because he has made it and because he can control (by maneuvering himself into the right position) its growth. His shadow is his first follower, one of the many subsequent nothings over which Richard will have dominion. It reacts totally to his whim, reflecting only the image he wants to project.

In Genesis, God gives Cain a motive, egging him on by making him feel less worthy than his brother. Here Richard spurs himself forward by pretending an inadequacy that leaves villainy as the only logical solution. He begins by placing himself in the psychological position of Cain, shrinking as he reiterates the privation attributed to a cause not his own. While Cain reacted to a situation beyond his control, Richard wills his reduction as the first step in the aggrandizement he seeks. His opening monologue represents a self-imposed diminution that leaves him no where to go but up. The figure he creates in the shadow he seeks is shrunken by an art seeking to place the blame on nature.

It is the same art that allows him to become the very lover he earlier claimed he could not be. Posing as the Petrarchan suitor, Richard succeeds by flaunting his weakness. In the first scene he plans murder to avenge nature; in the second, he excuses killing to quell love. Richard's defense lies in his appeal as victim. The neglected child of Nature, the rejected pursuer of Anne, he wins by proclaiming his loss. The first two soliloquies, coming so close together, reflect Richard's modus operandi:

I'll be at charges for a looking-glass,
And entertain a score or two of tailors
To study fashions to adorn my body:
Since I am crept in favor with myself,

I will maintain it with some little cost.
But first I'll turn yon fellow in his grave,
And then return, lamenting, to my love.
Shine out, fair sun, till I have bought a glass,
That I may see my shadow as I pass.

                                              (1.2.260–68)

In the second soliloquy he chooses to see his shadow only temporarily
while awaiting the mirror he earlier scorned. What accounts for the difference? Certainly Richard does not change his mind because Anne falls
for his pleas. Already here he declares he will not keep her long. The
reversal occurs because Richard begins to practice the process of self-
judgment he defined in the first speech. Pronouncing himself the loser of
nature and the failure of love, Richard finds the esteem he needs to
continue. What he discovers in winning Anne is that his method works.
Richard delights now because he is "crept in favor" with himself. The
word "favor" is telling because it suggests a state of good will on the part
of a superior power. Slowly, Richard ascends the ladder of recognition
that begins and ends with his own judgment. The looking-glass reflects
his private formulation. In the first soliloquy, when he rejected the mirror, he sought the "shadow" of a shape he himself would impose. Now he
seeks that darkness only as a temporary stopping point on his way to the
sun, which he (as Marvell's lovers do theirs) makes "run." His mandate to
the orb, "Shine out, fair sun," reflects not only a feeling of optimism but a
sense of control. If the mirror of the first soliloquy was contingent on the
movement of others (the woman in whose shining eyes he might see his
image, the children in whose similar features he could extend his lineage)
upon whom he could never depend, the looking-glass he here seeks needs
only Richard. If he can dominate the sun and command it to shine, he
feels confident enough to master himself. At this point, Richard sees the
mirror simply as a reflector of what he wants; in the tailor's glass he can
still be the designer of himself. Setting himself up at the Copernican
center of his fifteenth-century world, and peopling that world with the
Richards of his looking-glass, he becomes self-sufficient. No longer
courting the "favor" of a woman, he emerges the creator and governor of
his personal demesne.

If the first soliloquy has Richard seeking a cause for his villainy, the
second reflects his delight with what he found. Both speeches present
frames for behavior still to take place. The first ends with Richard's
reduction, the second with his growth as Richard transforms the shadow
of his fall into the shining of his triumph. But without the artificially
created initial cause of inadequacy, the subsequent exultation in evil

would have been impossible. The progression from shadow to sun occurs because of Richard's control over the body he now sees worthy to adorn. By freeing himself from an obligation to nature, Richard enables himself to become his own master. And, by emphasizing in the first speech how he has been cheated, he erases (in the second) any sense of guilt. Because he has arranged the conditions whereby the world rejected him, he can now create his own standard, regenerating his chosen vision in the mirror he buys. Such a license becomes identical to the comfort God gave Cain. Owing nothing to anybody, Richard raises his own "countenance," ascending, as Cain might have, into a domain he controls. From this psychological vantage point, Richard engineers his assault on the crown. The action of the play is premised on the logic of these two speeches. Both are set up as syllogisms: the first provides a motive; the second, a method for a deification of self, annihilating conventional notions of morality and familial solidarity. By treating his reflection in the mirror as if it were an individuated being he commands, Richard gives himself permission to carry out his plan. Able to feign, he is free to act.

That Richard derives his animus from a source similar to the one God gave Cain emerges clear in his final soliloquy, where the reflexive sense dominates:

> Give me another horse! Bind up my wounds!
> Have mercy, Jesu!—Soft, I did but dream.
> O coward conscience, how dost thou afflict me!
> The lights burn blue; it is now dead midnight.
> Cold fearful drops stand on my trembling flesh.
> What do I fear? Myself? There's none else by;
> Richard loves Richard, that is, I and I.[5]
> Is there a murderer here? No. Yes, I am!
> Then fly. What, from myself? Great reason why,
> Lest I revenge? What, myself upon myself?
> Alack, I love myself. Wherefore? For any good
> That I myself have done unto myself?
> O no, alas, I rather hate myself
> For hateful deeds committed by myself.
>
> (5.3.178–91)

As Richard wakes from the dream in which his demise is forecast, he seems to have forgotten his initial vision of power. His prayer—"have mercy, Jesu"—sounds automatic, spoken out of some prelapsarian, long-distant world where forgiveness might have been possible, uttered, like a faint cry out of the innocent realm he destroyed. When he recovers his senses, Richard analyzes his body from the distance he created: "Cold fearful drops stand on my trembling flesh." With that assessment, he acknowledges the separation of the calculating mind from the weak body it observes.[6] Once having detached himself he can logically ask: "What do I fear? Myself?" Alone in the world, he answers his question systematically, demolishing the self that believes in powers greater than his own. Richard acts as his own interlocutor, subduing his fears with declarative sentences that describe his physical scene ("it is now dead midnight") as a fact of time governed by nature and his psychological scene as a state of mind determined by him ("There is none else by"). Calming his body the way a father might console a child who has had a bad dream, Richard places himself at the apogee of his universe: "Richard loves Richard."

If Richard loves Richard and is (as most texts suggest) the "I *am* I" of this speech, then he, as God to himself, has wrought what Cain wanted. There is neither competitor nor judge. Richard the god and Richard the man are alone. When he comforts himself, Richard returns to the solidity of the first soliloquy where he emerged the wronged child of nature. There he had to cope only with a shadow over which he held complete dominion. His shadow self is the "poor child," the "trembling flesh" who can be forgiven by the god self who originally "abandoned"—and who now comforts—him.

But also unleashed here (in the "I *and* I" of the First Quarto) are the selves revealed in the mirror of the second soliloquy—those manifold replicas Richard sought as he multiplied his power. The shadowy self lies close to the bosom. It is one with its creator. The mirrored selves answer back, unpredictably returning, more sharply than Richard expected, what is there. And the selves (infinitely repeated—Richard and Richard and Richard) turn on their originator to expose what he could (in the comfort of the shadow) hide. The shadow is the conscious creation of the waking mind. It depends on daylight to exist. The mirror dredges up the unconscious that, once opened, pours forth uncontrollably. In the haze of the shadow image, Richard could hide his self-doubt. In the starkness of the mirror image, tiny complexities surface and reverberate. Those multiplying images seem to have a life of their own, overcoming the shadow self with evidence against the god self. If the shadow is guilty, so is the god who created him. And if the shadow is vanquished, the god loses control.

That loss is registered in the contrast between the high point of self-assurance at the middle and the low point of self-censure at the end. As he proceeds, Richard continues with the logic he has used so far, but it breaks down when he alternates between the desire pronounced, in the second soliloquy, to stretch his limits and the need affirmed, in the first, to limit his possibilities. He falls from the god who contains everything to the fool who can retain nothing, spreading himself thin with the tales of "several thousand tongues." His center cannot hold as the many facts condemn the single being and tear him crime by crime. Having willed himself into Cain's position, Richard discovers, as God reprimands in Genesis, that "sin lieth at the door":

> Murder, stern murder, in the direst degree;
> All several sins, all us'd in each degree,
> Throng to the bar, crying all, 'Guilty, guilty!'
>
> (5.3.199–201)

The one man Richard attempts to enclose with the "I am I" is threatened by the compound "all" (the "I and I") who, gathering near, vandalize the logic of his defense. The enclave is challenged by the multitude, the fortress of self so besieged that it can only surrender to what becomes the final fact of the speech: "There is no creature loves me." Richard emerges the abject being he pretended to be at the opening of the play. The story of his abandonment haunts him now, turning his fantasy into fact. The declarative statement of his isolation becomes the source of Richard's concluding interlocution:

> And if I die, no soul will pity me—
> And wherefore should they, since that I myself
> Find in myself no pity to myself?
>
> (5.3.201–3)

Like a disloyal soldier who deserts a losing army, Richard betrays his creation. Depleted of pity, he is emptied of self. Once the fiction is accepted as truth, the god game is over and the man's world begins.[7] At the opening of the speech, Richard begged Jesus for mercy; at the conclusion, he cannot even find it in himself. Having renounced the Christian God and erected himself in his place, Richard discovers, as he searches, that there is nothing to find. He is lost now, forsaken finally not by those powers—God, nature, other men—which he earlier scorned but by the self he created in answer to a fabricated deprivation.

Critics who regard *Richard III* as a history play argue, with E. M. W. Tillyard, that the restored order "is wrought by man's finding his rightful, and hence human, place in God's world."[8] Richard is, as C. P. Rossiter writes, "God's agent in a predetermined plan of divine retribution."[9] Such historical readings render the play parallel to Genesis. There God planned for Cain to be the scourge of the world, tantalizing him temporarily with sovereignty, but ultimately letting him know that there is only one Supreme Being. In *Richard III*, Shakespeare went behind the myth, exploring man's need to try on the suit of authority, not as Cain did, out of revenge for a destined inferiority, but as Richard did, out of a knowledge that a conscious expropriation might become the justification . and hence the source for a retributive annexation. The historical readings deny Richard's complicity in the original plot. While Cain reacted to a rejection imposed upon him, Richard chose to capitalize on his inherited flaws in order to free himself to act. The interest in *Richard III* lies in the exploration of power in the beginning rather than in the restoration of order at the end. Richard renders himself a god because he has mastered what Cain could not control. In exploiting his handicap, Richard emerges, for a while at least, the arbiter of his destiny. When he falls apart at the end, his dissolution reflects the limitations of his method. The art kills the artist, the design crumbling because its base is fictional. Lamenting "there is no creature loves me" (5.3.201), Richard absorbs the alienation of the foundling moment and emerges the pitiful child he at first pretended to be. His final loneliness repeats, in the reality of its enforced reduction, the invented deprivation he used to justify his early acquisitions. None of the inferior beings he subjugated remains to offer what he once refused. There are no comforters for the orphan of this privately caused, self-inflicted, isolation. *Richard III* concludes with its hero as tragically confined as he initially pretended to be. Having designed his abandonment, Richard discovers the reality of its fiction.

10

Romeo, Juliet, and the Art of Naming Love

As a comedy, *Romeo and Juliet* might have been a perfect foundling story. Like Florizel and Perdita, the lovers would have forced their feuding parents to reconcile, celebrate their marriage, and await the grandchildren who would perpetuate their strengthened dynasties happily ever after. The formulaic possibility makes the tragedy all the more devastating. Romeo and Juliet are so eminently findable partly because they are so willingly losable. They never hesitate to run away or to use the art of the adoptive interlude to satisfy their willing natures. It is nature that is unwilling in this play, failing to corroborate the lovers' faith in its foundation. They rethink their lives for love, expecting (as they do in the first balcony scene) that the cyclical structure of nature will support them, but finding (as they discover in the second balcony scene) that the cycle grinds away indifferent to their plight. *Romeo and Juliet* is structured around the art/nature controversy evoked in jest by Mercutio when he baits Romeo in act 2:

> Why, is not this better now than groaning for love? Now art thou sociable, now art thou Romeo; now art thou what thou art, by art as well as by nature. For this drivelling love is like a great natural that runs lolling up and down to hide his bauble in a hole. (2.4.88–93)

Mercutio maintains that the complete man uses art to implement nature. Reason distinguishes man from the beasts, raising him above all other creatures. Groaning, drivelling, and lolling are mannerisms of the "natural," a creature victimized by, rather than master of, his situation. Sociability—the art of applying art—signifies for Mercutio the measure of manhood. Conversely, love marks a retreat from the task of forming, and so becoming, fully what man was destined to be. To "hide" is to fail to evince the jewel of the realized self. The natural man, obsessed with baubles and holes, babbles. The artistic man is articulate, in control of both his desire and his tongue.

But Mercutio's ideal is threatened by forces that make him see how fragile is the art he praises. Announcing, in act 3, the gravity of his wound, Mercutio makes the figure of his speech literal by facing the very fate he feared:

> Ask for me tomorrow and you shall find me a grave man. I am peppered, I warrant, for this world. A plague o' both your houses. Zounds, a dog, a rat, a mouse, a cat, to scratch a man to death. (3.1.98–102)

Peppered, "sped" (3.1.92), and scratched (3.1.94) by Death, as he claimed Romeo had been "stabbed . . . run through" (2.4.15) and "cleft" (2.4.16) by love, Mercutio is badgered into the grave, rendered solemn instead of witty, the steward (an Elizabethan meaning of "grave") instead of the owner of his being. Nature retaliates against complexity with forthright thrusts, scratching at the artistic veneer, leveling everything. Mercutio's presence in the play demands that the flatness of nature be enriched by the fullness of art.[1] His injury—foreshadowing the heroes' fate—reduces him to the animal—dog, rat, mouse, cat—he hoped to overcome. For Mercutio, art is the opposite of death because it stabilizes the self, endorsing man's formulative power in the universe. Art makes the whole self visible by completing nature.

During the opening sequences, the lovers approach that completion. The introductory sonnet (1.5.92–105) and the balcony scene (2.2) manifest their wish to share an art that at first recognizes and then builds upon what they hope to be the solidly present natural cycle. The happiness in the early scenes stems from a belief found first in the lovers' creative capacity, evidenced in the Genesis allusions of 2.2.37–47, and second in the earth's created endowment, found in the references to its foundation in 2.2.133–35. They use art in the expectation that it will force nature to yield. Romeo and Juliet exult in the strength they impress upon each other and the support they derive from the world, fixing the metaphors for their love on the certainty of the constellations (2.2.184–85) and the reality of the senses (2.2.165–66). They move from moments of self-doubt to periods of self-confidence (2.2.28–34; 2.2.139–41) when they confirm their feelings in a natural setting. In the first half of the play the lovers cement their union with what they think is a firm physical bond. Their effort throughout the second half is to salvage what they made despite the inexorable retreat of the structure underlying their hope. In the aubade (3.5.1–35), they begin to see nature's indifference to their plight. Just before she takes the Friar's potion (4.3.15–59), Juliet envisions her physical end as a mental collapse, the animal in her destroying the reason earlier directing it. The edifice of love topples when she imagines her uncontrolled body "dashing" (4.3.54)—as Mercutio had seen the brutes "scratching" (3.1.102)—her defenseless brains. Nature obliterates in that scene the art that it had once sustained. The tragedy in the final acts is defined when the lovers witness the erosion of the foundation binding their union. Nature withdraws, leaving an empty art—hollow statues intead of supple bodies. Yet if Mercutio saw, in his gravity, the leveling power of the bestial, Romeo and Juliet remember in the vault the soaring strength of the creative. What remains in the enveloping gloom at the end is the recollected light of the beginning, the lovers determined to secure the golden vision originally inspiring them. Romeo seeks to preserve with a kiss (5.3.120), and Juliet to restore with an embrace (5.3.166), the image of the life they named together.

That sense of cooperation is apparent from their first encounter, where the ingredients of fairy-tale romance become the properties of actual experience. Their love begins with the Pygmalion formula—the melting of art into life. That fusion allows them in turn to live that life as art:

> *Romeo.* If I profane with my unworthiest hand
> This holy shrine, the gentle sin is this:
> My lips, two blushing pilgrims, ready stand
> To smooth that rough touch with a tender kiss.
> *Juliet.* Good pilgrim, you do wrong your hand too much,
> Which mannerly devotion shows in this;
> For saints have hands that pilgrims' hands do touch,
> And palm to palm is holy palmers' kiss.
> *Romeo.* Have not saints lips, and holy palmers too?
> *Juliet.* Ay, pilgrim, lips that they must use in prayer.
> *Romeo.* O, then, dear saint, let lips do what hands do:
> They pray: grant thou, lest faith turn to despair.
> *Juliet.* Saints do not move, though grant for prayer's sake.
> *Romeo.* Then move not, while my prayer's effect I take.
>   (1.5.92–105)

When Romeo calls Juliet a shrine, he makes her both the container of the saint and the thing contained, exalting and embodying her. Unlike the conventional sonneteer, he can touch the Petrarchan woman and yet not die of her. When Juliet takes his hand, she raises him to the level at which he has praised her, allowing him to join her on the same plane. The gratification is immediate. Through the submerged metaphor of the ladder, Juliet's indulgence emboldens Romeo to climb even one rung higher:

"Have not saints lips, and holy palmers too?" It is Juliet who maintains his equilibrium, keeping Romeo from toppling over with audacity or tripping out of dizziness. Like Rosalind with Orlando, she puts him "to entreaty," refusing him momentarily so that they can have more "matter" to discuss, letting him take the reins by giving him something to do. The lovers alternatingly provide tasks for each other, extending the arena of the possible to the height of the exhilarating. Demanding prayer, Juliet keeps Romeo looking up. Begging Juliet to join him in the name of balance, Romeo reminds her of the possibility, always near, of despair. If she falters now, things may reverse themselves. Romeo might slip into the void. Similarly, Juliet suggests the need for equanimity when she argues for continual vigilance. If Romeo stops praying to her, he becomes inconstant, himself subject to change. In concert they find a solution:

> *Juliet.* Saints do not move, though grant for prayer's sake.
> *Romeo.* Then move not, while my prayer's effect I take.

Permitting the kiss, Juliet bestows herself on Romeo, acknowledging her feelings by consenting, but encouraging his suit by permitting it "for prayer's sake." Such a constant coming-to-be and fulfillment is the promise of the sonnet, a mutual exchange to keep from changing. The gentleness (granting) of nature preserves the stillness (or permanence) of art.

The banter about movement anticipates Florizel's speech to Perdita in *The Winter's Tale:*

> When you do dance, I wish you
> A wave o' th' sea, that you might ever do
> Nothing but that, move still, still so,
> And own no other function.
>   (4.4.140–43)

When Perdita moves, she inspires Florizel to imagine the stillness (eternity) of her reproductive powers. Granting without moving, Juliet creates a different permanence. In the late play, Shakespeare's sympathies are clearly with the procreation Florizel equates to the sea. Perdita progresses toward maternal fulfillment to be achieved in future "stillness." In *Romeo and Juliet,* the young lovers attempt eternity through the art of their current lives. By allowing Romeo to imbibe the kiss, Juliet breathes life into him, becoming the muse of the prayers he formulates to get more. The lovers in this play find a state that is at once solidly unchangeable ("saints do not move") and softly yielding ("grant for prayers' sake"). They provide thereby the conditions—Juliet by imploring Romeo to pray afresh, Romeo by urging Juliet to kiss again—that foster both immediate gratification and persistent desire. They stimulate each other by coming to life, simultaneously as they guarantee each other by surfacing as art, in an abiding vehicle for love.

The continuity of speaking becomes the incentive for expansiveness as the lovers meet again in the Capulet garden. When Juliet sighs, Romeo soars. Yet, as he praises her, he places himself in the exigency of the moment prior to the initial sonnet. In the garden, separated from Juliet, he seems to have fallen off the imaginary ladder. It is only through the process of the balcony scene that Romeo finds the courage to climb to, and enjoy, the heights of their first encounter. Overhearing Juliet, he is overcome:

> O speak again bright angel, for thou art
> As glorious to this night, being o'er my head,
> As is a winged messenger of heaven
> Unto the white-upturned wondering eyes
> Of mortals that fall back to gaze on him
> When he bestrides the lazy-puffing clouds
> And sails upon the bosom of the air.
>
> (2.2.26–32)

Like the saint of the initiating sonnet, Juliet is a bright angel. But unlike the woman contained in the earlier metaphor, this Juliet is unreachable—a "winged messenger of heaven." She moves majestically in the spheres above, while Romeo, in typical Petrarchan fashion, falls back into the ground below. Bereft of energy, Romeo is overtaken, his eyes fixed on the soaring and powerful eagle of his image.

Juliet restores him, not out of the vacuous clouds in the sky but out of the solid substance of the earth. In the garden, she becomes a kind of Adam in reverse, unnaming the universe, decomposing—in order to re-compose—the world. Her language is reminiscent of Adam's dream in Genesis:

And the LORD God said, It is not good that man should be alone; I will make him a help meet for him.

And out of the ground the LORD God formed every beast of the field, and every fowl of the air; and brought them unto Adam to see what he would call them: and whatsoever Adam called every living creature, that was the name thereof.

And Adam gave names to all cattle, and to the fowl of the air, and to every beast of the field; but for Adam there was not found an help meet for him.

And the LORD God caused a deep sleep to fall upon Adam and he slept; and he took one of his ribs, and closed up the flesh instead thereof.

And the rib, which the LORD GOD had taken from man, made he a woman, and brought her unto the man.

And Adam said, This is now bone of my bones, and flesh of my flesh: she shall be called Woman, because she was taken out of Man.

Therefore shall a man leave his father and his mother, and shall cleave unto his wife: and they shall be one flesh. (Genesis 2:18–24)

The process of Eve's emergence is curious. First God forms every beast of the ground for Adam to name, so that he becomes the arbitrary and wholly conscious word maker. But the woman—the companion—was taken not out of the earth but from Adam's rib. He was made less in order to be made more. Further, the moment of Adam's greatest creativity occurs during a trance, the height of his powers realized during the depths of his sleep.

In the joy of Adam's awakening the two negative components—the usurping of the body, the surrender of the mind—do not detract from the pleasure of discovering the wholly made being. Adam still names the woman, as he had all the other creatures, but he names her after himself since she had been taken out of him. He feels a double triumph, returning to himself—the namer, discovering himself—the maker. The joy is immediate but it contains a sense of the past (*now*, in view of these accumulated facts) and the future (*now* in sight of these forthcoming events). It is temporary, preceded by Adam's absence in the conditions necessary for creation, and foreshadowing a future leavetaking (of mother and father) in the circumstances governing marriage. History surrounds the *now* with anterior and ensuing attrition, but it can never retract the exhilaration of believed-in power.

In the balcony scene, Juliet allows Romeo to experience Adam's moment of happiness by giving him, however fleetingly, a belief in his own creative and generative endowment. The scene in the Capulets' garden parallels the scene in Eden. At first Romeo is, through his own hyperbole, rendered as passive as Adam, while Juliet finds the means to bring him to himself. She begins by defining her terms:

> 'Tis but thy name that is my enemy:
> Thou art thyself, though not a Montague.
> What's Montague? It is nor hand nor foot
> Nor arm nor face nor any other part
> Belonging to a man. O be some other name.
> What's in a name? That which we call a rose
> By any other word would smell as sweet;

So Romeo would, were he not Romeo call'd,
Retain that dear perfection which he owes
Without that title. Romeo, doff thy name,
And for thy name, which is no part of thee,
Take all myself.

(2.2.37–47)

Juliet is in sequence God, then Adam, then Eve, until Romeo awakens, newly baptized, ready to act and name and be Adam to the Eve she has become. The exchange of roles continues throughout the scene as one enters the other and as each revels in the self the other made and found. At first Juliet reforms Romeo by unnaming him, starting with hand and foot, returning him, part by part, to the nature of his origin, and directing him, name by name, toward the art of his aspiration.[2] In the recreative moment she seems like the God of Genesis. But in the next line, she descends to the place of Adam:

What's in a name? That which we call a rose
By any other word would smell as sweet.

(2.2.43–44)

By equating Romeo to the rose, Juliet renders him part of the found universe that she, like Adam, merely names. The more she speaks the more she retreats, enlarging Romeo's promise as she diminishes her role. He is next the precious ("dear") beginning and the ultimate ("perfect") consummation of her life. When she asks him to substitute herself for his name, Juliet crawls into Romeo, emerging the nascent Eve of Genesis. She becomes in that act, flesh of the flesh, bone of the bone which is their mutual compound. With the command, "take all myself," she makes Romeo simultaneously the God who "took" Eve from man's rib and the Adam who named her because she was so taken. Through this bestowal, Juliet converts Romeo into the begetter of her life—"all." The mutuality of the exchange continues as the lovers toss each other compliments testifying to their power to rework the world. Romeo in turn makes Juliet his Adam and his God:

I take thee at thy word.
Call me but love, and I'll be new baptis'd:
Henceforth I never will be Romeo.

(2.2.49–51)

By taking Juliet at her word, Romeo credits her as mortal and believes in her as "saint" (2.2.55). She is, as he was to her, his origin and destiny. If she renames him, he will be reborn, no longer the old Romeo but the "new baptis'd" self. Such a rebirth is premised on a creative mutuality that neither is ashamed to call love. The Romeo who earlier lay gazing in passivity is now active in appreciation, ready to "tear" the word (2.2.57) Juliet cannot stand and prepared to dare the world (2.2.68) that tries to stop him.

Recovered, Romeo reveals how he entered Juliet's enclave. He compares himself retrospectively to the bird he called Juliet, flying in backward glances to the now attained heights:

> With love's light wings did I o'erperch these walls,
> For stony limits cannot hold love out,
> And what love can do, that dares love attempt:
> Therefore thy kinsmen are no stop to me.
>
> (2.2.66–69)

And Juliet, too, speaks in excess:

> My bounty is as boundless as the sea,
> My love as deep: the more I give to thee
> The more I have, for both are infinite.
>
> (2.2.133–35)

Both lovers emerge limitless, their happiness based on the illusion of strength (paralleling the moment after Adam's trance) inspired by the renaming process. Juliet's goodness (bounty) equals her generosity and that equals her boundlessness. Like the sea returning to the shore, she crests with still more to give, expressing, in the reference to the ocean, a metaphorical response in depth to Romeo's earlier bestriding bird. The extension builds on nature, stretching its limits to a vision of grandeur and moving from a fixed center to an unending circularity. Juliet's concluding expansion downward to the sea corresponds to Romeo's initial praise upward in the skies, rounding the universe now.

Having defined her fullness in her capacity to give, Juliet casts herself as the maker Mercutio praised. When she calls Romeo the "god" of her "idolatry" (2.2.113), she summarizes the progress of the scene where Romeo moved from passive worshiper to active Adam to idealized god. As god, Romeo is the object of her adoration; as idol he is the image she carved. The illusion of creativity satisfies their craving, forming a temporary frame of love around the core of nature. In the course of time, reality will break through with the dark truth of its unyielding presence but for the moment, at least, the lovers seem to be able to bend the lines of the world to the encircling purposes of their art. The process by which they fix their beliefs reaffirms the method by which they professed their love. They pull back, in their fear of losing, to the moment before the joy of finding, and surface redoubled in their faith. Immediately following the mutual discovery of power, Romeo, left alone, is afraid he imagined everything:

> O blessed blessed night. I am afeard,
> Being in night, all this is but a dream,
> Too flattering sweet to be substantial.
>
> (2.2.139–41)

Repeating Mercutio's admonition about dreams (1.4.54–94), Romeo tests his own expanded expectation against the inflationary process of wish fulfillment. All this is "too flattering sweet" he whines, worried that, inspired on insufficient grounds, he has been cozened into believing himself the hero of his own life. During that moment alone, Romeo loses faith in art because he has lost touch with nature. The sweetness of the night seems unsubstantial. It cannot be seen or smelled or heard.

Only by regaining his physical bearings can Romeo rekindle his artistic faith. When Juliet calls him back, he combines sight and sound by comparing her voice to music:

> How silver-sweet sound lovers' tongues by night,
> Like softest music to attending ears.
>
> (2.2.165–66)

Juliet's voice yields a light that awakens touch ("soft"), sound ("music"), sight ("silver"), and taste ("sweet") to the nature of the world. With the word "attending," Romeo pushes his present listening into a still-unrealized act. The sweetness premises more than a "now." It anticipates a "then," leading him to expect fulfillment because of an instantly realized substance.

Similarly, Juliet prolongs the word of departure so that it becomes the signal for return:

> Good night, good night. Parting is such sweet sorrow
> That I shall say good night till it be morrow.
>
> (2.2.184–85)

Sound restores Juliet's faith here just as it earlier bolstered Romeo's. If she continues calling it will, as surely as day follows night, be morrow. By centering her prolongation of the "now" on a permanently recurring cycle, Juliet attempts to guarantee her word. Her art is linked to nature, the sorrow of the parting "sweet" because the repetition of the sound will make Romeo return to her when the sun completes its journey in the sky. While the lovers rejoice in their own creative capacity, they hinge that potential on what they assume to be the firm foundation of nature's reserve. If they began the balcony scene with an imagined dream of love, they close it with a felt experience of life, reiterating with the sweetness a solid sight and sound and smell. That sweetness recalls Juliet's rose, which appeared as a promise of what nature, signaling its immutable "bounty," might give.

In the opening acts, the lovers feel confident that the shrine they build has the strength of a sympathetic cosmos at its center. They seek in the natural world the protection once supplied by the families they desert. But their early belief is fleeting. What they discover subsequently is that the center does not hold. The foundation keeps slipping out from under them. The last acts "scratch" away the illusion of art, leaving only—what Mercutio found—the indifference of nature.[3] In the first half of the play, Romeo and Juliet turned figurative flights of fancy into practical possibilities. The birds of their immediate imagination signified the high level of their ultimate aspiration. They gave to each other, when they exchanged vows, the capacity to realize a creative life. The more they touched, the more they sparked the universe with their desire, converting external objects into manifestations of their inner state. They named the world out of the selves they promoted in each other. But in the final acts, the bird songs of their early expansive similes are replaced by the death knells of reductive actuality.

The aubade begins with Juliet's attempt to transform the lark into the nightingale she covets, just as in the balcony scene she had reconstructed Romeo into the lover she desired:

> Wilt thou be gone? It is not yet near day.
> It was the nightingale and not the lark
> That pierc'd the fearful hollow of thine ear.
> Nightly she sings on yond pomegranate tree.
> Believe me, love, it was the nightingale.
> . . . .
> Yond light is not daylight, I know it, I.
> It is some meteor that the sun exhales
> To be to thee this night a torchbearer
> And light thee on thy way to Mantua.
> Therefore stay yet: thou need'st not to be gone.
>
> (3.5.1–5, 12–16)

Romeo's perception, she claims, is shaped by the pressure of a reality she fears, the hollow in his ear pierced by his failure to believe in love.

Sensing the vacancy, Juliet tries, as she had so successfully earlier, to stuff it with the bird of her imagination. In her efforts to prolong Romeo's stay, she asserts the logic of her calculations, rendering the light Romeo paints an exhalation of the sun, a torch left as a remainder from the day before instead of a signal sent as a herald of the morn ensuing. Such a wish to reverse time is based not, as her "sweet sorrow" speech was, on the certainly seen and solidly stable cycle of the fixed star but on the dubious gift and sudden miracle of the variable meteor. With the redundant "I know it, I" she desperately recalls the strength of her earlier intuitions about nature and her previous assertions of being, both of which empowered Romeo to find his way with her. Juliet clings to the assumptions of self and the vision of nature inaugurating her reformation of the world. It is Romeo this time who reminds Juliet that reality foils them:

> Night's candles are burnt out, and jocund day
> Stands tiptoe on the misty mountain tops.
> I must be gone and live, or stay and die.
>
> (3.5.9–11)

On the one hand, day flattens Juliet's heightened expectations, reducing her hopes to the mist of dreams. On the other, day stands ready, poised like a dancer, to begin the journey across the sky launching (with the tiptoe) the inevitable succession of the spheres and manifesting (with the jocund) the utter indifference of the planet. The aubade contrasts to the balcony scene, the lovers issuing to each other the responsibility for dealing with nature, the necessity of parting from their dreams.

Romeo commands Juliet to say what he has already seen; she orders him, in turn, to do what he himself has proposed:

> It is, it is. Hie hence, begone, away.
> It is the lark that sings so out of tune,
> Straining harsh discords and unpleasing sharps.
> Some say the lark makes sweet division.
> This doth not so, for she divideth us.
> Some say the lark and loathed toad change eyes.
> O, now I would they had chang'd voices too,
> Since arm from arm that voice doth us affray,
> Hunting thee hence with hunt's-up to the day.
>
> (3.5.26–34)

In act 2, the sound of voices signaled an awakening of the lovers' faith; now the rousing echo of nature initiates the destruction of hope.[4] With the line "arm from arm that voice doth us affray," Juliet acknowledges the defeat of the body through the devastation of the mind. Romeo and Juliet

are torn apart (physically frayed) by the voice that makes them psychologically fearful. Left armless (defenseless) they no longer can enclose
nature within the sphere of their desire. The sight of day increases the
sound of their lamentation (woe as exclamation), leaving them, as Mercutio had found Romeo in the beginning, subjugated by sound, overwhelmed by sight, the very forces they had, in act 2, so well mastered.
Their eyes are now turned downward toward the grave as they feel themselves betrayed by, rather than formulating, reality:

> *Juliet.* O God, I have an ill-divining soul!
> Methinks I see thee, now thou art so low,
> As one dead in the bottom of a tomb.
> Either my eyesight fails, or thou look'st pale.
>   *Romeo.* And trust me, love, in my eye so do you.
> Dry sorrow drinks our blood.
>
>   (3.5.54–59)

Parting this time, Juliet describes Romeo not as the enshrined saint she
might bring to life, but as the contained body nature has already cast in
marble. In the first balcony scene, the lovers instilled liquid life into each
other; here dry sorrow drinks their blood, sucking the life they had
formed, sapping the expectations they raised. Earlier, Romeo and Juliet,
the creative artists, felt themselves infinitely ready to give; now nature,
the controlling force, manifests itself as inexorably destined to take.[5]

While "dry sorrow" attacks from without in act 3, "cold fear" circu-
lates from within in act 4. When she imagines her death there, Juliet
extends the fear of the aubade until it reaches every part of her body,
moving from the torn arms to the frozen marrow of her being:

> I have a faint cold fear thrills through my veins
> That almost freezes up the heat of life.
>
>   (4.3.15–16)

The fear is active, penetrating Juliet's body, controlling her totally. In the
potion-taking moment, Juliet reverses the process of the balcony scene
where she used her mind to construct the Romeo she desired:

> O, if I wake, shall I not be distraught,
> Environed with all these hideous fears,
> And madly play with my forefathers' joints,
> And pluck the mangled Tybalt from his shroud,
> And, in this rage, with some great kinsman's bone
> As with a club dash out my desperate brains?

O look, methinks I see my cousin's ghost
Seeking out Romeo that did spit his body
Upon a rapier's point! Stay, Tybalt, stay!
Romeo, Romeo, Romeo, here's drink! I drink to thee!

(4.3.49–58)

Here death becomes all physical. It smells and shrieks and environs her until she sees herself madly playing with her forefathers' joints and in a rage dashing out her desperate brains.

While she speaks, Juliet turns the faith, for which Romeo prayed in the initial sonnet, into the despair he feared. The corpses closing in on her smash and depress her spirit. Having begun with a brain hopeful enough to create a body, she ends here with bodies powerful enough to unmake her mind. Death for Juliet, as it was for Mercutio, is "madness"—the dashing, the confounding of reason. Already in the throes of her anticipated derangement, Juliet imagines Tybalt's ghost avenging Romeo. As she drinks the potion, she bids Tybalt "stay," seeking to keep from her lover—in order to prevent him from feeling—the despair that has overtaken her. Similarly, Romeo will "stay" with Juliet to stop "Death's pale flag" (5.3.96) from advancing on her cheek. Faced with the onslaught of unavoidable fate, both lovers attempt somehow to preempt it, to overtake it before it unmakes them. They die in an effort to revive the image of the heroic selves they once made possible.

If, in act 4, Juliet contemplates the body quelling the mind, Romeo remembers, in act 5, the mind infusing the body. His famous dream speaks of the power they had together experienced:

I dreamt my lady came and found me dead—
Strange dream that gives a dead man leave to think!—
And breath'd such life with kisses in my lips
That I reviv'd and was an emperor.

(5.1.6–10)

Once more, Romeo turns Juliet into the goddess inspiring him to strength. She breathes "such life" into him that he feels, as Adam did for the moment of naming, the maker of the world. He gives her the ability to give him a life of creative power. In *Antony and Cleopatra*, Cleopatra dreams there was an emperor Antony who, after his death, becomes the energetic source of her final act. But here, the dreamer is the emperor, having already been granted ("leave to think") the energy to control his life. This mutual bringing to strength by memory (he dreaming her reviving him; she imagining him restoring her) counterbalances the encroaching leveling to weakness by destiny.

If Juliet sought to protect Romeo from Tybalt, so Romeo takes on death, finding in the tomb the same monster that Juliet saw. But if Juliet, with the potion, envisions a future based on dissolution, Romeo, in the vault, seeks to preserve a past premised on consolidation. Act 4 ends with Juliet feeling only the darkness. Act 5 ends with each lover recovering light. In his last speech, Romeo reverses the process by which he came to life in the early sonnet. There, the lovers kissed, advancing from stillness to movement. Here Romeo retains—with a kiss (5.3.120)—the beauty originally prompting him to move. Similarly, Juliet dies with "a restorative" seeing the kiss as a means for revitalizing the shrine of the self Romeo worshiped.

> I will kiss thy lips.
> Haply some poison yet doth hang on them
> To make me die with a restorative.
> Thy lips are warm!
>
> (5.3.164–66)

In actively stalking Death, the lovers deliberately revive the golden images inspiring their union.[6] The statues the Montagues erect are merely symbols of the conscious artifice their children, following Mercutio's philosophy, struggled to preserve.[7] Doing their own undoing, Romeo and Juliet retain the vision that enabled them, however briefly, to name and so reclaim their lives in love.

Acknowledging her fear in act 4, Juliet calls her family back to her and confesses that she misses the support sacrificed when she so willingly deserted them. Facing every aspect of that fear, she seeks to shield Romeo from it and to offer him, even in the grave, the hermitage of parental protection. Richard III became his own protector, creating a shadow self and a shielding self. This enclosed family gave him the motive and the license for unlimited expansion. But in the end he abandons even his own creation. When he claims "there is no creature loves me," he emerges the orphan of his own ambition. Similarly orphaned, Romeo and Juliet find in each other at least the buffer nature failed—in their parents and during the interlude of their escape from them—to provide.

A Womanly Discovery

I went deeper and deeper into the woods and some time at the height of the afternoon wandered into a stand of ancient pine with a porous forest floor of brown pine needles that was so soft you couldn't hear your own footsteps. It was dark in there, there was an umber twilight in lieu of the day, and there seemed to be no unusual busy life at all, no birds, no insects, just this dark place of unnatural quiet. Looking up, I could hardly find anything green. Yet it was not threatening, the solitude was so complete, the stillness so perfect that I felt as if I had come into some vast, hushed cathedral of peace. Not even a Father. I stopped walking and stood very still and listened for I don't know what. And then, right in my tracks I sat down and for a while was as still as everything else.

E. L. Doctorow, *Loon Lake*

In *Richard III* and *Romeo and Juliet*, Shakespeare mined the possibilities of art through characters who, by severing their parental ties, released themselves from the confines of nature. In both plays the family myth is abolished as each hero gives birth to the self he covets. But in *The Comedy of Errors*, *Pericles*, *As You Like It*, and *Antony and Cleopatra* the myth is revived and nature emerges the key to liberation. The heroines of those plays find what they want not by creating their own lives but by embracing what they were given—by approximating "everything else." *The Comedy of Errors* concludes after Adriana, comparing herself to a mother hen, accepts her part as errant wife; the ordeal in *Pericles* is over when Marina, equating herself to the "meanest bird," acquiesces to her minor role in a larger cycle. Similarly, in *As You Like It*, Rosalind is only fully able to arrange the outcome of her life when she admits that she is "many fathoms deep," overwhelmed by the uncertain bottom of love. Once the characters come to know the range and limitations of their own power, they can control the immense feelings and the dynamic forces setting them in motion. Though Cleopatra forfeits her life, she wins her love by acknowledging the element inaugurating her union with Antony. She advances to a "better life" by reexperiencing the "poor passion" of this one. Rosalind (exposed in childhood) and Cleopatra (abandoned as a woman) are analogous foundlings. Their understanding of sexuality—in both its elusive and its bestial aspects—anticipates the direction taken by the women (particularly Perdita and Hermione) who participate in the formulaic plots of the last plays. That recovery of nature includes a discovery of self central to the foundling experience. Despite their losses, Shakespearean heroines find their place in the larger universe, returning always, like the found child, to their reaffirmed origins.

11

Earned Reprieve in *The Comedy of Errors* and *Pericles*

When T. S. Eliot adopts the persona of Pericles in "Marina," he evokes the experience of Shakespearean romance:

> This form, this face, this life
> Living to live in a world of time beyond me; let me
> Resign my life for this life, my speech for that unspoken
> The awakened, lips parted, the hope, the new ships.
> What seas what shores what granite islands towards my timbers
> And wood thrush calling through the fog
> My daughter.[1]

Eliot celebrates the release of Shakespeare's elements—seas and shores—from the storm of uncertainty. The wood thrush parallels the noise that Pericles first, and then everyone else, hears at the conclusion. For Eliot that sound is a birdcall; for Shakespeare it is "the music of the spheres" (5.1.227). But for both poets it represents an awakening to the cycle of nature and the influence of the gods. The rediscovered child promises to "live in a world of time beyond" the narrow limits of the reigning generation. That survival is hinged on the return, through the fog, of the missing daughter.

In Shakespearean romance the discovery lies in a future founded so that the characters might await the word, as Eliot described, still "unspoken." Marina begets him that did her beget (5.1.195), atoning in her recovered presence for the absence of the lost years. Instead of the promised destiny of romance, Shakespearean comedy delivers a fulfilled moment. Rosalind wants neither her father nor her child, just her "child's father." Though *The Comedy of Errors* and *Pericles* are based, as Harry Levin says, on "the vicissitudes of a family progressing through misadventure by sea to recognition under religious auspices,"[2] the early work emphasizes a present realization, the later an ensured dynasty. The difference in the plays can be seen by comparing Adriana, who at the beginning knows neither herself nor her husband, to Marina, who has a center fixed from the start. Adriana develops into a woman aware of her responsibilities. Marina remains rooted to what she already understands herself to be, that "gentle kind and noble stock" (5.1.68) from which she originated. Marina finds the means to perpetuate, Adriana struggles to ameliorate, what was.

The reunion in *The Comedy of Errors* occurs because of lucky circumstances; that in *Pericles* because of divine (and perhaps predestined) intervention. But in both plays the denouement depends on a young heroine who appropriates the function of (in *Errors*) a husband and (in *Pericles*) a parent, an occupation allowing the heroes to experience the recognition for which they wait. In the early play, Adriana's conversion from jealous to loving wife coincides with the comic conclusion. In *Pericles,* Marina's emergence through self-definition heralds the appearance of Diana. The characters earn the good fortune they come finally to inherit. The transformation of the heroines centers on images evoked in Eliot's poem—that of the sea[3] and a bird. In *The Comedy of Errors,* Adriana finds herself by abandoning an unreasoned desire to be consumed by her husband, which she expresses in the famous water-drop image (2.2.126–28), for a realistic ambition to support him by assuming her own identity, a conversion embodied in the lapwing metaphor of 4.2.27–28. Marina, on the other hand, moves from an insistence on her uniqueness, fixed in her idea that the sea outdid itself at her birth, to a sense of her mortality, confined in her wish to be drowned and engulfed by water (4.2.63) or to be obscured, as is the "meanest bird" (4.6.100), by nature. Adriana grows as she finds her identity, Marina as she expends it. But the undertaking and the surrender are associated with an idea of wholeness that comes to Adriana after she pulls herself apart from her husband in order to let him be reborn, and to Marina when she is rejoined with her parents in order to be revitalized herself. Adriana actively negotiates her release by untying the man whom she confounded in her grip. Marina passively awaits the reunion by acknowledging the power of nature to unravel itself. In *The Comedy of Errors,* the recognition coinciding with Adriana's development emphasizes the present. The characters exit "hand in hand, not one before another" (5.1.426). In *Pericles,* the recognition extends into the future; the characters leave to "grace . . . a marriage day" (5.3.76).

Early in *The Comedy of Errors,* Adriana declares herself to be "undividable" from her husband. She establishes from the outset, as most critics agree,[4] her jealous nature, emerging too possessive. But because, through the water-drop image, she repeats Antipholus S.'s very words,

Adriana adopts unknowingly the search for selfhood that is the subject of the play.[5] The alienation imposed on the twins by a haphazard fate is simply appended to her by an erring husband. Thinking the Syracusan to be her Antipiholus, she complains:

> How comes it now, my husband, O, how comes it,
> That thou art then estranged from thyself?—
> Thyself I call it, being strange to me,
> That undividable, incorporate,
> Am better than thy dear self's better part.
> Ah, do not tear away thyself from me;
> For know, my love, as easy mayst thou fall
> A drop of water in the breaking gulf,
> And take ummingled thence that drop again
> Without addition or diminishing,
> As take from me thyself, and not me too.
>
> (2.2.119–29)

Expressing her connection to her husband with the same metaphor that Antipholus S. laments his immersion in the world,[6] she voices her affinity to his twin. In the reiteration she creates a consanguineous chain among the principal characters so that when she tugs at it by reacting, her motion rebounds. The domino effect makes Adriana the central character. When she reverses her position, the brothers fall in place. But this recognition can occur only by a radical change in everyone's direction. At the opening of the play, the characters seek self-knowledge by planting themselves in one another. Antipholus S. plunges in the ocean, hoping to extract the brother who would constitute his completion.[7] He discovers, in falling, that he loses himself in "quest." To surface, he needs to stand far enough away so that he can recognize a resemblance, rather than experience an identity, with his brother. Similarly, by clinging to her husband, despite her intuition that he wavers, Adriana lapses into a losing vein. She becomes, in her desperation, so closely attached that she cannot see herself.[8] As Musidorus urged the desperately in love Pyrocles, she needs to "separate [herself] a little from [herself] and let [her] owne mind look upon [her] own proceedings."[9] The search for identity, so crucial to the foundling formula, is incorporated by the water-drop metaphor. In order to find themselves the characters need to see their uniqueness, to establish their independence from the engulfing water that they view as an embryonic protection. They must surface from their immersions to be reborn. The necessary separation comes about when Adriana changes from passive recipient to active instigator of her fate.

She begins denouncing herself instead of criticizing her husband after she finds the infidelity she suspected verified by her own sister. That confirmation enables her to cut the chain of dependency on which she based her being. Instead of waiting for events to occur, she now will initiate them, adjusting her position from target to source. Expressing her altered spatial orientation in terms of a reversed temporal sequence, Adriana becomes the originator, rather than the subsidiary, of her husband. Pressed by Luciana who believes her invectives, Adriana replies:

> Ah, but I think him better than I say,
> And yet would herein others' eyes were worse:
> Far from her nest the lapwing cries away;
> My heart prays for him, though my tongue do curse.
>
> (4.2.24–27)

By distancing herself in her strategy from the object of her anger, Adriana commences the campaign that will enable her to win. Comparing herself to the bird who nurtures her brood not by smothering the young but by distracting the enemy, Adriana emerges the protector of her husband. In the analogy, she assumes for herself the origin he unknowingly seeks, asserting her responsibility for Antipholus's welfare.

Having retracted from clinging vine to supportive center, Adriana sponsors Antipholus's future by accepting a liability for his past. When the Abbess rebukes her for causing Antipholus's madness, Adriana replies, "She did betray me to my own reproof" (5.1.90). In that acknowledgment, she judges herself to be the victimizer, not the victim, of her husband. Further, when the Abbess attempts to separate the patient from the cause of his sickness, the fight seems an archetypal one of mother-in-law and daughter-in-law,[10] the older woman censuring the younger for the present demise. Adriana, however, refuses the separation, proclaiming herself, by right of "office," the proper minister to his sickness and the true agent for his deliverance:

> I will attend my husband, be his nurse,
> Diet his sickness, for it is my office,
> And will have no attorney but myself,
> And therefore let me have him home with me.
>
> (5.1.98–101)

With the double meaning of "attend," Adriana announces that she is willing to wait for and to serve her husband's release. She becomes both wife and mother, elected to the position by her anxiety to execute its prerogatives. Eager to perform the supportive tasks of her role, she is no longer interested in the reflected glory of her station. When Luciana suggests that she complain to the Duke, she promises:

> I will fall prostrate at his feet,
> And never rise until my tears and prayers
> Have won his grace to come in person hither,
> And take perforce my husband from the abbess.
>
> (5.1.114–17)

Imploring the Duke, Adriana creates a "scene" and thereby orchestrates the conclusion simply by commanding all the characters on stage.

Without her zeal to "take" her husband back to the restorative nest, the comic revelation might never have occurred. Having renounced everything by humbling herself to the Duke, Adriana wills the loss that permits the concluding discovery. The sacrifice of her self-denial prepares for the pleasure of everyone's self-recognition. Adriana successfully maneuvers into the antecedent position she sought, supervising her husband's recovery as she guides his renaissance. Once the past is rectified, the present can be reassembled. In the clarity of separation, the characters return to themselves. When Dromio of Ephesus meets his Syracusan counterpart, he acknowledges his innocence:

> Methinks you are my glass, and not my brother:
> I see by you I am a sweet-fac'd youth.
>
> (5.1.417–18)

Released at last, he sees in his detached brother a reflection of himself. Lining up hand in hand, the characters are ready in the present to find themselves as good.[11] But it is Adriana's acknowledgment of responsibility for her husband's mistakes that instigates the chain of events reflected in the now-clarified "glass." Having first viewed her own face in the mirror of self-judgment, she changes her "aspect" and manipulates the actors so that they subsequently appear in just the right place, at precisely the right time, for comic coincidence to occur.

In *Pericles*, Marina, too, acts as a compelling force—not by reversing herself to permit a new reflection but by maintaining herself so that the world is drawn to her, as the moon is to the sea.[12] She is Persephone and Demeter, mourning doubly, in the guise of both missed child and grieving parent:

> No, I will rob Tellus of her weed,
> To strew thy green with flowers; the yellows, blues,
> The purple violets, and marigolds,

> Shall as a carpet hang upon thy grave,
> While summer-days doth last. Ay me! poor maid,
> Born in a tempest, when my mother died,
> This world to me is as a lasting storm,
> Whirring me from my friends.
>
> (4.1.13–20)

In *The Winter's Tale*, Perdita strews lilies over Florizel to make her marriage bed, assuring the prince that the flowers will be like a "bank for love to lie on," promising him not death in love but life in marriage. Perdita is clearly Persephone, the maiden who plucked the flowers to awaken her physicality. But in this play, Marina is more complex, having strewn the flowers not to find her future but to celebrate her past. Like Persephone, she is "whirred" from her friends; but unlike Persephone, she finds no future in another world. Marina is relegated to this one, torn, but left behind to wonder about her origins. Aligning herself with Tellus (Demeter), she seems only aware of becoming her parent. Obsessed with her need to extend backward into her mother, she is unable to progress forward into herself.

The initial tempest becomes a lasting storm, removing her, through the whirlwind, from the source of her being. Because of the tempest she is, though actually on dry land, still at sea, left without meaning in the dynastic structure, insisting that the persistent recollection of that difficult time might lend her a safe harbor in this distant place. Mourning the loss of Thaisa, Marina becomes Demeter searching for her daughter, sensing at once that in order to find herself, she must be the mother of her mother. The recapitulation of her birth story is the central event of her life. She relives both aspects of the foundling event—experiencing the parent's desperation and the child's desolation—with the initiating rupture. Thus she gives herself a larger role, insisting on the mythical proportions of her story. When she walks along the shore inquiring of Leonine the direction of the present wind, she overwhelms the distracted servant (who is contemplating the moment of Marina's death) with information about the circumstances of her birth.

> When I was born.
> Never was waves nor wind more violent.
>
> (4.1.58–59)

Recalling the heroic action of her father during the storm, Marina proclaims the originality of a birth that occurred at an unprecedented moment in time.[13] Necessary to her sense of self is a concept of the uniqueness of her life. Child of a king who "galls" his royal hands to take on the sea, she emerges also a child of the elements, the tempest at her birth accompanying the labor pangs of her mother. The habitual pattern of the winds and waves—like the embryonic link between mother and child—was ruptured when she was born: "Never was waves nor winds more violent." Citing the unusual turbulence of the water, Marina asserts with the "never" that chronologically prior to, and immediately proceeding from, that moment, the earth behaved predictably. Only at her birth was it in extremis. If she is unable to reconstruct her origin, nature itself, similarly paralysed, is unable to repeat its unique moment of violence. In the certainty of that "never," Marina possesses not just the past but the future. Through the rhetoric of her injunction, she controls, as did Demeter during the period when she searched for Persephone, the cycle of the earth. In the opening sections of the play, Marina mothers herself, doubling her importance because of her disproportionate burden.

Yet, if Marina was eager, in Tharsus, to assert her aristocracy by telling her story, so is she anxious, in Mytilene, to preserve it by maintaining her silence. Determined now to be anonymous, Marina at first mourns that the pirates "had not o'erboard / Thrown me for to seek my mother" (4.2.63–64) and then prays that the "gods / Would set me free from this unhallow'd place / Though they did change me to the meanest bird / That flies i' th' purer air" (4.6.97–100). She moves from a compulsion (expressed in Tharsus) to make nature into the mirror of her situation, to a desire (in Mytilene) to make her situation the mirror of nature. If earlier she insisted that her birth coincided with an unheard moment in the earth's cycle, here she longs to be engulfed by the generalized, typified, pattern of it. To find her mother, she now chooses to be drowned by the sea; to escape, she would exchange her exalted state with the lowliest bird. Adriana finds herself by choosing the lapwing as a form that will reflect her mind; similarly, Marina is discovered after appropriating from nature a creature that her mind can become. Praying to be drowned, Marina uses the water as a protective embryo. She ends where Adriana began, with a metaphor from the sea reflecting her insignificance in comparison to the immensity of nature.

In *The Comedy of Errors*, Adriana changes and thereby allows the comic release to occur. Imitating the lapwing, she begins to assume a responsibility for her state. In *Pericles*, Marina acknowledges that she might need help to be set free. She is ready now to release the self to which she so tenaciously clung, and she prepares for that release by admitting to the power of nature. If earlier she tells her story in order to demonstrate her extraordinary presence in history, now, in Mytilene, she remains silent, yielding to the ordinary sequence of time.[14] She becomes simply a girl engulfed by the sea rather than the girl embodying its name. By waiting until asked to tell who she is, she passively allows the recognition that she formerly actively sought.

It is Pericles' command to tell her story, to "recount . . . speak . . . deliver" (5.1.141, 154, 168), that impels her to reveal her past. The story is inched out of her until finally all the parts are reconciled, the ends returned, by the proofs and talismen common to foundling plots, to the beginnings. Pericles' remark, "thou that beget'st him that did thee beget" (5.1.195), signifies not just a revival of faith in the future but a restoration of faith in the past. In the last scene the generations move backward, Pericles assuming center stage. The events now happen to him; he reigns. But it was Marina's compulsion to hold on, followed by her willingness to let go, that enabled Pericles to experience, once again, the commanding position of parental power. Once the parent/child sequence is rectified, so too is the god/human order restored.

As the sea is connected to the moon, Marina is linked to Diana. The goddess controls the people, ordering them to be themselves in order to find one another:

> Before the people all,
> Reveal how thou at sea didst lose thy wife.
> To mourn thy crosses, with thy daughter's, call
> And give them repetition to the life.
> Or perform my bidding, or thou liv'st in woe;
> Do't, and happy; by my silver bow!
>
> (5.1.240–45)

Earlier Pericles implored Marina to tell; here Diana orders him. The goddess urges the man and thereby legitimizes a return to the experience with which the whole cycle began. Pericles is told to mourn, as Marina had earlier, the events that destroyed his life. But Diana's final command is more complex: "Awake, and tell thy dream" (5.1.246). At first, she urges Pericles to relate what has transpired in his sleep—to carry out to the letter the spirit of her decree. But then she solidifies the joy of the reunion by calling the initiating events, rather than the concluding ones, a dream. If Pericles is to live and tell his dream, he is to foretell, anticipate, the future, as well as retell, recollect, the past. When Diana commands him to speak, she summons an awakening to the truth that nature gives as well as takes away, that in "the music of the spheres" is the possibility for reprieve.

For Marina, the reprieve involves more than a retelling of the past. She must relive it. The reunion recalls her compulsion earlier in the play to become her mother and fulfills her desire now to be released from that obsession:

> My heart
> Leaps to be gone into my mother's bosom.
>
> (5.3.44–45)

Marina literally expresses the wish of all foundlings to bring their parents back from the recesses of the dead—to restore their lives by an act of submersion ("being gone" into the other) that makes reparations for the years of separation ("being gone" away from the other). When Marina calls Thaisa "my mother," she converts the stranger before her into a member of the family. She qualifies as the restorer both by the persistence of her pursuit in the past and the insistence of her gallantry now. With her heart in Thaisa's bosom, Marina pumps her back to life. In the recognition moment, Marina enters her mother and then is reborn as herself. Rendering Thaisa as Demeter, she is singly Persephone. Having crawled back into the womb and been delivered, she is released of the burden of the past. When that happens her parents begin to function as parents, her father becoming the instigator, her mother the nurturer. It is Pericles who plants the seeds of the new order when he commands Thaisa to recognize, and accept, her daughter:

> Look, who kneels here, flesh of thy flesh, Thaisa;
> Thy burden at the sea, and call'd Marina
> For she was yielded there.
>
> (5.3.46–48).

Recalling the unity and separation, Pericles restores chronology, assigning the mother to her role in the past and surrendering Marina to her part in the future. With her benediction, Thaisa reenacts a biblical ritual. "Bless'd and mine own" (5.3.49) she says, standing as the intermediary, in the "bless'd," between the gods, whom she calls down on her daughter's head, and the child. Marina belongs to Thaisa as Thaisa belongs to Marina, the two experiencing, in the common bond of womanhood, not only the presentness of recognition but the process of history.

Such a bond enables mother and child to acknowledge both the powers behind time, evoked in the blessing of the gods, and their power in time, captured by their possession of each other. Having seen into themselves and through the boundaries of mortality, they have also seen into themselves within the limitations of nature. In *Pericles*, the future is made possible by the reconstruction of a past thought irretrievable; in *The Comedy of Errors*, the present is made enjoyable by the rectification of a past thought irremediable. But in both plays the ending is earned by women who prove their flexibility. Having found their centers (Adriana by judging herself against, Marina by immersing herself in, nature) they realign—and so affirm—their worlds. The recognition in both plays occurs because their protagonists find themselves through metaphors linking them to the natural cycle. In both, the goodness of art never even comes to the foreground. The adoptive interlude of *The Comedy* is mired in error and confusion, that of *Pericles*, in deception and betrayal. Thus the plays represent an unquestioning acknowledgment of the goodness of nature.

In *As You Like It* and *Antony and Cleopatra*, this endorsment comes only after a deeper probing. The heroines begin by denying their nature. They distrust it and so cannot fully experience the love that would link them to the larger cycle. Both are afraid of the vicissitudes of sexuality and so (Rosalind through her disguise, Cleopatra through her memory) both seek the permanence of art. Rosalind at first tries to extend the safety of the pastoral interlude; Cleopatra attempts to strengthen the certainty of the remembered moment. Finally, risking their security, the heroines accept their nature. In *The Comedy of Errors* and *Pericles*, sex is subsumed by the parental quest. But in *As You Like It* and *Antony and Cleopatra* sex is the subject.

12

The Dream of a Better Life in *As You Like It* and *Antony and Cleopatra*

Shakespeare describes graphically both the physical and psychological devastation of "lust" in sonnet 129, equating it with the Spenserian savagery of *The Faerie Queene* 4.10.46. But the sonnet is not just about the invidious anticipation of sexual encounters; it is also about their elusive aftermath. Through the process of his diatribe, the narrator discovers that nothing solid remains to verify the act, to make the experience less fleeting.[1] In the most revealing line of the sonnet, the man confesses his fear: "Before a joy proposed; behind a dream."[2] Anticipated pleasure is the joy proposed. The chase presents an object worth having. But the second half of the line is harder to gloss. Some texts footnote "dream" as nightmare,[3] a reading that makes sense in terms of the contrast between the expected delight and the disappointing act. But that definition denies the vehemence of the opening and the helplessness of the couplet. When he complains that "behind" lies a "dream," Shakespeare suggests that the proof of having becomes the woe of wanting again. Memory transforms the consummated hope into a new desire.[4] Once realized, the act itself becomes an insecurity instead of a foundation, a "dream" instead of a fact. The recollection of a sexual encounter stimulates the longing to have it once more, making it seem as if it had never occurred.

One way of holding the dream or of stilling the experience is to produce a child who would irrefutably testify that the consummation occurred. The foundling theme confronts the issue of confirmation through the progeny who serve as a verification (or, as in sonnet 3, a concrete mirror) of memory. Thus, the parental desperation with the initial loss becomes retrospective; the child is not only a link to the future but a "proof" of the past. In *As You Like It* and *Antony and Cleopatra*, Shakespeare reflects on a different angle of the loss. In sonnet 129 he explores it through a male narrator who apprehends, in the course of the poem, the bestiality and annihilation of the sexual act. In the last plays, he deals with parents who transfer those perceptions on to the children they expose and recover. But Rosalind and Cleopatra are, even before they start, exposed. Beginning where others leave off, their background is the "behind" of sonnet 129. Both analogous foundlings (Rosalind knows, but cannot be with, her father; Cleopatra has, but cannot keep, her lover), they face their abandonment alone. No one adopts them. Nevertheless, they use the art of the interlude to protect themselves; in fact, their art is the same. Each (Rosalind in action, Cleopatra in memory) wears a male disguise, becoming the other they pursue. In that becoming they overcome the brutality and nihilism the narrator of sonnet 129 describes, incorporating, by facing it, the psychological void that is equivalent to the physical loss in foundling stories.

At the opening of *As You Like It*, Rosalind is sad because of her missing past. Linking expectation to experience, she mourns her absent father and refuses to be merry:

> Dear Celia, I show more mirth than I am mistress of, and would you yet I were merrier? Unless you could teach me to forget a banished father, you must not learn me how to remember any extraordinary pleasure. (1.2.2–6)

Rosalind associates joy with a vanished time of innocence. As her father is banished, so too is her belief in fun. For Rosalind, "extraordinary pleasure" is connected to her missing childhood. To have her father gone from this place now is to be unable to recall that time when pleasure seemed possible.

In a scene parallel to this early one, Celia, again noting Rosalind's sadness, asks whether her sorrow is for her banished father. Rosalind's reply—"No, some of it is for my child's father" (1.3.11)—sets the play in a new direction, moving its scheme from remembered loss to anticipated discovery. But the shift in emphasis occurs only after the wounding initiation is fully taken into account. Rosalind's defense mechanism, heightened by the brutality of her father's banishment, keeps her from blithely falling, easily believing, in love. Because she cannot constitute a world where "extraordinary pleasure" is retainable, Rosalind doubts the possibility of reaching for it now. When she speaks of her future husband, her "madness" is precisely the same as the one she felt for her banished father:

> *Rosalind.* O how full of briers is this working-day world!
> *Celia.* They are but burs, cousin, thrown upon thee in holiday foolery; if we walk not in the trodden paths, our very petticoats will catch them.

Rosalind. I could shake them off my coat: these burs are in my heart.
Celia. Hem them away.
Rosalind. I would try, if I could cry hem and have him.

                                                          (1.3.11–20)

Rosalind's sense of possibility is based on her knowledge of history. Given her present situation, how can she command a union that would somehow entail a rebirth? When Rosalind thinks of Orlando, she sees only briers in her way. The rose at the center is surrounded by a barrier of the "working-day," thrusting happiness too far away in the past, and therefore too inaccessible in the future, to pluck. The pain of not having is lodged in Rosalind's heart; it constitutes her dramatic situation. She can neither tuck Orlando away from her mind nor cough him up. Rosalind is caught because she cannot ease the pain of love's absence and succeed in winning the "pleasure" of its presence. Because she sees the connection in time between a secure past and a stable future and because she knows that both states are somehow obscured by the pressures of the immediate, she has no illusions about how difficult it might be to find release ("hem") and hold on ("have him"). Even when she reaches the Forest of Arden, Rosalind seems constantly aware of the fallen world she cannot evade.

The most important fact about the forest for Rosalind is that it is postlapsarian. It contains winter and rough weather. It includes Jaques for cynical melancholy, turns natural trees into artistic books,[5] and provides the identical fodder for the love game in all the Petrarchan (Silvius and Phebe) and lascivious (Touchstone and Audrey) gamuts she knew before. The ostensible escape route, which Celia so hopefully advocates, simply provides a setting for the real world to play. The Arden of *As You Like It* is not the Bohemia of *The Winter's Tale;* there occurs here no transformation because of location. Nature does not heal the suffering that might occur at court.[6] When Rosalind soothes Silvius, she discovers more of the same: "Searching of thy wound / I have by hard adventure found mine own" (2.4.41–42). Attempting to escape, she returns all the more heavily home. What should be the pastoral enclave of an adoptive interlude merely hits her with an originating pain. But though the world affords no refuge, she creates her own protective artifice: the disguise. With it, she manages to "hem" and "have him" using a combination of rueful remembrance and preemptive worrying. In short, she escapes by hitting where it hurts most. Emboldened by the armor of her disguise, she puts herself in the psychological position where she can forge an inward estate that defies, and so is fortified against, the outward world she seems to scorn. This revolution takes place, at the very moment Rosalind seems most unwilling to believe in it, immediately after she minimizes romance in act 4, when she equates her private sense of its dismal history and depressing destiny to her public ridicule of past and future lovers. Rosalind's confession to Celia about the depths of her love (4.1.195–206) provides the audience with the assurance that the dream of achieving it prevails despite her denial of its feasibility.

In her proviso scene, she stretches the working-day world back to its beginnings, setting up the briers even as she reaches for the rose. When Orlando threatens to die in his own person at Rosalind's refusal, she answers:

> No faith, die by attorney . . . men have died from time to time and worms have eaten them, but not for love. (4.1.89, 103)

Her banter is hedged with legalities. Taking love to the bar, she sentences it to oblivion because, in the timed sphere of the brier, it cannot survive. The working-day world is one of humiliating accident not exalted heroics. Rosalind's final appraisal measures the life span in terms of the death span. The past inched forward from "time to time" (4.1.103), each generation merely breeding more food for worms. Men end, despite their noble endeavors, like animals. Similarly, the future is predictable. When Orlando swears he will love her "for ever, and a day" (4.1.137), she counters that he should "say a day, without the ever . . . Maids are May when they are maids, but the sky changes when they are wives" (4.1.138, 140–41). If the past is boring because of its inevitable decline, the future is frightening because of its anticipated sophistry. In her revisionist archives, death is unavoidable; in her mapped-out future, infidelity is inescapable. The past is dwarfed because everything (great lovers, "foolish swimmers") seems the same; the future is depreciated because everything (lovely maids, laughing hyenas) dwindles into a meaner shape. To exalt history is to be misled by man's inflated image; to bank on time to come is to be gulled by woman's painted face. In her analysis, Rosalind arrives at the position of sonnet 129. Love appears incredible as retrospect, futile as prospect; base (a worm) in its history, savage (a hyena) in its future. When yesterday is banished, tomorrow seems untouchable; the briers of the foreseeable eclipse the rose.[7]

Accused by Celia of having maligned her sex and destroyed her nest, Rosalind counters that she merely protects her center:

> O coz, coz, coz, my pretty little coz, that thou didst know how many fathom deep I am in love! But it cannot be sounded. My affection hath an unknown bottom, like the Bay of Portugal. . . . No. That same wicked bastard of Venus, that was begot of thought, conceived of

spleen and born of madness, that blind rascally boy that abuses everyone's eyes because his own are out, let him be judge how deep I am in
love. I'll tell thee, Aliena, I cannot be out of the sight of Orlando. I'll
go find a shadow, and sigh till he come. (4.1.195–98, 201–6)

With the simultaneous movement inward (toward the oceanic depth of
the Bay of Portugal) and outward (toward the imagined heights of Mount
Olympus), Rosalind escapes the boundaries of the world she mocked,
entering the wilderness of an uncharted place and an undetermined time.
Spatially and temporally she evades both the court, which everyone else
scorns, and the forest, which she alone penetrates. However, in maintaining that the depths of her love are to be neither sounded by man nor
measured by time, she buttresses her feelings from the enemies she anticipated. In making her love into a dream so deep that no one can fathom it,
Rosalind casts herself as a dreamer, sighing in the shadows. She turns
herself inside out, trading the snappy persona of the proviso for the
soppy victim of this confession. But even as she keeps her love far away
(so many thoughts beyond) from the outside world, Rosalind outlines the
scheme of her recovery. When she tells Celia that she cannot "be" out of
sight of Orlando, she defines her existence as a revelation she will have to
arrange. To "be" she must be seen. Her task is to bring the speculative to
the working-day—to make the imagined viable, the unsoundable audible.
Rosalind in the shadows of retirement is where the narrator of sonnet 129
is only after his worldly consummation. For the moment, she holds her
life in suspension, waiting until she comes within the visual range of
Orlando. Then she will make the abstract concrete despite her premonition that coming out might initiate the cycle of disintegration she mocked
in her proviso. But because she is already immersed now—so deep in
love—even a temporary surfacing later seems worth the risk.

Orchestrating the recognition, Rosalind grants to everyone, and especially to herself, the sight lost in the gap of absence. When she speaks of
magical restoration, she means the coming-to-be that will occur when she
beholds Orlando and is beheld by him. While, in her "fathom" speech,
she allies her love with unreachable places, in her conclusion she thinks
only of precise location. Promising Rosalind's return, she maintains:

I know into what straits of fortune she is driven, and it is not impossible to me, if it appear not inconvenient to you, to set her before your
eyes tomorrow, human as she is, and without any danger. (5.2.65–68)

To emerge "human" as she is, she must be set before Orlando's eyes; she
must, in short, be seen by him. When she commands the time and place

of the reunion, she vows to come out of the arena of her dream and face the test of its possibility:

> Tomorrow meet me all together. . . . As you love Rosalind meet.
> (5.2.113, 119)

The "meeting" she arranges forces the visible public world and her inviolate private one to collide. Encountering Orlando, she agrees to confront ("meet") the enemy, time, as it exists in the working-day world. She will then find ("meet") the love she declared could never materialize there. The meeting becomes that mutual accord that brings her into being and validates her existence. The final recognition is phrased in terms of sight. In defining herself as already belonging to her father and lover, Rosalind presents herself within the parameters of a past and future she thought unattainable. With that presentation she comes into existence for the others. The Duke and Orlando respectively declare:

> If there be truth in sight, you are my daughter.
> If there be truth in sight, you are my Rosalind.
> (5.4.116–17)

As daughter and wife, Rosalind fulfills the promised meeting by appearing as herself. When Hymen sings of "earthly things made even" (5.4.109), she speaks of antonement as the unity of vision that Rosalind, by believing in both the depths and heights of her love, has made possible. Though Hymen is present at the end, it is Rosalind who is the comic engineer of her life, having called the meeting to order and having brought her dream into the open. In the equalization process, Rosalind has descended from her reverie, not with the expectation of recapitulating "extraordinary pleasure" in a banished pastoral, or of realizing impossible joy in an unreachable utopia, but in the assurance of sharing with her lover the inner vision that earlier she kept hidden. With her love in full sight of everyone, she is ready to reveal and be revealed, to come into the promised being she left languishing in the shadows.

When *As You Like It* opens, Rosalind lacks a past and a future; both seem to be banished with her father. It is only in the course of the play, as she opens up her self to an imagined and boundless world deep within, that she gains the strength to test it out in the limited and imperfect sphere outside. Rosalind begins without a beginning, having lost faith in proposing hope because for her there never was a joy behind. But she concludes with a vision she is willing to share with everyone so that, for a moment at least, they might see with her, human as they are, the fathoms she has

found in the prospect of Orlando. Cleopatra, on the other hand, begins
with a joy she wants constantly to renew. She fears losing the moment of
initiation, that bud upon which she has grounded her existence. Both
Rosalind and Cleopatra accept the fleeting dream of sonnet 129 as a fact
of humanity. Rosalind is the ingenue too cautious to try; Cleopatra the
aging woman afraid of not having another chance. But both are able,
through the experience of their plays (Rosalind by sharing Orlando's
persuasion in love, Cleopatra by feeling Antony's desolation in death), to
follow and so actualize their dreams. They dream of what they lost before
they began: the protective nurturing of love. And they find it because
they are willing to accept its fleetingness. In brief, they take what they
can get, and that suffices. For Rosalind, the dream world lies within the
confines of her heart. Full sight of Orlando bares it before the world. For
Cleopatra, it lies without the borders of this life. Full sight of Antony will
wait until she leaves behind the flesh she thought so vital to her being.
Once having formulated the rose of their desire, they pluck it shame-
lessly, embrace it wholly. For Rosalind, the quest involves an admission
that, to realize her dream, she must allow it to wallow in the less-than-
perfect present; she must "meet" it in this world and at this time. For
Cleopatra, the dream becomes something she, at the end of the play, is
about to receive. She will experience then what she had before: the presence of Antony. If Rosalind at first doubts the possibility of love because
it was heretofore snatched from her, Cleopatra begins with a memory she
longs to bring forward into the present, having found so often in the past
Rosalind's "extraordinary pleasure."

At the start of the play, Cleopatra attempts to prevent herself from
seeing what, by the end of act 3, she acknowledges on a public scale: her
immersion in nature, not just in its sensuality but in its permutation.
When Caesar's messenger intrudes upon her court without advance
notice, Cleopatra acknowledges her diminished state as the decline of the
very flower Rosalind longed to touch:

> Against the blown rose may they stop their nose,
> That kneel'd unto the buds.
>
> (3.13.38–40)

Comparing herself to the tainted blossom that cloys the appetite, she
recalls how the bud of herself commanded homage. In her image of what
she has become to Caesar, she expresses what, earlier in the play, she
feared she might emerge to Antony: too old to be desired. But her tone in
act 3 has changed. Here she philosophically admits, as she formerly had
hysterically denied, the inevitability of decline. If, in *As You Like It*, the

rose was idealized, too obscure, in *Antony and Cleopatra*, the rose is realized, too accessible. Rosalind at first pushes her desires into an abstraction that kills them off as possibility. Cleopatra acknowledges that, by experiencing them as fully as she did, she unknowingly partook of the death she attempted to evade. In accepting herself as part of the nature she so much enjoyed and so much believed she could exploit, Cleopatra assumes, and hence is prepared for, the death she fears. The fate terrifying her has, by the end of act 3, already occurred. Once she learns to accept change—and to understand her connection to an evolving world— Cleopatra is ready to enter the dream that sets her free. Her suicidal longings do not spring suddenly out of an apprehension of her link to Antony in death, but arise gradually out of an extension of her relationship to him in life. She moves from an early desire to be immortalized by an art of love, expressed in 1.3.33–37, through an intermediary wish to be involved in the volatility of love in act 2, to a final willingness to be dissolved in a proof of love in act 4. It is Antony's absence in Rome, not his death at the end, that prepares Cleopatra for her final triumph.

Cleopatra at first idealizes the past because it seemed to preclude transformation:

> Nay, pray you, seek no colour of your going,
> But bid farewell, and go: when you sued staying,
> Then was the time for words: no going then;
> Eternity was in our lips, and eyes,
> Bliss in our brows' bent; none of our parts so poor,
> But was a race of heaven. They are so still,
> Or thou, the greatest soldier of the world,
> Art turn'd the greatest liar.
>
> (1.3.32–39)

The lovers of this description appear divine in origin and artistic in perfection, escaping the "poor" lineaments of their "parts" by the exalted state of their pursuit. To keep those parts eternal (still forever), Antony and Cleopatra must retain the enthusiasm through which they caught each other. Without that preservation, the past is untrue and Antony is "turn'd," at once altered in shape and reversed in direction. To move now is to negate the divine origin of his former cast (part). In the opening scenes, Cleopatra clings to a "fairer former fortune" (1.2.33), lauding it over what she senses to be the lesser present of diminished love. She seeks, through the "stillness" of art, to preserve her initiation in love. By evoking the eternity of their statuesque race of heaven, she attempts to still the dimensions of the past. As Antony leaves, that fear of gradual diminishment intensifies into a terror of losing all.

Delaying Antony's departure for Rome, Cleopatra reveals not only her sense of present abandonment but her idea of retroactive annihilation; the destruction of the picture of love she held as emblematic looms before her eyes:

> Courteous lord, one word:
> Sir, you and I must part, but that's not it:
> Sir, you and I have lov'd, but there's not it;
> That you know well, something it is I would,—
> O, my oblivion is a very Antony,
> And I am all forgotten.
>
> (1.3.86–91)

Acknowledging her future ("Sir, you and I must part") and recalling her past ("Sir, you and I have loved"), Cleopatra can find no present. As Rosalind seeks a "shadow" until Orlando reappears, Cleopatra finds no being when Antony is gone. In her ploy she describes the conditions under which she waits. Antony causes her both to forget and to be forgotten. Without his presence as a possibility, the heavenly race of which she spoke is wiped from memory. Without his active desire to recollect their past fulfillment, the eternal bliss for which she lives is lost as hope. Commenting on these lines, Rosalie Colie argues that "part of [the lovers'] tragedy lies in Antony's feeling himself dissolve when he is with her and Cleopatra's feeling her nothingness when he is not with her."[8] Her oblivion here matches Rosalind's "boundlessness" in the "fathom" speech. Both women fear the loss—the void—of love. In Antony's absence, Cleopatra loses the "all" of memory. Because nothing will *now* happen, nothing ever did *then* happen. By removing himself, Antony destroys the "behind" Cleopatra thought imperishable. Having immersed herself in Antony, she has no separate past, no reserves against the present loss, to command his remaining. Her obscurity bears the exact dimensions ("very") of her departing lover.

But when he is actually gone, Cleopatra recreates a past and plays with a future she previously thought impossible. Already here she establishes love as a dream, preparing herself psychologically through this change in life for her later transformation in death.

> Give me mine angle, we'll to the river there,
> My music playing far off. I will betray
> Tawny-finn'd fishes, my bended hook shall pierce
> Their slimy jaws; and as I draw them up,
> I'll think them every one an Antony,
> And say "Ah, ha! y'are caught."
> . . . .

> That time? O times!
> I laugh'd him out of patience; and that night
> I laugh'd him into patience, and next morn,
> Ere the ninth hour, I drunk him to his bed;
> Then put my tires and mantles on him, whilst
> I wore his sword Philippan.
>
> (2.5.10–15, 18–23)

Cleopatra is shameless about her desires, assuming (through her projection and remembrance) the male role. In her fantasy of anticipation, she is both pursued object (tawny-finned fish) and pursuing subject (drawer up). In her recollection, she betrays feminine wiles and masculine stratagems, laughing Antony out and into patience, teasing and holding him, pinning him down with conquering sword as he held her quiet with male penetration. Erased in the hermaphroditic image is the terror of the present, the fear that she cannot hold the slimy fish, the satisfied lover, with her bait. In her planned expedition and recomposed "time," Cleopatra playfully overcomes oblivion, contemplating and recalling what she fears irretrievably lost. The past and the future become, via the recapitulation in expectation of an experienced substitution of gender, interchangeable. Such a projection into fluidity, through the slime of the water, the release of the parts, prepares for the imaginative leap Cleopatra will make as she simultaneously accepts and unravels her nature in the vision of act 5. Already in act 2, Cleopatra frees herself from the desire for the assurance of "stillness" and so moves into an understanding of the pleasure of mutability. As the disguise did for Rosalind, so Antony's armor enables Cleopatra to accept the uncertainty of sexuality. The remembering queen of act 2 becomes the anticipating woman of act 5. In the early metamorphosis, she and Antony change places; he became her, after she became him. In the later dream, following his lead, she extends her memory into a future of exchange that both stems from and enlarges their earlier transformation. Thus her period of loss—the time of Antony's departure from Egypt—prepares for her moment of discovery—her final recovery of him. At first, referring to her "oblivion" (1.3.90), she played the part of lost child to the hilt. But, with the remembrance of 2.5.10–23, Cleopatra takes the sting out of her abandonment. And, when Antony abandons her a second time by leaving this world, she is prepared (partly because she has accepted mutability in act 2) to come out of the shadows. Refusing to stay behind helplessly, she will—as she did with his sword Philippan—actively pursue him.

Her willingness to accept a disappearing vision in act 2 enables her to glide easily into a reappearing fantasy as she awakens to Antony in act 5:

I dreamt there was an Emperor Antony.
O such another sleep, that I might see
But such another man!
. . . .
His legs bestrid the ocean, his rear'd arm
Crested the world: his voice was propertied
As all the tuned spheres, and that to friends:
But when he meant to quail, and shake the orb,
He was as rattling thunder. For his bounty,
There was no winter in't: an autumn 'twas
That grew the more by reaping: his delights
Were dolphin-like, they show'd his back above
The element they lived in: in his livery
Walk'd crowns and crownets: realms and islands were
As plates dropp'd from his pocket.

(5.2.75–77, 83–91)

When she dreams of Antony, Cleopatra makes him into a place as well as
a man. He becomes both the *locus amoenus* of pastoral and the entrance
to it. By mounting his dolphin-like "delights," Cleopatra elevates Antony in prospect as she had enjoyed him in memory. He is energy (the
male principle) and harbor (the female principle), transporting her to the
place "cresting the world" and forming a bridge of pleasure to the gate of
heavens. Bestriding the ocean, Antony straddles the sexes, leaping over
the depths with vigor even as he forms a protective arch for Cleopatra to
enter. He is now parallel to the remembered and projected fantasy of act
2, evolving into the object of her desire and the subject of her inspiration.
As she was fluid there, he is hermaphroditic here. When she declares that
his "bounty" grows "the more by reaping," she announces the success of
carnality and its triumph over death. In making Antony a heavenly harvest, she overcomes her fear of diminishing love by the possibility of
increasing fruits. The more she enjoys him, the more he replenishes her.
She converts the stillness of act 1 into a future "always," not by freezing it
in artistic perfection but by reaping it in perennial pleasure. No longer
needing the opening bud of youth and spring and "salad days" to retain
love, she evokes the full flower of age and fall and ripeness as the state in
which she awakens. Antony ascends because of his inexhaustibility; he is
capable of giving satisfaction constantly and endowed to renew it continually. The dream validates Cleopatra's experience, making the source
of her regeneration not the withholding of joy but the indulging in it. The
means of fulfillment becomes an end in itself, replacing both the "before"
and "behind" of sonnet 129 with an abiding presence of desire, eternally
renewed, and hence, constantly renewable. In recreating Antony,

Cleopatra calls him the creator of herself. As lover, he is the parent of her fantasy: the dreamer in the dream. Antony becomes the muse of her life, arousing her to name him as the source of their mutual fulfillment.

When she declares to the skeptical Dolabella that his doubts are a lie, she defends her inspiration. Spurred by the Antony she anticipates, Cleopatra speaks with the authority of her experience. The dream heads off winter by extending the autumn in which she dwells. Such an extension includes, rather than denies, the found universe. Thus Antony, giant man, shows his back above the elements, but is absorbed, in part, by them. He constantly rises above and descends into the place where Cleopatra is fulfilling herself by recalling the past she enjoyed and extracting from it the future she expects. Her vision is couched in temporal language: "Think you there was, or might be such a man" (5.2.93). "If there be, or ever were one such" (5.2.96). She moves from fantasized past to possible future, back to hypothetical present and theoretical past, rendering measurement speculative and dream calculable. Converting time into the questionable element, she makes her image fathomable (one step larger than the expected magnitude or size), moving by her logic into the scheme of Rosalind's enlarged universe of love. In challenging Dolabella, she emphasizes the reasonableness of her speculations. Antony did exist. There was "one such." The extended Antony, based on the real one (simply beyond him in size) must, by her calculation, also prevail.

Anticipating Prospero in *The Tempest*, she affirms that the lovers become a source of generative power:

> Nature wants stuff
> To vie strange forms with fancy; yet to imagine
> An Antony were nature's piece, 'gainst fancy,
> Condemning shadows quite.
>
> (5.2.97–100)

In Prospero's apparition, we are such "stuff" as dreams are made on; man is merely the disappearing fabric upon which a divine fabricator imprints and then destroys its changing and whimsical vision. In this dream Cleopatra begins, like Prospero, claiming that there is no substance in nature equal to the fancy she has just presented. But she reaches a different conclusion from Prospero because her mental image (fancy as imagination) is based on her bodily love (fancy as yearning). Her rebuttal is not a refutation of nature but final defense of it, as the means of transforming the Antony she knew. When she argues "to imagine / An Antony were nature's piece, 'gainst fancy / condemning shadows quite," she affirms that, in conceiving the Antony that "was," nature created the conditions allowing her to extend him beyond the confines of space and time. Antony's "piece" becomes for her not simply the creative source of an abstract design but the procreative resource of a felt love; her craving for the "piece" (as sexual organ) already created by nature becomes the inspiration for the masterpiece (as perfected being) she here describes. The power to deify Antony by enlarging him in size evolves out of her acceptance of him as he was and herself as she is—part of the nature that earlier, through her evocation of an artistic permanence, she attempted to evade. The masterpiece here moves her to want it and inspires her to describe it in the dream sustaining her. But the process of the harvest of recurring desire stems from the substance of the cycle of diminishing forms through which nature premises death as well as life. It is in nature's "piece" that Cleopatra finds the peace she always wanted, creating out of the magnificent Antony of her speech the ultimate vehicle against Caesar's leveling of her life.

If, in act 1, Cleopatra wanted to hold time still with her "race of heaven," here she and Antony race *to* heaven. In the rush to anticipate each other—he overtaking her (4.14.44), she taking him (5.2.310)—they thrive on the memory that was their desire. Cleopatra's dream fulfills Antony's last request:

> But please your thoughts
> In feeding them with those my former fortunes.
> (4.15.51–52)

Antony leaves Cleopatra nurtured. She becomes the active memorializer rather than the passive recipient of his bounty. He gives her the freedom to take what he once proffered so that, in feeding, she eats the him that became her "in pleasure." If his "former fortune" was *her,* so *he* now is her present estate. Further, Cleopatra follows Antony in death, as he, in dying, had followed her in life. Their metamorphosis is imitative.

But the race to become each other is part of a larger imitation already realized in the flux of nature. She mounts the dolphin when she sees herself as part of the element he surfaces, when she accepts the bestial aspect—the lower status—of her womanhood. In her last speeches she acknowledges not that she is "royal Egypt" but that she is an ordinary subject:

> No more, but e'en a woman, and commanded
> By such poor passion as the maid that milks,
> And does the meanest chares.
> (4.15.73–75)

Cleopatra becomes, finally, so much a part of nature as to be obscured by it, assuming now the oblivion she at first feared. No longer an empress, she is commanded. The poor "parts" exalted in her early speech are now governed by a "poor" passion—an overwhelming grief for, and a complete predilection toward, her lover. She mourns in his passing and reaches for his destiny, cast down into coarseness even as she moves up beyond it.

Incorporating passion as the form of earthly suffering and the state of heavenly aspiration, Cleopatra becomes what she dreamed Antony to be—both an emanation and an extension of nature. Her final speeches echo the dual elements she envisions, expressing a simultaneous desire to embody forms and to transcend them. When she prepares to leave the earth behind, she fixes immortality in terms of a "longing" (5.2.280), at once the yearning for, and the prolongation of, the pleasure principle inspiring her life. To embrace the change she earlier feared is to espouse those elements—"fire and air"—(5.2.288) which leave not a trace behind. Cleopatra enters the dream world because she has the courage to accept the unsolid aspects of her being. She opts for the instant regeneration of love over the extended prospect of survival. To choose death is simply to continue accepting, as she has learned in the course of the play to appreciate, the mutability of her being.

The dream in *As You Like It* enables Rosalind to capitalize on the present without worrying too much about the vanishing past and unstable future she outlined in her proviso scene. The dream in *Antony and Cleopatra* allows Cleopatra to escape the present as she accepts the past mutation and future transmutation Rosalind held at bay. Both women promulgate the dream the speaker in Sonnet 129 fears. Rosalind realizes it by bringing an inward rose outward; Cleopatra by reaching for one that already lies beyond. To live as a woman means that Rosalind allows the world to "meet" the wilderness of her heart. To die as a woman means that Cleopatra prepares the world for the unknown territory of her lover. When she declares to all around her that she is "again for Cydnus, / To meet Mark Antony" (5.2.227), Cleopatra parallels, even in her word, Rosalind's carefully staged "meeting." Returning to the river of their first moments, Cleopatra accepts its volatility, allowing it to transport her, not to some newly created sphere, but back to the eternally established element. In moving forward she revives her initial anticipation, finding in death the exhilaration of beginning again. She "meets" for all the empire to see, as Rosalind unveiled for Arden to know, the dream of a better life, composed of and composing, created from and expanding, the passion of this one. Both women recognize that there are no emblems against oblivion, nothing to ward off wanting again what they struggled to realize.

In *As You Like It* and *Antony and Cleopatra*, Shakespeare raises a question that the myths take for granted: Why does the lost child even want to become part of the sexual cycle that lies behind the dream of sonnet 129? Why risk it when it leads to either a brutality or an oblivion they have already experienced? The narrator's discovery in Sonnet 129 and Perdita and Hermione's trial in *The Winter's Tale* are Rosalind and Cleopatra's given. Yet they emerge from their abandonments prepared to accept a nature that includes the kind of dream haunting those biblical moments (Enoch, the tribe of Korah) where there is no "proof." In "meeting" their lovers (Rosalind in this life, Cleopatra in the next), they answer the existential question by absorbing its challenge. They love without "proof." They succeed because, like Pyrocles and Musidorus, they become the other—Rosalind in disguise, Cleopatra in Antony's armor—and that becoming helps them accept the nature they desire and the desire of their natures. Both, alone, do for themselves what is done by foster parents or a benevolent pastoral during the adoptive interlude. They create a protective art that allows them to realize their natural selves, even if those natural selves include the bestial and the ephemeral. In likening themselves to their lovers, they share a vision that is "likable" enough; satisfying a longing they know cannot be prolonged, they emerge confident enough to pursue what they want.

A Manly Loss

From his dragonboat, he looked down at his home and realized that escape and return were equally impossible.

Maxine Hong Kingston, *China Men*

Rosalind and Cleopatra emerge from their experience aware of their natures and of the larger nature to which they must submit. They face the bestial and the abstract in terms of their desire for love. Hamlet and Lear gain a similar awareness, but they define it in terms of their desire for power. Unlike the heroines who cope emotionally with the void, Hamlet and Lear attempt to deal with it philosophically. They are, then, one step behind the women, waiting too long in the arena of thought. The heroes seem stymied in childhood. Hamlet has his thrust upon him; Lear imposes it on himself. If the heroines grow steadily in the course of their plays, the heroes change only briefly—Hamlet in the brave acknowledgments leading to his duel, Lear in the short interlude transpiring on the heath. Finally, if Rosalind and Cleopatra anticipate Perdita and Hermione, Hamlet and Lear explore tentatively what Prospero and Leontes will realize in the formulaic foundling stories of the last plays.

13

Hamlet's Story; or, The Child's Refusal to Man the Father

When he confronts Polonius in act 2, Hamlet, obsessed with the feeling that he is an exposed child, alludes to legends that describe parental exploitation—that of Erysichthon who, in Ovid, calculatedly sold his daughter to save himself and that of Jephthah (2.2.174–84; 400–415) who, in Judges, unwittingly offered his child to keep a promise to God. In both myths, the maiden is used to further the parent's cause.[1] Hamlet has properly perceived that Ophelia is manipulated by Polonius to please Claudius and thereby to enhance his standing in the royal court. In the assaults against Polonius, Hamlet deals with his own feelings, transferring his guilt about surviving his father's violent end by converting all parents into the perpetrators of evil against their children. As Ophelia is Polonius's pawn, Hamlet is his father's. The play is not so much about "time out of joint" as it is about the "cursed spite" of being required by birth to set it right.[2] The child who survives in an evil world feels doubly burdened: first by a blow coming from those outsiders who commit the crime; second, by a curse inherited from inside the family, from the actual victim. How can Hamlet go on living after his father was poisoned? On the other hand, how can he not feel that his own life—like that of Jephthah's daughter—is consumed by his obligation to settle past accounts? Like Una, Hamlet is held back, forced to be the "man" in his father's revenge plot rather than the hero of his own life. But he is also pushed forward, compelled to go beyond this life into "the undiscovered country" of death.

Hamlet exists on a level still more terrifying than Una's. He must face not only the evil of this world but the mystery of the next one. Writing about that "undiscovered country," Jean Kerr asks:

Now what does this character mean, "no traveler returns"? His own father, dead as a cod, has been steadily returning all night. In fact the

159

ghostly old boy has been virtually commuting between Elsinore and that bourn.[3]

Kerr is not wrong. Hamlet is being sucked across the border into death by a father who will not let go, will not stay where he belongs. He is an unusual foundling. Most are snatched from their parents and discover unexpected life in the adoptive interlude. They are saved from a realization of their mortality by a second—often a better—chance. Hamlet is stolen by a father who demands the sacrifice—a death before dying. He is condemned to contemplate all the ramifications of what that death entails. Hamlet forfeits even his memories. The Hamlet early in act 1, grieving for his father, is different from the Hamlet later in that act, living for his father. He becomes the ghost's ghost,[4] obliterating with that commitment both his recollection of the past and his expectation for the future. When he meets his father, Hamlet ceases to mourn, as he did in the unweeded-garden speech (1.2.130–42), a vanished innocence; he assumes thereafter that good never existed. His father's insistence that he eradicate "all . . . fond records" (1.5.99) inspires a seemingly irradicable belief in retrospective evil. The command to "remember" leaves Hamlet philosophically bereft of innocence, as he demonstrates in his confrontations with Ophelia (3.1.105–34). The undiscovered country overpowers the childish gardens Hamlet once recalled and effaces the youthful love Ophelia remembers. The soliloquies explore the mandate of familial obligation; in them, Hamlet denies his own life and defines himself only as his father's son. A student of philosophy, Hamlet at first treats the mandate philosophically, attempting to deal rationally, as Rosalind and Cleopatra dealt psychologically, with his fear. In the course of the play, Hamlet twice changes—once (in 1.5) to become the sacrificial pawn of his father's poisoning, once (in 4.4) to free himself from that victimization. In act 4, Hamlet grows out of the role of child, condemned by his father to perform in a remote revenge plot, to play the part of a man, pushed by his desire to live in and act out a personal scenario. The reversal (in 4.4.65) coincides with Hamlet's consciousness, in his vow to have "bloody thoughts," that he is no longer spurred by a philosophical command to die; rather, he is prompted by a physical need to realize his being. Such a realization is contingent upon Hamlet's restoring and setting "right" the vision, held before he met the ghost, of the "goodness of good."[5] No longer dictated by a ghostly compulsion, the story he bequeathes to Horatio at the end records Hamlet's life, Hamlet's death. Hamlet is a foundling who escapes from, rather than finds, his father. Like the restoration in formulaic foundling plots, the deliverance purges the contaminated past and makes the future (for others, at least) possible again.

In his first soliloquy, the as-yet-unghosted prince recalls a better garden, a time of vanished innocence. His bereavement is conventional. Despite the burden of what *is*, he has the consolation of what *was*:

> How weary, stale, flat, and unprofitable
> Seem to me all the uses of this world!
> Fie on 't! ah fie! 'tis an unweeded garden
> That grows to seed; things rank and gross in nature
> Possess it merely. That it should come to this!
> But two months dead—nay, not so much, not two—
> So excellent a king, that was, to this
> Hyperion to a satyr, so loving to my mother
> That he might not beteem the winds of heaven
> Visit her face too roughly. Heaven and earth,
> Must I remember?
>
> (1.2.133–41)

His recollection consists of a contrast between past promise and present waste.[6] The garden of the world is unweeded, grown "to seed." This early speech is based throughout on an assumption that Denmark once was inhabited by great men and that it was a good place. His father, an excellent king, is now replaced by a satyr. The golden, growing pasture has turned rank and flat. To see the world as an unweeded garden is to presuppose that formerly it existed without tarnish. To recall the past so longingly is to assume that it was once a happier place. Hamlet's past is the pleasance of the pastoral interlude in foundling plots. His present is the unweeded garden.

The ghost deprives Hamlet of the opportunity to mourn his father by taking away his remembrance of a better past. That deprivation can be seen in act 3 as the depressed Hamlet seeks to transpose his gloom onto Ophelia. There, he casts a shadow over the garden and a pall over the future, transposing his resentment at being the child of a victimized father into a hesitation to father still another victimized child. In act 1, Hamlet's philosophy includes a past innocence, a weeded garden. In act 3, the very existence of that garden is challenged. Two things happen between those speeches to turn Hamlet against Ophelia—the first is the encounter with the ghost; the second, his realization of what that encounter means in the "to be or not to be" speech. With the retrospect of the ghost's mandate, and with the knowledge of not-being acquired in the famous soliloquy immediately preceding this confrontation, Hamlet denies his childhood belief in good:

The power of beauty will sooner transform honesty from what it is to a bawd than the force of honesty can translate beauty into his likeness.

This was sometime a paradox, but now the time gives it proof. I did
love you once. . . . You should not have believed me; for virtue cannot
so inoculate our old stock but we shall relish of it. I loved you not.
(3.1.111–16, 118–20)

The "time" Hamlet speaks of erases the "sometime" (or particular occa-
sions) Ophelia remembers. The happy moments of the past have been
drowned out by the engulfing evil of the present. When Hamlet declares
that he did love Ophelia "once," he speaks as if trying to recall for himself
that time of innocence when love and a belief in beauty, now seen as
merely translatable, seemed possible. When he immediately contradicts
himself and declares, "I loved you not," he speaks out of the knowledge
of his present philosophical position.

From the perspective of the unweeded garden, he might have said to
Ophelia, "I loved you once; I do not love you now." Here he attests that
in a fallen world there never could have been a time of innocence or a
place of love. The inheritance of the "old [sinning] stock" relegates all
presumed beauty into an illusion never to be believed possible. Hamlet's
truth eradicates good in the past and eliminates hope for the future.
Ophelia should remain chaste because the only sexual option available is
to breed more of the same generation of sinners. Hamlet reveals, then,
not only the existence of evil that he suspected before but the obliteration
of good that emerges as impossible. He nullifies the garden of the opening
because in the meantime the ghost has taught him a revisionist history,
one that takes away any sense of a prelapsarian—sheltered—past. The
ghost keeps Hamlet from Ophelia. When he rejects her here, he is merely
repeating his vow to erase the "fond hope" of love, the innocent
memories and expectations of youth. Hamlet's cruelty to Ophelia, voiced
in philosophical paradoxes, is the direct result of his promise to love his
father, as Lear will later demand, "all." One of the animating factors in
the foundling formula is the parental desire for continuity fulfilled by the
child's marriage. One of the signs of Hamlet's possession by the ghost is
his rejection of a love that normally would gratify the dynastic impulse.
Ophelia represents a dissipation of his energy, a diversion from his sole
purpose: the reparation of his father's murder. He cannot love Ophelia
because he has promised, in the flush of his encounter with the ghost, to
become his father.[7] In terms of this duty, Hamlet's obsession with Gertrude is partly a reflection of moral rectitude. How can she, by remaining
with Claudius, continue night after night to betray her husband? He is
outraged at her on behalf of his father; but he is also (for the same reason)
drawn to her. His attachment is not merely an infantile sexual craving. It
is also an expression of manly responsibility.

The ghost commands and Hamlet follows, blindly obedient. He must stand in—stand up—for his wronged parent. When he learns of Claudius's murder and Gertrude's betrayal, Hamlet repeats the ghost's injunction as a rhetorical question:

> Remember thee?
> Ay, thou poor ghost, whiles memory holds a seat
> In this distracted globe. Remember thee?
> Yea, from the table of my memory
> I'll wipe away all trivial fond records,
> All saws of books, all forms, all pressures past
> That youth and observation copied there,
> And thy commandment all alone shall live
> Within the book and volume of my brain,
> Unmix'd with baser matter.
>
> (1.5.95–104)

Promising not only to recall his father's presence in the past but to anticipate his anguish in the future, Hamlet vows to wipe from the table of his schoolboy memory all beliefs that presupposed a time of innocence. They were, he now sees, merely youthful impressions formed without the knowledge of experience. Honoring his father involves ignoring any evidence of former happiness, any shred of hope for good. Thus Hamlet pledges himself totally, recompensing his father's death with the gift of his life. The vow to reconstitute his father depends upon eradicating a past when Hamlet, allowed to think about himself, was Hamlet. Ophelia belongs to that past. The promise leaves Hamlet no other life but that commanded by his father's charge to remember him.

The "to be or not to be" speech, culminating in Hamlet's denunciation of Ophelia in 3.1, is a response to that promise; in it Hamlet wrestles with the philosophical sacrifice imposed on him, following it to its logical conclusion in a state of terrifying abstraction.[8] The speech has two phases: the first, in which Hamlet poses false alternatives only to discover that they both lead to the end of his life;[9] the second, in which he explores the literal dimensions (the exact locale and the precise sensations) of the death he is forced to face:

> To be, or not to be, that is the question:
> Whether 'tis nobler in the mind to suffer
> The slings and arrows of outrageous fortune,
> Or to take arms against a sea of troubles
> And by opposing end them.
>
> (3.1.55–59)

To accept the slings and arrows of outrageous fortune is to acquiesce to the high rank of his birth obligation. To take arms against the sea of troubles—the flood of his father's demands—is to be overcome, as was Ajax fighting the waves, by the hostile element.[10] In either case he sees the inexorable demise of his personal aspirations. In being what "outrageous fortune" imposed on him by birth,[11] he endures quietly the end of individual choice.[12] In opposing the sea of troubles—in not being his father's man—he loses sight of his own thoughts because he must subdue them, spending his energy in the struggle for release. Being and not-being lead to a similar denial of individuation. The "native hue of resolution," the desire to think on his own behalf, is stifled by the command to follow through, and accept, his father's burden. Hamlet realizes at this moment his role as sacrificial child. He can go nowhere on his own. He is condemned, and it is Ophelia who receives the fallout of that condemnation.

Having obliterated choice (with the conclusion that being himself or not being himself leads to the same consummation), Hamlet then explores the details of his sentence, pursuing the death awaiting him at either end of the forked road. Though Hamlet thinks in terms of philosophical beginnings, he is forced to contemplate his physical end:

> Who would fardels bear,
> To grunt and sweat under a weary life,
> But that the dread of something after death,
> The undiscover'd country, from whose bourn
> No traveller returns, puzzles the will,
> And makes us rather bear those ills we have
> Than fly to others that we know not of?
>
> (3.1.76–82)

Hamlet steps into the metaphor he uses, describing himself in the skin he surrenders and in the land he envisions with identical imagery. Like the shedding serpent, he opens up—with the mortal coil—a self tender to the touch. Similarly, the undiscovered country has a snakelike bourn, undulating and undefined.

Through the image of the undiscovered country, Hamlet emerges the exposed scion, abandoned by a relentless parent in some remote place, sacrificed by his father's demand for reparation. Hamlet is the Mordred of this play. The head and tail of the snake emerge at either end of the spectrum, both in the self he reveals, shuffling off his mortal coil, and in the territory he envisions, reaching his final destination. Even in the sleep from which he expected relief, Hamlet simply exposes himself, through the death he risks, to a place beyond his control and to the dream that might overcome even the most resolved of men. By being, Hamlet risks not being and finds himself moving beyond the present he knows into a place totally outside his capacity. In the very act of moving forward to assume his parent's cause, he is pushed backward, shaking adulthood, to emerge the unprotected child in the wilderness. The conscience that makes Hamlet a coward in the third section is the wavering cry of a frightened son, exposed too early to a world beyond his ken. Hamlet sees ("the native hue of resolution / Is sicklied o'er with the pale cast of thought") that his trap is set not by an externally imposed evil but by an inwardly expressed duty to lose himself in a battle inherited by birth. The serpent lurking in the design of the undiscovered country lies inward in the complexity of the unexplored self. Hamlet unravels a coil that resembles George Herbert's collar; he cannot shake it without feeling even more aware of his position as child. To act for Hamlet is to die, first to the self and whatever ideas of innocence or pleasure it had and then to the flesh and whatever notion of solidity or permanence it fostered. His "native hue" is usurped by his resolution to be his father's child.

Most foundlings awake in an undiscovered country that turns out to be better than the known country from which they are exposed. But for Hamlet that better garden only existed in an imaginary golden time—wiped out now by his second realization that such an innocence could never have been possible. His vision of the borderland includes the monstrosity of his own annihilation. With the "to be or not to be" speech, Hamlet, plagued by the anxiety of an overwhelming responsibility, recognizes the limits of philosophy and the loneliness of his position. Like Una, Hamlet has to fight a monster—and the monster happens to be his own father. The fact that his father is dead does not change the nature of the compulsion. It intensifies it, forcing Hamlet not only, like Una, to set this world right; he must explore too early yet another world—the undiscovered country of death. At the end of thought is the unthinkable, the realization that the "being" who gave him life is the very source of a "not being" for which he is unprepared. Because thought excises past innocence, Hamlet has to change—to stop thinking. His only hope now is to try the tactic of the Shakespearean heroines, to move from thought to feeling. And he succeeds in this conversion in act 4 when, inspired by Fortinbras, he seeks a new mode of action.

Observing Fortinbras's army marching toward its death, Hamlet determines to reverse himself:

> From this time forth
> My thoughts be bloody or be nothing worth.
>
> (4.4.65–66)

He is spurred by a desire to be more substantial than Fortinbras, by a determination to validate his motive and make his mind reflect the anguish that has already aroused his being. Earlier, Hamlet tried to forge an abstract idea into a concrete action. The system of the "to be or not to be" speech depended on a movement from idea to idea, from palpable life to insubstantial death. Here another connection occurs. When Hamlet commands his thoughts to be bloody, he inaugurates a physical action that influences his mental intention.[13] Hamlet's resolution springs neither from intellectual calculation nor divine ambition. Rather it spreads, as the family "stain," inherited from his father through his guilty mother, permeates his being, like the dyer's hand in sonnet 111. To have bloody thoughts is to "think" passionately, to let the body (blood) infiltrate the mind.

With that resolution, Hamlet turns toward the future, "from this time forth," quickening himself through a combination of reason and blood and thereby mobilizing his formerly paralyzed parts. If, in the "to be or not to be" speech, he separated his mind from his body, here there is a unity of being enabling him to see that the end he fears has already happened. Previously he called himself the "tardy son / laps'd in time and passion" (3.4.107–8). Now he thinks of himself as the nascent man— ahead, rather than behind, anticipating action "from this time forth." The Hamlet of act 5 emerges increasingly responsive to the reality of death. He no longer views it as an ambassador from the "undiscovered country." It will not come to kidnap him to a place he has never known. Death is something he has already—on his own—touched. With that acceptance he awakens his memory to a time of innocence. As his body comes into closer contact with physical decay, his mind returns to a tighter hold on remembered good. When he jokes about the noble Alexander (5.1.200– 210), reminisces over the playful Yorick (5.1.178–89), and waxes poetic over the dead Ophelia (5.1.265–86), he restores the vision of the better world he had previously annulled. The recovery occurs because Hamlet no longer sees death as a monster waiting to reduce him to a quivering shadow. Rather, death emerges as part of the known and solid substance of the self. Like Cleopatra, he has preempted the enemy and so conquered his fear of it.

Following his imagination in the grave-diggers' scene, he revitalizes history:

May not imagination trace the noble dust of Alexander till a find it stopping a bunghole? . . . But to follow him thither with modesty enough, and likelihood to lead it. Alexander died, Alexander was buried, Alexander returneth to dust, the dust is earth, of earth we make loam, and why of that loam whereto he was converted might they not stop a beer barrel?

> Imperious Caesar, dead and turn'd to clay,
> Might stop a hole to keep the wind away.
> O, that that earth which kept the world in awe
> Should patch a wall t' expel the winter's flaw.
>
> (5.1.200–210)

Death no longer brings him beyond the border into uncertainty but back to the originating and palpable dust. Such a reversal promises no strange and frightening new world; instead it presents the all-too-familiar present one. Hamlet seems here to echo his sadness over the "quintessence of dust," but there are two differences. When he baited Rosencrantz and Guildenstern, Hamlet voiced a philosophical position denying his body. Here, his "gorge rises" (5.1.180) to stimulate his imagination. The physical being now ignites his speculative preoccupation. Further, in the comic-logical cause and effect, Hamlet begins with the noble Alexander of Greece, as he had in his unweeded-garden speech referred to the Hyperion father of Denmark. He restores the memory—even while he restates a present bleakness—of a bright beginning. With the skull of Yorick he traces a better time:

> Alas, poor Yorick. I knew him, Horatio, a fellow of infinite jest, of most excellent fancy. He hath bore me on his back a thousand times, and now, how abhorred in my imagination it is. My gorge rises at it. Here hung those lips that I have kissed I know not how oft. Where be your gibes now, your gambols, your songs, your flashes of merriment, that were wont to set the table on a roar? Not one now to mock your own grinning? Quite chop–fallen? (5.1.178–88)

Recalling a playful era of gambols and merriment, Hamlet resurrects the happy world he had, in the scene with the ghost, wiped from the tables of his memory. Similarly, when he competes in theatrics with Laertes, he shouts for everyone to hear (as earlier all had overheard his scorn), "I lov'd Ophelia" (5.1.264). Declaring "This is I, / Hamlet the Dane" (5.1.250–51), he resumes the faith he held before he knew how his father died. His announcement of selfhood presupposes that initial psychological state where love seemed—if only for the interlude of Ophelia's life—possible. Thus, Hamlet defies his father's hold, affirming with his restated love for Ophelia, his freedom from the ghost's mandate. With the vitality of Hamlet's self-assertion and the insistence of his love vow, Hamlet resumes his old identity. The source of Hamlet's new found "being" is a physical motivation. Hamlet feels, then thinks, and then is able to act. He has assumed, in his vow to have bloody thoughts, the destiny he earlier felt was designed to fit someone else.

That sense of having absorbed in advance the dreaded end goads him into the final fight. When Horatio asks him if he wants to postpone the duel, Hamlet replies:

> The readiness is all. Since no man, of aught he leaves, knows aught, what is't to leave betimes? Let be. (5.2.218–20)

With the phrase "readiness is all," Hamlet asserts that what matters is that he is inwardly braced for the coming of a fall, that he has been previously shaped by the divinity for the moment of destiny. With the calm "let be," he denies the inclination not to be and so thrusts his own, rather than his father's, presence to the foreground. No longer representing a thought controlled puppet or an anxiety-bound rebel, the "being" that surfaces here reflects a newly discovered calm. In declaring how prepared he is for the fight, Hamlet also acknowledges how accepting he is of the death to which it might lead. Claiming that he does not care when it happens, Hamlet admits that the fate terrifying him has become, without fanfare and without constraint, at last his own. The readiness for the future involves something that transpired in the past. That something is an acceptance of death that renders its actual occurrence casual. Because he is so concerned in the second half of the play with a mortality he can touch—as he does when he fingers Alexander's clay, fondles Yorick's skull, weeps over Ophelia—Hamlet seems to have felt beforehand the force, which in the "to be or not to be" speech he thought destined, afterward, to take him irrevocably away. Hamlet's contact with death in act 5 returns him to a past—noble history, childish laughter, experienced love—he has known. His readiness now converts the undiscovered country, the unthinkable event, into a familiar place, a palpable moment.

In the final scene, Hamlet quietly announces "I am dead, Horatio" (5.2.338), "Horatio, I am dead" (5.2.343), repeating that the state for which he has prepared himself has at last arrived. Drawing Horatio away from "felicity" (5.2.352), Hamlet asks him to set the record straight—to trace, in the demoralized present, the existence of a nobler past. From the vantage of his physical end, Hamlet restores his philosophical beginning. The wounded name passed on to him by his father will be healed even as the injured body has surrendered to its destiny. With his recovered history, Hamlet renders the story Horatio will tell triumphant. No longer the sacrificed child, he is a man "ready" for, and attending, his own awaiting end. Hamlet has, in short, and only in his death, unleashed himself from the compulsion to be his father's man. In seeing death not as a ghostly "other" but as an already present part of his nature, Hamlet finds his place in the larger cycle the Shakespearean heroines accept much earlier. Unlike Rosalind whose understanding promises a bright future on earth, or Cleopatra whose vision anticipates yet a better life, Hamlet is left with neither earthly pleasure nor heavenly prospect. But by accepting his mortality, he has incorporated the undiscovered country into his own experience. Without living the adoptive interlude literally, Hamlet has given himself the freedom it offers. He has escaped the confines of his father's demands and found a way "to be" on his own. He has stopped thinking and started feeling. Through that transition, he has set right the history of the race (his recollection of the noble Alexander), the memory of his love (his shouting over the grave of Ophelia) and the biography of his family (his evocation of the playful Yorick), creating a psychological analogue for the foundling recovery.

14

A World Within: Found Enclosure and Final Exposure in *King Lear*

King Lear twice comes close to the foundling experience, nestling a small haven of reconciliation between the larger contexts of exposure in the opening and concluding acts. The larger story reverses the order of the formula. It begins with the art of the adoptive interlude—in Lear's wish that his daughters would mother him while he, infantile, "crawl[s] . . . unburthen'd" (1.1.41). It ends with the voracious nature usually inaugurating foundling plots (in the final sacrifice of Cordelia). At first Lear creates a fictional pastoral, demanding that his daughters fulfill his philosophical concept of love. The nature he denies with that artifice comes back at the end to assert itself all the more cruelly.

But between that artificial beginning and the brutal end is a foundling story based on the role reversal of Lear and his daughters. On the heath, Lear is the exposed child who experiences a more persuasive semblance for the adoptive interlude—both its primitive surroundings and, with Edgar and Kent, its nurturing humanity. After his humbling conversion, he is reconciled to the daughter he condemned and restored by her to his former stature. For a moment in act 4 and the beginning of act 5, the man who at first sought to be a child and give away his power becomes once more a father and a king. The happiness of that restoration is only momentary, partly because of the all-pervading violence at the end and partly because Lear is blinded, as he was earlier, by his need to possess Cordelia in a world he imagines. Thus, the second foundling story climaxes in the original artifice of Lear's dominion as he anticipates an extended prospect of "blessing" and "forgiveness" (5.3.10,11) in prison. Seeking again to monopolize his child, Lear stymies the dynasty that would complete the formula. If, in the enclosed story, Lear becomes the abandoned child, experiencing, on the heath with Edgar and Kent, the pastoral renewal that enables him to become the found parent of act 4, in

170

acts 1 and 5 he is the arbitrary father, exposing Cordelia to the fantasy of his dominion. As father and as king, Lear believes that he can—by an art he invents (in act 1 through an arbitrary command, in act 5 through a pathetic dependency)—force his vision on the world.

During the opening moments of the play, Lear places himself in a fictional country, trusting in the dream of a supportive realm as he releases the remnants of his personal power. The dream is based not on created reality (nature) but on invented substance (art). Lear confers on his children the land of his mind in exchange for the love of their devising. If Goneril and Regan vie for the opulence of "shadowy forests with champains rich'd / With plenteous rivers and wide-skirted meads" (1.1.63–64) never seen in the play, they match in hyperbolic gesture the poetic vistas they receive. What Lear gives is what he gets—an art of nature, a pastoral world of "shadowy forests and plenteous rivers" for a romanticized sign of filial devotion.[1] He bequeaths an imagined territory; he accepts a professed love—because both fit a picture he wants to believe. Fantasizing about his kingdom and making his children his parents, he invents the pastoral realms and the nurturing substitutes of the adoptive interlude. Promising "our largest bounty may extend / Where nature doth with merit challenge" (1.1.52), Lear speaks of what is given ("bounty") in terms of what is earned ("merit"). Such a philosophy finally discounts an externally created universe, making man's words equal in their seminal power to God's.

Lear's quibble about nothing manifests this philosophy. When Cordelia is silent, Lear answers with the famous rejection: "Nothing will come of nothing" (1.1.90). Threatening his daughter with extinction, Lear places the source of her failure to acquire in the obstinance of her refusal to utter the words reaping riches. The context for creativity is the mind, out of which words flow and empires follow. Without those words, Cordelia's sphere is barren. She can pull nothing to her. No thoughts (no words) equal no worlds (no things). Lear repeats this position in response to the Fool's questions about practicality:

Fool. Can you make no use of nothing, Nuncle?
Lear. Why, no, boy; nothing can be made out of nothing.
                                                            (1.4.136–37)

Man's intellect propels the idea that forms a concrete entity, just as in Genesis God's spirit "moves" on the face of the waters to make land. Lear considers himself the guiding force in his firmament.[2]

The Fool mocks this belief when he shows Lear how he squandered his dominion:

> *Fool.* Nuncle, give me an egg, and I'll give thee two crowns.
> *Lear.* What two crowns shall they be?
> *Fool.* Why, after I have cut the egg i' th' middle and eat up the meat, the two crowns of the egg. When thou clovest thy crown i' th' middle, and gav'st away both parts, thou bor'st thine ass on thy back o'er the dirt: thou hadst little wit in thy bald crown when thou gav'st thy golden one away.
>
> (1.4.160–71)

Having given away his crown and the concrete wealth it represented, Lear cut out his brain (crown) and the abstract ideas it formulated. Since the land, as Lear defines it, is measured by the mind that makes it, to empty the container (crown) is to flush out the thing contained (wit). The egg white corroborates, in its absence of color, the truth of Lear's hollowness. He has destroyed the golden—the substance—and is left with only the blankness—the abstraction.

Without his crown and its accompanying power, Lear is bald, shorn of the wit he once had because his center—as the vanished egg yolk shows—is eaten. In the voracious image that follows, the Fool ties the eaters to the daughters:

> For you know, Nuncle,
> The hedge-sparrow fed the cuckoo so long,
> That it's had it head bit off by it young.
> So out went the candle, and we were left darkling.
>
> (1.4.222–26)

Like Error's children devouring their dam in *The Faerie Queene*, Goneril and Regan swallow Lear, reversing the process of confinement he initially imposed on them. Reduced, he is left groping for wit, searching for love, emptied of the enlightening power out of which his world grew. If Lear believes the world to be made by man, the fool convinces him that without evidence "out there" to objectify it, nothing remains "in here" to originate it. Having snuffed the candle of reason, Lear is left "darkling," deprived of the light in the self that would in turn illuminate nature. To be witless is to be worldless. Strengthening his daughters, he weakened himself, converting them into the custodians of his life:

> *Lear.* I should be false persuaded I had daughters.
> *Fool.* Which they will make an obedient father.
>
> (1.4.241–42)

Goneril and Regan emerge mothers to his self, definers of his being. Reduced to nothing, Lear becomes the controlled object of his daughters' imaginations. Having cast himself out, Lear wills his decline. He has been taught by the Fool, forced by his daughters, to pronounce the failure of his art.

When he understands his diminution, the first frame of the play ends and Lear—the proud parent—becomes the humbled child of the enclosed story. Forfeiting his crown of art, he has lost his power in nature. The second story begins on the heath as Lear reaches the bottom he feared and discovers, in accepting the nature he formerly denied, that he can touch and be touched. In his defense of the storm, Lear's new being surfaces:

> But where the greater malady is fix'd,
> The lesser is scarce felt. Thou'ldst shun a bear;
> But if thy flight lay toward the roaring sea,
> Thou'ldst meet the bear i' th' mouth. When the mind's free
> The body's delicate.
>
> (3.4.7–11)

Formerly a believer in absolutes ("all" or "nothing"), Lear affirms the relative. While the sea can overwhelm, the bear might still be tamed, cajoled. When the mind is free from raging passion, the body emerges "delicate," trainable, young. Thus, what at first seemed impossible (the wild animal) becomes containable—not so threatening. Meeting the bear in the mouth, Lear promises to "endure" (3.4.18). Taking his chances with the bestial he finds, as the rain pelts and pours, what remains when everything seems to have slid over the cataract: that something in himself existing to fight back. He comes to rest with the strength of the human form, what it suffers, what it fears, what it touches. The Lear who started out as a god, making and measuring the world, begins as a child. In the storm, Lear earns his position as foundling. Lost on the heath, he acquires a radical innocence and establishes his brotherhood with man. When he promises to "endure," Lear, like Cleopatra, recognizes humanity at its simplest level. The "poor naked wretches" are Lear's equivalent to the milkmaid Cleopatra tried to become. Befriending poor Tom, Lear defines man as one rung lower on the chain of being:

> Thou wert better in a grave than to answer with thy uncover'd body this extremity of the skies. Is man no more than this? Consider him well. Thou ow'st the worm no silk, the beast no hide, the sheep no wool, the cat no perfume. Ha! here's three on's are sophisticated; thou art the thing itself; unaccommodated man is no more but such a poor, bare, forked animal as thou art. Off, off, you lendings! Come; unbutton here. (3.4.103–12)

When he asks, "Is man no more than this?" he mediates between the death of self he saw as the nothing and the new something he finds—the thing itself. Man is more than an extension of the gods (the trembling extremity) and more than the things he adds from nature (the temporary lendings). The first image denies man's wit by making him the bearer of a foreign internal force; the second hides his substance by transforming him into the wearer of an appropriated external trim. To add is to detract from the self, to confuse the subject with the objects it manifests. Calling Tom a beast, Lear aligns himself with him. To be the thing itself is to be undisguised by show, unswayed by force. The poor bare animal is steadfast, planting himself with "forked" legs in the earth, enduring because he can, an animal himself, confront the bear. Unbuttoning, Lear removes the accommodations of man and emerges "delicate." Ridding himself of "lendings," Lear finds new origins, establishing himself—with the forked animal—on the ground he earlier denied.

This alliance with the earth and unaccommodated man provides the adoptive interlude that makes possible the actual reconciliation within the play. Joining with Edgar, Lear is nurtured by the minimalist surroundings—the bare animal, the plain heath—that contrast to the false opulence (both of the wealthy court and of the adorned mind) with which he began. Promising to endure, Lear recognizes in the bear a nature from which he initially thought he was exempt. This double opening, both to the existence and experience of the animal, helps Lear become the chastised man Cordelia protects. When she finds him, she restores him to that better place he has learned, through what he has lived, to appreciate. Removing his thorns and changing his clothes, Cordelia attempts to revive in her father the eminence he lost in the duration of his trial. Cordelia's rage translates into more than a praise for endurance; it resounds with an insistence on reparation. If Lear on the heath was reduced, through his relationship with Kent and his "unbuttoning" with Edgar, to the naked babe of fortune, Cordelia gives him back his former prowess, taking him in four steps beyond the stage of childhood and into his present age. When she ascends in her appellations (first) from "poor perdu" (4.7.35) to (second) "poor father" (4.7.38), she transforms Lear from child lost to man loved. When she insists (third) "No, Sir, you must not kneel" (4.7.59), she reminds him at once of his position as royalty and his role as parent. Blessing him, she begs Lear, as Joseph did Israel, to bless her, returning to her father the kingdom of supremacy he thought long ago vanished. Fourth, she places him once more on the royal pedestal, advancing in her address from child, to father, to Sir, to "Highness" (4.7.83), even as she assures him with the full force of her presence—"I am, I am" (4.7.70)—of his majesty as king.[3]

And when the recovered Lear, in turn, commands Cordelia to "bear with" him (4.7.83), he turns to the future, imploring her to endure at his side the burden of humanity that might make it possible to bloom to-gether ("bear") in a revival he henceforth can anticipate. That shared expectation is what Lear sought on the heath and what he finds now. Finally, when he prays to Cordelia, empowering her to act as God, commanding her to obey as child (4.7.84), he removes the past, lifting with the "forget and forgive" any burden of personal guilt. If he is now old and foolish, perhaps he was so "then." The release makes it possible to see his daughter at once as young child he can direct (bear with) and as fellow creature who can help (bear him up). A "fool" (4.7.60), Lear arrives at the stage of helplessness that still has hope, having survived the tears of birth and reached ancient renewal.[4] The enclosed story ends there. Restored to his kingship, Lear returns, in act 5, to his early self.

When Cordelia revives her father, she reinstills his initial posses-siveness; bolstered by the exhilaration of his recovery, Lear imagines his independence by denying Cordelia hers. Even as he vows to defy his enemies by creating a psychological freedom within the prison's confines, he deprives Cordelia of her own voice. Her future, her capacity to bear her own life, have her own children, is forgotten. She can now only "bear with" (sustain) her father:

> Come, let's away to prison;
> We two alone will sing like birds i' th' cage:
> When thou dost ask me blessing, I'll kneel down,
> And ask of thee forgiveness: so we'll live,
> And pray, and sing, and tell old tales, and laugh
> At gilded butterflies . . .
> . . . .
> Upon such sacrifices, my Cordelia,
> The Gods themselves throw incense. Have I caught thee?
>   (5.3.8–13; 20–21)

With the redundant "two" of his opening he reveals how Cordelia fortifies him. With the "alone," he speaks as if the two of them were the last people on earth, on yet another island of imposed love. After he assures Cordelia of the gods' assent, Lear turns and asks, "Have I caught thee?" With that question, he confesses how his vision of protection is buttressed by his daughter. If Lear is imprisoned by Edmund, Cordelia is confined by Lear. He captures his bird, enticing it into the cage by a combination of rhetorical logic and physical embrace.[5] Lear has "caught" Cordelia, inspiring her and holding her with him as a wall within the enclave of the world he now anticipates. There, he seeks to preserve the "blessing and forgiving" of his recovery by perpetually repeating it. He creates a tableau, a picture of kneeling parent and importuned child, which will "wear out" those who "ebb and flow by the moon." Those who so ebb and flow are those whose earthly fortunes change—the gilded butterflies and the court fools. But they are also those who live by the changing process of time and seek, in the generational cycle, a continuance that also depends, in its monthly progress, on the moon. In his image of what he and Cordelia will do, Lear creates an artistic empire (tiny as it is) that transcends (in his mind) both the peaceful flow—and the flooding tides—of nature outside. As Spenser "holds" his characters, Lear "catches" his daughter in a moment of reconciling arrest that impedes the dynastic renewal so important to the foundling formula.

In his exaltation Lear, returned to his beginnings, reiterates the fatal flaw of his initiation—the belief in a picture of love that is self-sustaining. For the rich pastures of the opening, he substitutes a little cage, content with the simplicity he has learned to endure during his trial. But that happy isolation sets him off once more into a false pastoral interlude, a fantasy realm within the same court he initially transformed. No wonder, then, that the beast he originally denied rises once again to its monstrosity, leaving (as it did in *Hamlet*) a stage of corpses and raising (as it did not in the end for Hamlet) the specter of nothingness. When Cordelia is hanged, Lear's faith is wrenched away. He ends where he began, discerning neither object in space—"no, no, no life" (5.7.305)—nor proof in time—"never" (5.3.308). If Cordelia does not breathe, what is left is carnivorous nature—a dog, a horse, a rat—obliterating living man. There is no thing in itself, no returning sign of the humanity Lear lost and then found. He has not caught Cordelia; he cannot hold her still in his arms. Nothing remains to face the bear in the mouth. Believing, as he once did, in the goodness of art, even if it is a better art than he earlier espoused, Lear is left with only the evil in nature—an evil, moreover, that he, both through paternity and philosophy, engendered.

Lear at the end is to Cordelia what the ghost was to Hamlet in the beginning, imposing on her a vision of filial forgiveness as the ghost forced on his son an obligation for familial revenge. Like the ghost, Lear calls his child back to himself, "catching" her without casting her forward into the generations. Both tragedies end in lost dynasties. Each hero is given a moment of recovered beginnings (Hamlet's restoration of his childhood, Lear's reconciliation with Cordelia) that cannot last. The generational continuity—so vital to the foundling formula—is left for someone else to fulfill. The vision of *King Lear* is barren, its emptiness heightened by the false hopes of the temporary reconciliation. Lear's tragedy is precipitated in the first act by his failure to appreciate the needs of his children. When he demands that Cordelia love her father "all"

(1.1.94), he denies her the right, as she answers, to make a future with her husband. When the restored Lear ignores that future again by reviving the parental possessiveness that caused his downfall in the first place, he destroys the dynastic sequence that should follow the forgiving and blessing in the foundling experience. Proselytizing the fictional realm of "old tales" (5.3.12), as he had earlier boasted about his "champains rich" (1.1.64), Lear reverses the foundling formula. The art of the lost interlude rises at the beginning and at the end, both times unleashing an absolutely savage nature. The relatively benign nature of the enclosed story, a nature that could sustain the belief in return corroborated by Cordelia's coronation speech in act 4, will "come no more" (5.3.307) to sustain Lear. Despite the brief recovery of his child, he is left with "nothing." He cannot keep—or be kept by—his family.

15

Becoming the Story in *The Winter's Tale*

In *The Winter's Tale* and *The Tempest*, the dynasties denied Hamlet and Lear are recovered. After the suffering of the tragedies, Shakespeare offers a reprieve based on the very deprivation his earlier work involved, as if the canon were waiting for the last phase to close a circle opened in the comedies. The restoration in these plays contains a living legacy given to the characters by themselves. Hamlet and Lear salvage elements of their pasts, but Hermione and Prospero get back most of it, partly because they care so much about the future symbolized by Perdita and Miranda. The protagonists of both plays use the foundling conventions as models around which to shape their lives. Hermione and Perdita remember myths to inspire them, Prospero anticipates stories to occupy him, in newfound life. Opting for the generational cycle, they choose the good of nature; but they also use the good of art to facilitate their participation in that cycle.

In *The Winter's Tale*, Shakespeare defines art in terms of its imitative rather than inventive function, and in *The Tempest*, he sides with the generalized larger cycle, rather than the particularized individual aspect, of nature. Allowing his characters the full process of the foundling experience, he recharges its categories to emphasize the wonder of the found universe, downplaying with Prospero man's capacity to change, extolling with Hermione his ability to pursue, all the "issues" of "being" (*The Winter's Tale*, 5.3.128, 127). Spenser offers his solution to the Renaissance poetic dialogue by redefining nature and imitating a system of duplicative succession over a process of sexual generation. His idea of reproduction is artistic in its progression. That definition denies the communal impulse of the foundling plot and accounts for his failure to complete it in *The Faerie Queene*. In the last plays, Shakespeare denigrates the invention Spenser admires. He finds social and natural answers to death.

He broadens his concept of story in *The Winter's Tale* to include (through his use of gossip, history, myth, and fiction) plots designed both for edification and entertainment. This broadening corresponds to the attenuated role of art in the play. Since all the tales are equal there is no grand art that might elevate one teller, as major artist, above the rest. All the characters contribute to the evolving concept of narrative through the small "tellings" that comprise the larger "tale" of the play's title. Polixenes thinks first of legends of childhood and later about whisperings of state. Leontes is spurred by fables of cuckolds, Paulina by those of tragedies, Florizel by those of Ovid, and Hermione by that of the oracle. But, if the tales motivating the older generations force them to anticipate conclusions commensurate with their fictionalized expectations, so too does the tale governing Perdita. She lives her name, becoming the found "lostling" everyone awaits and embodying the formula upon which her fiction is based. Her recovery indicates that the tale has a reasonable ending; her impending marriage promises a viable future. At the opening of the play, the characters subvert real events into fiction but in the final scenes fiction is consumed by life. The purpose of the tale emerges finally as a modest one: to propound the generational continuity that the reconciliation of the foundling plot ensures. The ending is plausible partially because the process of the play diminishes the grandeur of its art, rendering it merely functional. In this play about playing, Shakespeare proposes that truth is stranger than fiction and that the rehearsal of fiction makes it possible to believe not only in vision (sight) but in visions (or dreams) when they are grounded in fundamental reality.

As victim of the "tales" of cuckoldry motivating Leontes' revenge in the first act, Hermione acknowledges that the romantic past she believed in no longer exists:

> The Emperor of Russia was my father:
> O that he were alive, and here beholding
> His daughter's trial! that he did but see
> The flatness of my misery, yet with eyes
> Of pity, not revenge!
>
> (3.2.119–123)

The open-air courtroom provides both a literal judgment (trial) and an endurance test (trial); the "flatness" of her misery describes not only the dreariness of her present existence but the extent of her fall. Without Leontes' love, without Mamillius's presence, without the child she has just borne, Hermione's life (as described in those lines) is nothing. She may as well be "flat," prostrate, lifeless. In response to Leontes' baseless accusations of infidelity, Hermione invents her death as an instinctively protective device. Innocent, she has nevertheless been tried and found guilty. Her only answer is to retreat from her accuser and withdraw, folding up like an animal that has been mercilessly beaten. If the world refuses refuge, she must find it alone, hibernating, as would the bear in the stage direction, from the fire and ice that threaten. "Suicide" appears as the only way to fight back, a suggestion of her power and a demonstration of the strength she will verify in the incredible denial of self for which the sixteen-year pretense (Hermione's version of a winter's tale) is designed. If Lear meets the bear and endures, Hermione imitates the bear and retreats. But the retreat becomes a form of *reculer pour mieux sauter,* a pulling back into nature in order to sustain the art (the tale of her death) that will in turn serve her revitalization. In most foundling stories, the bereft parent gives up on the child's life. Hermione does not. She withdraws—like Demeter; but unlike Demeter, she has no bargaining strength. What can she withold to force the Fates? How can she stop the consequences of her husband's story? The only possible answer to his active hostility is the passive resistance she invents. In her story, Hermione imitates nature in order to abet her belief in the return promised by the oracle. To become like Demeter—to experience the resurrection the goddess receives—Hermione seeks the lowest escape route; she mimics an animal and then resembles a goddess in what she gets back at the end.[1] Like the bear in winter, her aim in retreat is to awaken safe and restored to what she was. While she feeds Leontes' guilt, she feeds herself (as she says in 5.3.126) on the hope of divine, Demeter-like, return. Her "story" provides her with the means to "preserve" herself and "punish" Leontes, a punishment reinforced by Paulina.

Immediately summarizing the preceding events in terms of conventionally hyperbolic tragic speech, Paulina builds her tale as the logical extension of the earlier ones. She enters crying what she knows to be (and what the audience and Leontes do not recognize as) false tears:

> What studied torments, tyrant, hast for me?
> What wheels? racks? fires? what flaying? boiling?
> In leads or oils? what old or newer torture
> Must I receive, whose every word deserves
> To taste of thy most worst? Thy tyranny,
> Together working with thy jealousies
> (Fancies too weak for boys, too green and idle
> For girls of nine), O, think what they have done,
> And then run mad indeed: stark mad! for all
> Thy by-gone fooleries were but spices of it.
>
>   (3.2.175–184)

The speech refers to traditional punishments—wheels, racks, fires—the heat of tragic passion and the intensity of tragic suffering. All these torments, however, are understatements for the pain of the present situation, which Paulina knows is an invented one.[2] Yet, she goes on from there, pairing Leontes' early fury with Polixenes' speech about youthful innocence (1.2.62–79). It was merely, like his boyhood, green and idle, fanciful, when compared to what she will now relate. Tragedy evolves out of contrasts—"this once was; this now is"—and Paulina draws the oppositions to emphasize what becomes an increasing level of horrors, a further ascent from the fictional base of Leontes' story. Her definition of the tragedy is couched in deliberately literary terms. And the effect of this hyperbole is to render all that has happened, all that the audience saw and will see, into the realm of story. Leontes' tyranny together with his jealousies—the substance of the first three acts—are merely fancies or preludes to the actual suffering that will take place in the purgatorial future of Paulina's rhetoric. But the tragedy itself, both Leontes' revenge plot and Hermione's pretended death, appears as little more than something that might have come from Mamillius's "sad tale." What the audience witnessed were "sprites and goblins" for grown-ups told in terms deliberately reminiscent of already-familiar stories.

The real tragic suffering occurs offstage in what is related, first as proposed occupation and then, in the fifth act, as remembered occurrence. Leontes here designs his winter in "shame perpetual" (3.2.231–42) through the pilgrimage that will become his future life. In his daily excursion to the chapel, living as he will so close to it, he appears to be precisely the hero of Mamillius's earlier untold tale:

> There was a man . . .
> . . . .
> Dwelt by a churchyard.
>
> (2.1.28, 30)

Leontes ends where Mamillius begins. One of the myriad stories of *The Winter's Tale* is the saga of that man as he lives by the churchyard where he presumes his wife lies buried, a tale untold by Mamillius and only indirectly told by Shakespeare in the ensuing drama. Having pushed Hermione away, Leontes is kept outside now, dwelling "by" (next to) the sanctuary into which his wife has crept. His agony lies in his enforced celibacy so close to the center—the holiness and wholeness—that Hermione, defensively retreating, refuses to yield.

The audience never sees the daily repentance or the constant flow of Leontes' tears, and the details of Hermione's sixteen-year swoon are

barely explained. In stories such lapses are taken for granted. The tempest
and the bear are needed to underline the contrast between things dying
and things newborn, between the sorrow of the first acts and the joy of
the forthcoming sequence. The storm, as a heavenly rage, and the bear, as
an animal one, suggest that the rebirth in the last acts will come through a
proper fusing of the heights and depths of nature—the divine strength
and animal instinct in which Hermione persists and whereby her daughter flourishes.[3] With the tempest and the bear, Shakespeare introduces
Lear's two monsters, both of which are assuaged (the one through the
passage of time, the other through the softening of man) in this play. The
storm, as Ben Jonson was quick to point out,[4] is a storybook device, part
of the "machinery" of tales. So too is the introduction of Time. Time's
argument is a justification of artifice, an effort to convince the audience
that what it does not see is as true as what it does:

> Impute it not a crime
> To me, or my swift passage, that I slide
> O'er sixteen years and leave the growth untried
> Of that wide gap, since it is in my power
> To o'erthrow law, and in one self-born hour
> To plant and o'erwhelm custom.
>
> (4.1.4–8)

Referring at once to the traditional theatrical unities and to the overthrow
of those unities for the present plot, Time defends the story about to
unfold. If the audience accepts, as part of Time's action, the sudden,
inexplicable, and unfounded jealousy of Leontes and the subsequent
"trial" of the opening of the play, so too must it accept the sixteen-year
lapse as part of the actual trial of life. By establishing (through the delu-
sions of Leontes, the hyperbolic speech of Paulina, the bear sequence,
and the figure of Time) the tale in the truth of what the audience saw,
Shakespeare prepares his audience for the truth in the tale it is about to
see.

The Winter's Tale opens with a sequence of witnessed events that are
turned through the characters' own rhetoric into a series of fictionalized,
or exaggerated, occurrences. The drama in the final acts centers on Perdita's desire to dismantle all the literary illusions and allusions of the
opening. The most complex exploration of story occurs in the adoptive
interlude where Perdita, who benefits from its art (she is saved by kindly
peasants, raised in pastoral Bohemia), defends the nature that would have
undone her *then* (had Leontes prevailed) and will undo her *now* (if Polixenes wins). In the famous love battle, she insists that she cannot be
transformed by Florizel's wishes. In the famous art battle, she rejects the

amelioration Polixenes advocates. She denies Florizel at first because his belief in transformation precludes the death that she sees at its base. She dismisses Polixenes because his idea of changing nature undermines the generational process that she wants as its end. In her argument with Florizel she refers to the Christ myth—a story based on the foundling recovery. In her argument with Polixenes she alludes to Persephone— whose story is also based on resurrection. Though she speaks against art she uses it anyway, not as a philosophical premise but as a testament of faith in the possibility for a happiness based on an acceptance of nature. Though the Christ and Persephone myths involve resurrection, Perdita applies them to enforce her belief in earthly continuity. The analogous foundlings in those myths are converted by her imitation into formulaic ones. When she becomes them, Perdita substitutes her earthly dynasty for their supernatural perpetuation.

Perdita and Hermione are mirror images of each other. They seek opposite routes toward the same end—each choosing a different side of the same myth and each following a different path to realize that choice. Hermione imitates nature and waits for mythic recovery. Perdita, imitating the myth, pins her hopes on natural return. The story that supports her surrender to Florizel is Christ's; that invigorating her retort to Polixenes is Persephone's. But the commitment can occur only after she accepts the death that precedes the resurrection, when she makes Florizel see, and Polixenes feel, the natural process the myths transcend.

To Florizel's playfully Ovidian defense of transformation, she responds with a dark truth:

> O, but sir,
> Your resolution cannot hold when 'tis
> Oppos'd, as it must be, by th' power of the king:
> One of these two must be necessities,
> Which then will speak, that you must change this purpose,
> Or I my life.
>
> (4.4.35–39)

While he has elevated her to the level of a goddess, overpraising her in much the same way as Astrophil apotheosized Stella and Colin Clout deified Rosalynde, Perdita reminds Florizel of three facts. First, he is not a god and can, therefore, be thwarted by a greater "power," his father. Second, he cannot—godlike—affect her social standing or undo her lowly past. And third, he cannot metamorphose her by deeper means. The only way possible to change her life is to transform it totally through death. Florizel's proposals are for gods and dead men, not for life unchanged. Eternal pastoral play and joyous equality appear impossible in a mutable world. Perdita has identified the two battles in which she is engaged. The first reminder refers to her struggle against Polixenes' interference and the final arguments to her defense against Florizel's temptation. In her last point, about changing her life, spoken as much to herself as to the prince, Perdita acknowledges that sexuality involves death. According to her own stipulation Perdita can grant Florizel victory only after she has defended herself from the onslaught of Polixenes' prattle about art and nature. By that time she is prepared to "change" her life and give it all to Florizel.

She offers him the traditional flowers for victorious soldiers when she admits that in wooing her he is already triumphant. Her confession emerges from her final argument with Polixenes and is rooted in it. Beginning her flower speech with the death of winter, she stops at Easter to express her own resurrection in love, an announcement that takes Florizel off guard. Complaining that she lacks "lilies of all kinds" to strew over Florizel, she proclaims his victory. But when Florizel reverses their roles, asking about "corpses" (4.4.129), she replies, steadfast in her conviction:

> No, like a bank, for love to lie and play on:
> Not like a corpse; or if—not to be buried,
> But quick, and in mine arms. Come, take your flowers:
> Methinks I play as I have seen them do
> In Whitsun pastorals: sure this robe of mine
> Does change my disposition.
>
> (4.4.130–35)

Once having confessed her willingness to surrender, Perdita creates her own bower of revitalizing bliss for love to lie and thrive in. Sexual love connects with an apprehension of death as inevitable in the way that flowers are thrown indiscriminately on marriage beds and corpses. The idea of resurrection is suggested in her word "quick," associated by the apostles with the ascent of Christ and the descent of the Holy Ghost on Whitsunday, a feast celebrating the abiding spirit and the marriage of the heavenly and earthly—an impossible union, like Florizel's and Perdita's—involving a metamorphosis that is for the players, as believers in stories and Christians, already an historically confirmed fact. Perdita uses the story of Christ to enforce her faith in procreation, substituting her earthly continuity for his heavenly perpetuation. In the course of time, from her declaration that the only way she can have Florizel is to change her life to this passage where she has him "quick" and in her arms, Perdita prepares herself to die the death connected to the transforming power of her robe. Playing in Whitsun pastorals changes, as she admits, at least her "disposition" (4.4.135), her willingness to endure what she understands to be the process of love. Like Rosalind and Cleopatra, she changes her mind by changing her clothes, allowing her disguise to confirm her hope that mythical regeneration provides a model for human reproduction.

When the lovers' quarrel is over, the argument with Polixenes resumes, threatening to destroy the engagement so firmly established in Perdita's "I'll swear for 'em" (4.4.155). Polixenes alludes to place and earthly realities with "This is the prettiest low-born lass that ever / Ran on the green-sward" (4.4.156–57). Even in that reminder he seems already to contradict the basic tenets of his earlier dispute with Perdita, where he presented what most critics agree are versions of Shakespeare's or Sidney's or Puttenham's defense of poetry. Northrop Frye sums up the critical agreement about Polixenes' speech: "This is the sound humanist view: it is the view of Sidney who contrasts the brazen world of nature with the golden world of art but also speaks of art as a second nature."[5] Defending what amounts to a democratic position, one in which the prince (as "gentler scion") can marry a peasant girl ("wildest stock"), Polixenes answers Perdita's praise of "great creating nature" by claiming that art "mends" nature (4.4.89–96). Denying Polixenes' logic, Perdita maintains:

> I'll not put
> The dibble in earth to set one slip of them;
> No more than, were I painted, I would wish
> This youth should say 'twere well, and only therefore
> Desire to breed by me.
>
> (4.4.99–103)

G. Wilson Knight suggests that Shakespeare gives Polixenes the speech for the sake of irony so that he might here argue against his own later behavior.[6] Harold Wilson proposes that Shakespeare is dramatizing a Socratic dialogue about Elizabethan views of art and that he is not taking sides.[7] Yet each critic explains away Perdita's impact either by ignoring her vehemence or by arguing, as Knight puts it, that she reasons in petty terms, those of artifice as opposed to art, makeup or "paint," in contrast to Polixenes' more fundamental transplant.[8] What they fail to see is that Perdita refuses to accept Polixenes' "profundities" because they are not profound enough. He talks superficially about "changing" nature when for her, in view of her previous contention with Florizel, change is not just repairing, but something much more demanding: a matter of life and death. Polixenes implies that nature can be improved upon; Perdita argues that nature suffices, proves itself in its fullness and sets an example that man, at his most noble, might emulate, not "mend." Though Polixenes seems to be saying that art transcends death by providing another, the "bud" of a "nobler," life, Perdita suggests that the only life to give and reproduce is her own unmended one. On a more personal level, she maintains that there can be no substitute for the real child she is and the real child she might unpainted "breed." Even in her use of the word "breed," she defends the animal in her nature, accepting the procreational future of love.

But her argument does not quite end there. For, though she is reluctant to "set one dibble in earth" for the artificial flowers Polixenes glorifies, she is quite willing to use the real ones she has as emblems for the people around her. Identifying her friends, she comes to the central foundling story:

> O Proserpina,
> For the flowers now that, frighted, thou let'st fall
> From Dis's waggon! daffodils,
> That come before the swallow dares, and take
> The winds of March with beauty; violets, dim,
> But sweeter than the lids of Juno's eyes
> Or Cytherea's breath; pale primroses,
> That die unmarried, ere they can behold
> Bright Phoebus in his strength (a malady
> Most incident to maids).
>
> (4.4.116–25)

In using the Persephone myth, Perdita emphasizes its floral aspects; the seeds of earthly plants become the source of regenerated life. As part of the life-and-death cycle, the earthly flower maidens surface sweeter than the power of heaven (Juno's eyes and Cytherea's breath) through their potential (these tiny violets) for soaring love. Their sexual longings raise them to the heights Perdita reveres. Like them, Perdita possesses the gift of life inherited through the suffering from which she emerged. Newborn as foundling, she transforms the brutality of her parents into the grace of knowledge.[9] In linking herself to Persephone, Perdita connects Hermione to Demeter, alluding again to the tale of deprivation and salvation she will embody. Though the flowers in her speech are emblematic, they end up being real and functional ("a bank for love to lie and play on") when the play is seen not as acting but as game, the inevitable gambol and gamble of life. In arguing against Polixenes' transplant, Perdita acknowledges that she must risk everything, including her life, which she is now "disposed" to "change." Through her allusions to Christ and Persephone, Perdita aligns herself to the foundling story that she will live. Her connection is based on a faith that what happens in stories (resurrection through miracle) might happen in life. While Polixenes argues that man can interfere with nature (mend it and make it better), Perdita believes that nature can only be altered by those greater powers who brought it into being. Her faith in breeding ties her to a cyclical structure. Her faith in miracle allies her to a mythical structure, an inspiration that she can imitate by participating in the cyclical structure.

The carefully nestled tales within *The Winter's Tale* condition the viewer to believe the final reconciliation. Either he must refute everything by "hooting" (as Paulina might put it) at all stories or he must accept what ensues as just as real as, no more a contrivance than, what has preceded. The structure of the statue scene follows the pattern of earlier crucial ones. If Leontes precipitated the trial and Paulina was its tragic chorus, here Paulina initiates the action and Leontes is its chorus, each participating in Hermione's story. Paulina begins by gently leading her audience into the act she directs, playing with one of several meanings of "mocked," a word often echoed in the dialogue that follows:

> Prepare
> To see the life as lively mock'd as ever
> Still sleep mock'd death.
>
> (5.3.18–20)

Obliquely hinting at Hermione's bearlike retreat, Paulina calls her audience to attention by boasting about the verisimilitude of the art she is about to unveil. But her metaphor reflects the scheme of the play, rendering the wondrous sight unfolding no more spectacular than the process of ordinary experience. In the very act that separates him from nature, man appears, through her metaphor, as an animal in hibernation ("mocking death"), awaiting the revitalization of spring in its inevitable return to earth. Art emerges, finally, as a protective device, serving man in his need for continuity and linking him, as spring follows winter, to the seasonal rebirth that is the natural equivalent of mythological resurrection. Through her stagecraft, Paulina draws a line leading always back to the real center she will divulge. She suggests, in her introduction of the mockery theme, that art imitates life and in that imitation also laughs at (mocks) man by revealing his weakness, his desire to believe the imitation is life itself.[10]

Leontes will turn that weakness into a strength, transforming it into the inspiration for the action he takes. Showing at once his awareness that the art he views has a message meant for him, he concludes:

> The fixture of her eye has motion in't,
> As we are mock'd with art.
>
> (5.3.66–67)

The art ridicules (mocks) his desire to have it melt into the life it so accurately imitates (mocks). But the mockery is linked to memory, pricking Leontes into assuming his own guilt. The word itself recalls his jealousy, "rebukes" him as he says earlier (5.3.37). One of the justifications Leontes offered for the burning of Hermione and the banishing of her child was the thought that Camillo and Polixenes were gossiping about his stupidity, that they were "laughing" at him, making "their pastime at his sorrow" (2.3.24). In the course of the play, however, he comes to understand that the public tale-telling (mockery) once so important to him is insignificant in comparison to the private story of his tragic passion. Like Prince Charming or Pygmalion, his only desire now is to become the hero of a fable, to do the ridiculous and love the art into life by wooing Hermione once again. He defies his past as well as his future in his pledge to act:

> Let no man mock me,
> For I will kiss her.
>
> (5.3.78–79)

Leontes not only accepts the vision of his fancy but is willing to risk anything, even the ultimate reprobation (mockery) for the life of his desires. His final vow, emerging in the context of a word so closely connected with art and its credibility, defines the reconciliation necessary for comedy. It is Leontes' command, "Proceed" (5.3.97), which releases the queen. He is "prepared" (as Paulina has demanded) to act in the name of love quickening him. While Lear seeks to hold Cordelia in a still-life picture, Leontes prods the still life before him into movement.

Once she is certain of Leontes' commitment, Paulina is free in turn to command Hermione:

> Bequeath to death your numbness; for from him
> Dear life redeems you.
>
> (5.3.102–3)

The "dear life" as savior and redeemer is simultaneously all of nature and one particular dear life, Leontes, who sacrifices himself, his public self ("let no man mock me"), for her. As stage manager, Paulina brings to Hermione the things the queen holds dearest—her husband and her child—declaring triumphantly the ultimate message of the play about the relationship between art and reality:

> That she is living,
> Were it but told you, should be hooted at
> Like an old tale: but it appears she lives,
> Though yet she speak not. Mark a little while.
> Please you to interpose, fair madam, kneel
> And pray your mother's blessing. Turn, good lady,
> Our Perdita is found.
>
> (5.3.115–20)

She mocks the final mockery, that of disbelief or the "hooting" at an old tale by presenting this specific child to this particular mother. The story the characters live is "like an old tale." The fictional narrative of their aspirations and the historical narrative of their experiences are the same, "like" each other.

Perdita, as Paulina declares, is "ours." She belongs to everyone who has discovered through her an "awakening of faith" in himself and in the possibility of finding what was lost. Hermione's words make the miracle in the miracle story logical, tearing down all the carefully constructed artifice of the play:

> You gods, look down,
> And from your sacred vials pour your graces
> Upon my daughter's head! Tell me, mine own,
> Where hast thou been preserv'd? where liv'd? how found
> Thy father's court? for thou shalt hear that I,
> Knowing by Paulina that the Oracle
> Gave hope thou wast in being, have preserv'd
> Myself to see the issue.
>
> (5.3.120–27)

The end seems so simple, all the complexities gone, as the mother, placing her hand on her daughter's head, invokes the gods. The blessing connects one generation to the next and sanctifies the mother's wish to see her daughter alive and grown. The tenacity of her preservation appears at once superhuman and subhuman. What brute strength could have kept Hermione hiding so long, what "monstrosity," as Paulina calls it (5.1.41), brings her forth now from the grave? Perdita is "ours," but she is also for Hermione "mine own," a double possessive indicating that the story is not just a fable; its scope is at first personal. Hermione kept herself alive because the oracle's story gave her hope that the word might indeed be made actual and that her daughter might find that promised "being." The queen has waited to see the "issue" and the word itself, because it was used so often earlier in the play, conjures up a past now surmounted. The plot is fulfilled as the queen "sees" and is herself seen, touches and is touched, lives and revives the truth in the light of what is essentially a man-made (her "own") experience. Like Perdita, Hermione believes that the gods might bring to man, through the "issue" of generation, the resurrection of heaven.

The Winter's Tale absorbs the art/nature controversy into its dialogue—and it does so not to create a philosophical treatise but to provide a context for a larger controversy: the sexual/generational struggle. Though Polixenes may be logically right, he is dramatically wrong. Perdita wins the debate in act 4 when she defends nature. Hermione supports her in act 5 when she redefines art. Art does not provide the means, as Polixenes claimed, to improve the world; rather it emerges, more simply, a way to perpetuate it. Thus, the bear mocks sleep, Hermione mocks the bear, mocks her death, mocks (finally) herself; in that mockery, art emerges a mirror, not a mender, of nature. In a play based on fiction (Polixenes' pastoral childhood, Leontes' imagined cuckoldry, Hermione's pretended death, Paulina's tragic interpolation, Mamillius's sad tale), the stories the audience accepts as fact become no less believable than those it interprets as myths: the legends of Christ and Persephone. These stories gave Perdita the strength to believe in breeding; they gave hope (through the oracle) to Hermione that what she bred "wast in being." Hermione and Perdita imitate those stories emerging, through their generational potential, the earthly equivalents of the supernatural myths inspiring them. Unlike Lear who got the world back and then had it taken away, Leontes finds it and is allowed to keep it. He is granted this renewal partly because his daughter and wife (like Rosalind and Cleopatra) believe so strongly in what he so easily dismissed: natural continuity. What makes the experience of *The Winter's Tale* so satisfying is the return of everything, not as it was but as it might be in the normal human cycle, preserved (albeit aged). Hermione in her anger and Perdita in her faith come to understand that nothing in nature can be mended. But their belief in stories indicates that, though things cannot be made better by man, they can be healed. The foundling plot always takes time; it wipes out an entire childhood but returns with the "being" of that child (in the reconciliation) and the promise (in the marriage) of another one. That process—the taking away and the giving back again—is the process of nature; the story of Demeter and Persephone, which follows the cycle of the seasons, is the appropriate one for Hermione and Perdita to pursue.

Shakespeare's use of the foundling theme and all its rituals makes it possible to align the mythical story to the human plane. Defining art as mockery, his characters simulate both the lowest element in nature (the bear) and the highest characters in myth (Persephone and Christ) in order to fuse their lives to the stories they want.

In *The Tempest*, nature is demythologized, and the hero hinges his belief in return on the daily rising and setting, the nightly ebb and flow, of ordinary experience. Perdita and Hermione come to terms with death and find their faith in dying and rising gods. Prospero, himself a dying god, recognizes that the only hope for continuity is to follow nature and align himself with what is made. Thus, he does not become a story; he becomes a storyteller. His art does not imitate nature; it still more primitively describes it.

16

Telling the Story in *The Tempest*

Like so many other Renaissance works, *The Tempest* has two stories: the first, one Prospero attempts to shape; the second, one he resolves to tell. Both revolve around the foundling formula. In the first story, Prospero melodramatizes his past so that he might be seen as the poor outcast logically avenging those who long ago exposed him. He begins—like Cain—seeking to eliminate his ascendant brother. His first story defines his power as maker. When, in the "revels" speech (4.1.146–63), he discovers the limits of invention, he ceases to call himself an inventor and begins the second story. Echoing Joseph,[1] similarly an analogous foundling exposed by his brothers, he acquiesces to a still-higher Maker, crediting the happiness he creates to God, not himself, and letting the others think that it was "meant" (Genesis 50:20) rather than wrought. What compels finally is not the storyteller but the story, the life experience itself. The concluding scenes summarize Prospero's transition from creator to raconteur of his adventures. Whereas his early and tear-jerking sagas inaugurate (as 1.2 demonstrates) the vindictive plot he later relinquishes, his concluding and modest tales are (as the last scenes reflect) self-fulfilling. In them Prospero becomes the paterfamilias gathering his relatives round to hear their history. His final telling records the past and reflects a future made possible by the transition from the first to the second story.

That second story reveals a power of its own as, in the fifth act, Prospero oversees its foundation. He succeeds so well at hiding his art that Gonzalo, witnessing the recognition, attributes it to a divine origin. Blessing Ferdinand and Miranda, he sounds like Hermione:

> Look down, you gods,
> And on this couple drop a blessed crown!
> For it is you that have chalk'd forth the way
> Which brought us hither.

> (5.1.201–4)

Like Hermione, he sees in the rediscovered lovers a continuity thought to be lost; like Hermione, he believes the marriage represents an event predetermined by the gods who laid down the path the court has followed. Gonzalo fails to perceive that the instigator of the foundling recovery is Prospero, whose real art lies in his ability to relinquish his craft.[2]

The stage direction that precedes the recognition scene is telling: "They all enter the circle which Prospero has made" (5.1.55). Like the nymphs dancing around the garland formed by Colin Clout and his shepherdess in *The Faerie Queene,* the courtiers form a circle ordained by Prospero at the helm. He chalks the way that both reveals the inner sanctum and controls the outside parameters, causing the spell that precipitates the recognition. Prospero's circle constitutes his final fling at magic before he gives up the books empowering him to create it. In that moment, the court is forced to attend the story he tells. But by the last scene of the play the story itself possesses the compelling power previously wrought by Prospero's magnetic charms. Alonso, earlier coerced, then listens freely:

> I long
> To hear the story of your life, which must
> Take the ear strangely.
>
> (5.1.311–13)

He admits his willingness to suspend disbelief and "to be taken" with Prospero's tale. Prospero uses this "longing" in the last lines of the play, softening his imperatives:

> I'll deliver all;
> And promise you calm seas, auspicious gales,
> And sail so expeditious, that shall catch
> Your royal fleet far off. My Ariel, chick,
> That is thy charge: then to the elements
> Be free, and fare thou well! Please you, draw near.
>
> (5.1.314–17)

Promising to "deliver all," Prospero combines a rescue, the safe return to Milan, and an explanation, the chronicle Alonso demands. When he beckons the court to "draw near," he commands yet another circle. This time they gather round, pulled by the strength of the narrative that traces (draws) their lives while it compels (draws) them to listen. Bereft of divine power, as he confesses in the epilogue, Prospero moves in the end within the confines of his limited sphere and commands the court because he has found a ground of mutual suffering on which to build. The story emerges for Prospero, as did poetry for Sidney, a way of forestalling the inevitable ravages of time and age and death. Like Sidney's poet, Pros-

pero comes "with a tale forsooth . . . with a tale which holdeth children
from play, and old men from the chimney corner."[3] In its capacity to
"draw," Prospero's account equals the power of Sidney's poem to "hold"
children and old men. The image of the circling listeners emerges as a
moment of arrest. Prospero's group, like that gathered around Sidney's
poet, forms a temporary fortification, whereby time, though it cannot
stand still, is momentarily outfaced. Like Hermione and Perdita, Prospero attempts to prolong the life he has. But whereas their prolongation is
based on a faith that the futurity they want is corroborated by divine
resurrection, Prospero relies for his security on something more mun-
dane—the return of day, the ebbing tides. The story becomes the
heroines' end as Hermione and Perdita are absorbed by the myths they
parallel. They see the proof for what they want in the gods' one-time
triumph—in what they do for themselves. Prospero finds it in the perennial manifestation—the constant recurrence—of what they make for the
world. His second story marks his new beginning, as he plans (in the
"drawing" of the epilogue) his telling of it.

   If Prospero's second story makes him the recorder, not the designer, of
what transpires, his first one places him at the center of the action. In his
second story he will retell for his captivated audience the events that led
to their presence in his circle; thus, his view there is retrospective. In his
first story, his aim is projective; he will use history, yes, but only as it can
be incorporated into his plan to shape destiny. He tells Miranda the cruel
events that forced them onto the island in order to precipitate the crueler
acts that will lead to their departure from it. His telling helps him launch
with Ariel the revenge drama about to unfold. In the autobiography
Prospero spins, father and daughter are both exposed children, banished
not by a cruel parent but by an ambitious brother. Attempting to remember and trying to understand, Miranda demonstrates that the "given" of
the play seems, to her at least, fabulous. Her past appears "like a dream"
(1.2.45) rather than a building block with which to construct a picture of
reality. Prospero's lesson invites incredulity. Miranda is hesitant to accept
the distant world, questioning (as well she might) whether her father
could have been both Duke of Milan and lord of this island (1.2.55).
Calling her life a fiction, she reports that her "heart bleeds" (1.2.64). "Oh
the heavens!" she twice exclaims (1.2.59, 116), exhibiting the hyperbolic
extremity reserved for parables rather than the measured response appropriated to history. She listens "heedfully" (1.2.78), clamoring for more
information even as she labels Prospero's truth "strange" (1.2.309), a
chronicle exoteric to the life she knows and a "tale [that] would cure
deafness" (1.2.106). Like Gonzalo at the end, Miranda at the beginning
reacts to the truth as if it were fantasy. Prospero's first story renders the

real world unbelievable and initiates the train of events he needs to turn
that world to his advantage.

He justifies at once his purpose in the telling and his aim in the action:

> By accident most strange, bountiful Fortune,
> (Now my dear lady) hath mine enemies
> Brought to this shore; and by my prescience
> I find my zenith doth depend upon
> A most auspicious star, whose influence
> If now I court not, but omit, my fortunes
> Will ever after droop.
>
> (1.2.178–84)

Prospero recalls the "then" in order to precipitate the "now." An auspi-
cious star lies in his way, one whose influence he feels ordained to woo as
Rosalind feels destined to pursue Orlando once having found him in the
forest. If he fails to seize the opportunity, his own circumstances will
correspondingly falter. In the revenge story he initially designs, Prospero
catapults himself to the upper pole of the horizon, a hero doomed to
plunge ("droop") unless he uses his power to maintain his ascendancy. It
is as if the loss of status in the story he has just told raised Prospero to the
zenith where he presently stands. Prospero admits to such a possibility in
the play on "foul" and "fair" (1.2.63) when he acknowledges to Miranda
that their arrival on the island was blessed, and confirms it when he urges
Ariel to perform his bidding "now" (1.2.187) and "to the point"
(1.2.194). Prospero's exile with the books he prized above his dukedom
allowed him to develop and so raise his powers. Secluded from the realm
of ordinary men, Prospero stands close enough to Fortune to pay her
proper "court."

In the opening sequences Prospero's pronounced sense of a pressing
present opportunity spurs him to manipulate the moment, but in the final
scenes his sense of an immense future expanse forces him to recognize the
limitations of such action. In the first story Prospero is Fortune's equal;
in the second he emerges, by his own surrender, her pawn. The "revels"
speech marks the turning point from story 1 to story 2, as Prospero
comes to see the failure of human thought and the consequent danger of
his art:

> You do look, my son, in a mov'd sort,
> As if you were dismay'd: be cheerful, sir.
> Our revels now are ended. These our actors,
> As I foretold you, were all spirits, and
> Are melted into air, into thin air:

And, like the baseless fabric of this vision,
The cloud-capp'd towers, the gorgeous palaces,
The solemn temples, the great globe itself,
Yea, all which it inherit, shall dissolve,
And, like this insubstantial pageant faded,
Leave not a rack behind. We are such stuff
As dreams are made on; and our little life
Is rounded with a sleep. Sir, I am vex'd;
Bear with my weakness; my old brain is troubled:
Be not disturb'd with my infirmity:
If you be pleas'd, retire into my cell,
And there repose: a turn or two I'll walk,
To still my beating mind.

                                        (4.1.146–63)

Prospero moves from an acceptance of finality to a terror at its prospect. He appears as a man grasping for a foothold that keeps slipping out from under him. His tone shifts while he talks from that of a man calmly calling attention to his prophetic powers to that of a man made suddenly aware that he, too, may be included in the prophecy.[5] While he can transform an idea into a reality, and while his power to do so has caused the action of the play, what he sees is the inevitable converse of that gift: the annihilation of an idea through its substantiation.[6] When thought becomes action, that action eliminates, by realizing it, the image it represents, grinding up, in the moment of embodiment, its formulating apparatus and creating a hollowness in which "death keeps [his] court." Once an idea is materialized, its purpose, its exhilarating premise, becomes extinct. Contemplating his mind and its creation, Prospero sees them as extensions of a process leading only to evaporation. Noting the wisp of air into which his pageant has faded, Prospero reasons by analogy that all forms will so dissolve and "leave not a rack behind." If man is like God, then the converse is also true. What Prospero does to the revelers might similarly be done to him. If a thing is called into being from nothingness, it can be returned from being into nothingness.[7] Prospero is at a different point now from his earlier "zenith." When he projected his revenge he was on a mountain seeking ways to avoid a fall. Reviewing that revenge, he moves not from heights to depths but into the heights, stretching his thoughts to their logical conclusion. Prospero ascends from actors created by him, to palaces envisaged by architects, to the globe designed by God. Part of the same process, all stem from ideas that are as vaporous as the air into which they dissolve, and hence, all end not as proven substances but as evanescent visions. Contemplating man as the created product of a divine originator like himself, he finds only a temporary shape embossed on a disappearing "fabric." Hamlet sees the dreamer *in* the dream as a castaway exiled to a permanent borderland. Prospero sees the dreamer *of* the dream as the cause of his own disappearance. In his view of concentric shapers, man represents merely the whim of some constantly changing mind, one of many dreams that, like the thin air, are refined until they disappear. He is "rounded with a sleep," as the gorgeous palaces are encompassed by the globe, engulfed by a voracious Maker eager to create new forms. Because nothing solid remains to testify to a life led, man and his work may be illusory. If the substance eliminates the generating idea, when the substance fades nothing is left. The only alternative is to quit playing God, to assume that the divinity differs from the magician.

That assumption launches the second story. By divesting himself of the capacity to reach the visionary heights, Prospero attempts to forget what he has learned there. Having seen through his own capriciousness, Prospero chooses to separate himself from God, to opt for the merely human. Such a choice does not eliminate the vision on the mountain; it simply allies Prospero with the made rather than the Maker, with the creature of Genesis 2 rather than the Creator of Genesis 1. The great globe may eventually vanish as it does in this vision; for the time being, however, Prospero espouses the solidity of the earth, basing his allegiance on a public and no longer isolated truth. He accepts now what Northrop Frye calls "some kind of force or power or will that is not ourselves, an otherness of spirit,"[8] fixing his belief in that deity by acknowledging that he partakes in the regular cycle of human life and that (by extension) all men participate in the cyclical patterns of the earth. He supports the first proposition when he decides to forgive his brother (5.1.20–31), the second when he determines to forgo his books (5.1.32–85). Earlier he felt compelled to manifest the creativity and singularity of his art; now he needs to demonstrate the fraternity of his nature.

Ironically, Prospero learns how to be human from Ariel, who announces his sympathy for the distracted prisoners. Amazed, Prospero replies that he too will be moved:

> Hast thou, which art but air, a touch, a feeling
> Of their afflictions, and shall not myself,
> One of their kind, that relish all as sharply
> Passion as they, be kindlier mov'd than thou art?
> Though with their high wrongs I am struck to th' quick,
> Yet with my nobler reason 'gainst my fury
> Do I take part: the rarer action is
> In virtue than in vengeance.
>
> (5.1.21–28)

Continuing in the same vein as the speech in which he followed the wisp of air into nothingness, Prospero observes that Ariel, though "but air," acquires substance in the assumption of human afflictions. If Ariel is capable of descending, so too is Prospero. Though Prospero has brought his plot to life ("to th' quick") in order to punish his brother, he can still change the conspiracy so that its outcome is both human (kind) and gentle (kindlier), realizing Lavinia's unrequited wish in *Titus Andronicus*. Prospero shows his awareness of story by describing his real-life mercy in terms of its fictional uniqueness. Calling it a "rarer action," a more unique narrative, he substitutes Joseph's concept of forgiveness for Cain's revenge plot. Like Joseph, Prospero will become his brother's keeper (preserver), answering the question raised by Cain in terms of the evil (vengeance) and good (virtue) with which Genesis closes. At the moment he is most in control, Prospero includes himself (as "one of their kind") in the company that expelled him and to which he felt, until now, superior. Like Joseph, Prospero manifests his humanity and his modesty. In Genesis, Joseph presents himself to his penitent brothers as the instrument of God rather than the source of their deliverance:

> And Joseph said unto them, Fear not: for am I in the place of God?
> But as for you, ye thought evil against me; but God meant it unto good, to bring to pass, as it is this day, to save much people alive. (Genesis 50:19–20)

Like Joseph, Prospero reverses the order of things. Both were the original victims of human, not divine, evil. Both were the subsequent agents—not the recipients—of salvation. But both, in the end, deny the guilt of their victimizers and the art of their "saving" under the guise of divine "meaning." Prospero, the divinity who shaped the end, claims no credit. Though he remains, throughout the play, the perpetrator of the foundling plot he tells, Prospero obscures his own role in that story. He does so not only as a sign of a Joseph-like forgiveness but also because he wants very much to believe that there exists a larger design. By acknowledging his "brotherhood," he calls himself a character in the tapestry—not the weaver of its threads—the stuff, not the stuffer, of life. Further, by affirming the regularity of nature and by "abjuring" his ability to alter its course, Prospero connects himself to a pattern upon which he can depend.

The moment he allows his enemies to recover their senses, he accepts the possibility of the fall he was so anxious, in that earlier scene at the zenith, to avoid. With a final salute to the ministers who helped him control the forces of nature, Prospero descends from the hills of the opening "deeper than did ever plummet sound" (5.1.56). He falls voluntarily now, freely abandoning the powers previously propping him up. As he moves in this speech, he unravels the circles of his art, "breaking" his staff in order to rupture his charms. If earlier he sought grandeur in the mystical aspect of nature (the midnight mushrooms and the elves), he now finds consolation in the predictable sequence of its ordinary forms. In the first part of the speech he demonstrates how he bedimmed the light of the sun; in the second he uses the expected order of day to signify the dawn of sense:

> And as the morning steals upon the night,
> Melting the darkness, so their rising senses
> Begin to chase the ignorant fumes that mantle
> Their clearer reason.
>
> . . . .
>   Their understanding
> Begins to swell; and the approaching tide
> Will shortly fill the reasonable shore,
> That now lies foul and muddy.
>
> (5.1.65–68, 79–82)

Earlier the elves mysteriously (with printless foot) chased the "ebbing Neptune"; here the morning renders the night invisible, "melting" it away as previously Prospero's spirits disappeared. In relinquishing the magic of his extraordinary powers, Prospero discovers the wonder of the ordinary dimension. But by fixing the approach of "clearer reason" on the diurnal pattern of the sun and the habitual motion of the tides, Prospero also finds in nature the proof that what disappears can also reappear, that light can overcome darkness and so return. In the "revels" speech he saw that the impetus of magic lies in the volatility of things—on the premise of ultimate dissolution; now he sees that the power of nature lies in the stability of return—on the promise of eternal recurrence. The knowledge that nature provides the solace of recapitulation makes easier Prospero's vow to abandon forever his capacity to toy with it.

His farewell to that power is also a last flourishing, a eulogy of renunciation that finally hinges on the foundling formula. At the close of Malory's *Le Morte d'Arthur*,[9] the confines of time are forced upon the heroes by the gods who gave them, through the magic of Excalibur, a sense of unendingness symbolized in the circle of the Round Table. Spurred on three times by the king, Sir Bedewere finally throws the sword deep into the water. The narrator then accounts for the divine role in human affairs by describing the hand that snatches it up:

And there cam an arme and an honde above the watir, and toke hit and cleyght hit, and shoke hit thryse and braundysshed, and then vanysshed with the swerde into the watir.[10]

The tautology in the passage is similar to Prospero's farewell to his book. The divine hand first took, then clasped, then shook, and, finally, flourished the sword. The redundant verbs extend the power of the goddess wielding it, as if, in taking back the sword, the deity puts on a final show for the world, dangling four times before it the magic she must take away. Bidding farewell to the elves of hills (5.1.32, 37), Prospero likewise flourishes his once-proud feats and gloats in his bygone tricks. But there is a difference between the conclusion of *The Tempest* and that of *Le Morte d'Arthur.* In Malory's work, the goddess appears and then vanishes with the sword into the water. In Shakespeare's, the instrument of rough magic is voluntarily revoked and the enchanter leaves the enchanted island to enter the world of men. Arthur, "the once and future king,"[11] removes himself to the vale of Avalon; the "sometime" (5.1.86) Duke returns to Milan and restores the dynasty of the foundling formula. Choosing to appear not as the god who chalked forth the way that brought the court to the island, but as the man he once was and now will be again, Prospero vows to "discase" (5.1.85) himself. Divested of his magical raiment, he assumes the guise of the court, following the inclination of nature to return, as do the dawn and tides, to their source. That pattern of loss and recovery provides the assurance that the foundling plot that he has chosen to tell has a ground in reality. Because part of him remains in Miranda, the child lost and then redeemed, Prospero will not entirely vanish from this earth. Such a hope lends light to the diminishing plain and leveling descent of his mountain vision. By fixing his metaphors on the phenomenological universe and by choosing for his plot a formula proclaiming the advancement of the natural, Prospero renders the merely human powerful enough to compose a story "drawing" everyone "near."

When he responds to Miranda's renowned wonder at seeing the court party, Prospero's quip—" 'tis new to thee" (5.1.184)—expresses not only the cynicism of his experience but the assurance of his discovery. The world appears new to Miranda but Prospero relishes the solidity of its age. As the waves prove when they lap against the shore, as the sun verifies when it dispels the darkness, things do not always disappear. They also return. Such is the peekaboo magic of existence for the child when he takes away his hand from before his eyes. He squeals with delight not because something remarkable has come but because something wonderful—the world that for a moment he thought gone—remains.

The Tempest ends with what comes back: in the plot, with a restored Duke and a recovered child; in the language, with a resurgent sea and a circling sun. Everything is returned after Prospero links himself, by an act of will, to the larger cycle of nature where nothing goes away forever. That connection removes the individual so starkly isolated in the tragedies from the pain of finality. The particular leaf does not reappear; the lonely man does not live perpetually. But the tree and the dynasty prevail. When Prospero bases his story on forgiveness rather than revenge, when he moves in his self-conception from Genesis 1 to Genesis 2, in his plot projection from Genesis 4 to Genesis 50, he reflects a changed use of the foundling formula. In the initial story he tells Miranda with haste (the one about her history), the two of them are clearly "lost-lings"—castaway on the island by a heartless brother. In the last story (the one he proposes to tell the court "at picked leisure"), he and Miranda are "foundlings"—having recovered the lost brothers and having regained the missing dynasty. Prospero's stories emphasize two phases of the foundling plot: the first, a missing past that must be returned; the second an ensured future that must be guaranteed. In the first phase, the individual is of vital importance: Only the missing child or the exposed Duke will suffice. In the second, that child and that Duke become part of a long history where the wronged family made right again will reign. For Prospero that history, like the eternal rising and setting of the sun, the diurnal ebb and flow of the tides, is a comfort. The world will not disappear as it did in the "revels" speech; it will come, in tiny happenings, again and again.

Shakespeare's use of the foundling conventions (Perdita's recovery and marriage in *The Winter's Tale,* Miranda's recognition and ensured dynasty in *The Tempest*) is made possible by his accommodation of the art/nature controversy. By reducing the role of art (through Hermione's imitation of natural survival and reinterpretation of mythic recovery in *The Winter's Tale*) and expanding the role of nature (through Prospero's acceptance of ordinary return and rejection of magical impulse in *The Tempest*), he allows his characters the deepened knowledge of the tragedies and the victorious élan of the comedies. Shakespeare confirms finally what Wallace Stevens calls poetic "confidence in the world."[12] Such a confidence is at the center of the foundling convention, an understanding that the return signals a bequest to the dynasty of a known, tried, and proven-precious experience.

The Findings of Loss

In a poem about deprivation, Jean Valentine writes about the sustaining power of memory: "Even in prison you would have your childhood."[1] The speaker's sense of what "is enough" echoes Lear comforting Cordelia in act 5. Valentine renders experience inviolable—so much a part of the individual that it can never be taken away. "The child is father of the man," Wordsworth claims, positing a little person inside the outer self whose mere presence assures continuity. The past is an internalized center from which the future grows. This view leads logically to the Freudian emphasis on childhood, where every parental mistake produces a predictable neurosis.

Such a connection does not exist in Elizabethan literature. While the foundling theme is optimistic in its concluding recognition, the exposure suggests that childhood is not impregnable. The initiation premises what Prospero feels in the "revels" speech: nothing is solid. Yet the loss at its base is liberating as well as terrifying. When Malory, Sidney, and Spenser emphasize (or when Shakespeare in *Romeo and Juliet* and *Richard III* explores) the freedom of the adoptive interlude, they write about their pleasure in an Ovidian volatility—in the *abandonne* (license) of abandonment. And, when Shakespeare concludes in the last plays that a return is possible, he forgoes individual creativity, opting instead for the always-returning, and therefore secure, generational cycle. The theme allows the writer to experiment with the possibilities of what he might invent (art) and the rudiments of what he was given (nature).

Elizabethans see childhood as a "province of the imagination,"[2] a place earned by the writer's struggle rather than a stage preserved through the rites of passage. In all the works of this study the early years are never described. Modern man takes for granted an organic self formed by sequential and interrelated events. For Elizabethans that progression could only be affirmed by penetrating the darkness of separation. Sometimes, as in *The Comedy of Errors* and *The Old Arcadia*, the void seems easy; the world just needs to be turned around a bit to come to its senses. Sometimes, as in Shakespeare's last plays, the severance provides a time where the initiating fury can be healed. Sometimes, as in the tragedies, nothing is saved. And occasionally, as in *The Faerie Queene*, that loss inspires the regenerative energy of the poet's song.

Peter Coveney argues that "in the Elizabethan drama, in the main body of Augustan verse, in the major eighteenth-century novel, the child is absent, or the occasion of a passing reference, at the most a subsidiary element in an adult world."[3] Coveney is right that children do not appear in Elizabethan literature. The number of foundling stories written during the period implies, however, that while children were not important as psychological beings in themselves, their physical "being" was an emotional necessity to their parents. Lost-child plots serve that necessity by working, as Leslie Fiedler claims about myths throughout the ages, "both ways."[4] The opening moments respond to doctrinaire Puritanism with a monstrous thrust that verifies the innate existence—and eliminates the future occurrence—of original sin. The exposure short-circuits the dynasty that transmits it. Yet the returned child signals that sinners can be healed and that the restored family might live, as part of a continuing cycle, forever. Having it both ways means "killing . . . kids and keeping them too."[5] By killing and keeping, the parents get their families back just when they need them—when they are ready to become their children's children. Thus Perdita struggles unconsciously, while Una and Hamlet strive deliberately, to protect injured parents. But, if the foundling theme makes reparations to the parents, what about the killed/kept kids? For them, those lost beginnings become the source of a pain setting Rosalind and Marina on guard, both Antipholuses into error, and the Red Cross Knight on his quest. All these characters share a sense that they missed out on something—a security, a warmth—that others, not so deprived, take for granted. And then, in those instances where the broken threads of the past are joined, their stories convey the double joy of a restoration only experienced through the fertile lack that brings them into being.

Notes

2. The Affinities of Kind: The Renaissance Context

1. David Kunzle, "William Hogarth: The Ravaged Child in the Corrupt City," in *Changing Images of the Family*, edited by Virginia Tufte and Barbara Meyerhoff (New Haven: Yale University Press, 1979), p. 99.
2. Ivy Pinchbeck and Margaret Hewitt, *Children in English Society* (London: Routledge and Kegan Paul, 1969), 1:4.
3. Lawrence Stone, *The Family, Sex and Marriage in England, 1500–1800* (New York: Harper and Row, 1977), pp. 42–43.
4. Miles Coverdale, *The Christen State of Matrimony*, translation of H. Bullinger, *Der Christlich Eestand* (London, 1541), unpaginated.
5. John Rogers, *The Glasse of Godly Love*, edited by Frederick J. Furnivall (London: Ludgate Hill, 1876), pp. 186–87.
6. Ibid., p. 187.
7. *The Sonnets*, edited by W. H. Auden and Sylvan Barnet (New York: Signet, 1966), p. 43.
8. Thomas Becon, *Prayers and Other Pieces*, edited by John Ayre (Cambridge: Cambridge University Press, 1864), p. 490.
9. Joel Hurstfield, *The Queen's Wards* (London: Longmans, Green, 1958), p. 3.
10. See Pinchbeck and Hewitt, *Children in English Society*, 1:27–30.
11. Roger Ascham, *The Schoolmaster*, edited by Lawrence Ryan (Ithaca: Cornell University Press, 1967) pp. 35–36.
12. Ibid., p. 36.
13. Stone, *Family, Sex and Marriage in England*, p. 175.
14. Ascham, *Schoolmaster*, p. 36.
15. "The Ypres Scheme of Poor Relief, 1531," in *Some Early Tracts on Poor Relief*, edited F. R. Salter (London: Methuen, 1926), p. 49–50.
16. Ibid., pp. 53–54.
17. Gervaise Babington, *Certaine Plaine Briefe and Comfortable Notes upon Everie Chapter of Genesis* (London: Thomas Charde, 1592), pp. 89–90.

3. Finders Keepers

1. "To Aphrodite," in *Hesiod, the Homeric Hymns and Homerica*, translated by Hugh G. Evelyn-White (Cambridge: Harvard University Press, 1914), p. 407. All quotations are from this edition.

2. "The Theogeny of Hesiod," in ibid., p. 91–93.

3. "To Demeter," in ibid., p. 295.

4. Pausanias, *The Description of Greece*, translated by W. H. S. Jones (Cambridge: Harvard University Press, 1935), 4:89.

5. "Epilogemena," in Carl Jung and C. Kerenyi, *Introduction to a Science of Mythology*, translated by R. F. C. Hull (London: Routledge and Kegan Paul, 1951), p. 254.

6. Ovid, *Metamorphoses, The Arthur Golding Translation*, edited by John Frederick Nims (New York: Macmillan, 1965), p. 34.

7. See Arthur O. Lovejoy and George Boas, *Primitivism and Related Ideas in Antiquity* (New York: Octagon Books, 1965), pp. 389–420.

8. Ibid., p. 447.

9. Ibid., p. 450.

10. Ernst Robert Curtius, *European Literature and the Latin Middle Ages*, translated by Willard R. Trask (New York: Pantheon Books, 1953), p. 192.

11. Longus, *Daphnis and Chloe*, translated by Paul Turner (Baltimore: Penguin Books, 1966), pp. 17–18.

12. Heliodorus, *An Aethiopian History*, translated by Thomas Underdowne (London: David Nutt, 1895), p. 288.

4. Finding and Losing "Beaulté and Noblesse"

1. Thomas Malory, *Works*, edited by Eugène Vinaver (London: Oxford University Press, 1967), p. 1240. All quotations are from this edition.

2. Of the changed world of the quest, Muriel Whitaker notes that "whether waking or sleeping the Grail knight sees visions of a kind that never troubled him in the world of Camelot" ("Christian Iconography in the Quest of the Holy Grail," *Mosaic* 12 [1979]: 13).

3. T. F. Wright calls Merlin both the agent through whom God's will and "grace are expressed" and "an omniscient strategist who leads Arthur to victory over the rebel kings" (see "The Tale of King Arthur," in *Malory's Originality*, edited by R. M. Lumiansky [Baltimore: Johns Hopkins University Press, 1963], p. 23). But in citing the "two important offices" of Merlin, Wright does not stress quite enough Merlin's reluctance to be the "agent of God." He may see the divine will, but that will seems often to be in conflict with his desires. See also Eugène Vinaver's comments on this matter in Malory, *Works*, p. 1286.

4. C. S. Moorman writes of the yearly pledge that "the Round Table has in the end failed in trust because the code which Arthur outlined for its maintenance in the very beginning . . . could not support it. Instead of providing the knight with a shield to protect him from the onslaughts of his own fallen nature, Arthurian chivalry attempted to disguise the ugly facts of that nature" (see *The Book of King Arthur* [Lexington: University of Kentucky Press, 1965], pp. 73–74).

5. Describing what it means to belong to the fellowship, Mark Lambert notes that "place, time, weather, quotidian activities are peripheral to the reality of *Le Morte d'Arthur*, and Malory does not want our eyes drawn away from the center. Individuality is also peripheral, with man as with things what matters is the norm" (see *Style and Vision in "Le Morte d'Arthur"* [New Haven: Yale University Press, 1975], p. 92).

6. Of Malory's changing the events of the story from those of the French original, where Pelleas and Ettard are united, P. E. Tucker claims, "Malory produces a not very coherent compromise" (see "Chivalry in the Morte," in *Essays on Malory*, edited by J. A. M. Bennett [Oxford: Clarendon Press, 1963], p. 704). In viewing (as F. Whitehead also did in *Medium Aevum* 2 [1933]: 99–208) this story as simply an exemple of Malory's

misunderstanding of the courtly-love theme, Tucker misses the centrality of Malory's treatment of grace.

7. On the history of this theme, see Larry P. Benson, _Malory's "Le Morte d'Arthur"_ (Cambridge: Harvard University Press, 1976), pp. 92–108.

8. Vinaver writes of the Gareth story:

> While dispensing with the subtleties of the courtly code, the French Gaheret propounded the theory that a man of low birth cannot defeat a nobleman except by accident or by guile and so championed the claims of knighthood as an aristocratic institution. For once Malory found himself in harmony with this French model. (Malory, _Works,_ p. 1434)

Launcelot's joy here, however, lies not so much in Gareth's verified birth but in his proven worth. The Gareth story emphasizes that the concept of aristocracy needs to be embodied in act as well as inherited through blood.

9. On the notion of adoption as used here, Wilfred Guerin writes, "Mutual love, not kinship is the essence of this relationship; Launcelot's worth, necessary for Malory's general purpose, is made clearer by his friendship for and fostering the young Beaumains" (see "The Tale of Gareth" in _Malory's Originality,_ edited by Lumiansky, p. 114).

10. In the French text, the decay of the familial relationship is underlined by a passage claiming that, in those days, if a son were to find a father dying in bed, the child would thrust the old man out, killing the parent (see _La Queste del Saunt Graal,_ edited by Albert Pauphilet [Paris: Librarie Ancienne Honore Champion, 1949], p. 95).

5. Transformation in Sidney's _Old Arcadia_

1. Jon S. Lawry writes, of the reflective importance of Strephon and Klaius, that they "have fairly distinct characters corresponding to those of Musidorus and Pyrocles" (_Sidney's Two Arcadias_ [Ithaca: Cornell University Press, 1972], p. 130).

2. On Philisides as Sidney, see A. C. Hamilton, _Sir Philip Sidney_ (Cambridge: Cambridge University Press, 1977), p. 35; Richard Lanham, _"The Old Arcadia," Sidney's Arcadia_ (New Haven: Yale University Press, 1965) p. 228; and Neil Rudenstine, _Sidney's Poetic Development_ (Cambridge: Harvard University Press, 1967), p. 107.

3. About Sidney's initial sense of his work Lanham argues that "a perceptive reader of the _Arcadia_ . . . cannot escape the evidences of Sidney's strong sense of the ludicrous, in both love and war" _"The Old Arcadia,"_ p. 403).

4. Citing the connection between poet and heroes on the subject of regeneration, Dorothy Connell writes, "If the poet shares with the lover a delight at the perception of earthly beauty, he also shares the lover's desire to propagate that beauty" (_Sir Philip Sidney: The Maker's Mind_ [Oxford: Clarendon Press, 1977], p. 45).

5. Philip Sidney, _The Countess of Pembroke's Arcadia,_ edited by Jean Robertson (Oxford: Clarendon Press, 1973), p. 328. Future references are to this edition.

6. David Kalstone, _Sidney's Poetry_ (Cambridge: Harvard University Press, 1965), p. 79. Kalstone's influence is evident throughout this reading of the sestina.

7. Commenting upon the relationship between landscape and psyche in the double sestina, Arthur K. Amos, Jr., writes that "Urania's symbolic function, then, shows the power of love in spatial terms and shows how a psychological state influences one's perception of space" (_Time, Space and Value: The Narrative Structure of "The New Arcadia"_ [Lewisburg, Pa.: Bucknell University Press, 1977], pp. 33–34).

8. Kalstone writes of Philisides fall from philosophical contemplation: "Like Marvell's thoughtful pastoralist, he is to learn that "Two paradises 'twere in one / to live in paradise alone" (_Sidney's Poetry,_ p. 57).

6. Two Irreconcilable Foundlings

1. Edmund Spenser, *Poetical Works*, edited by J. C. Smith and E. de Selincourt (Oxford: Oxford University Press, 1975), p. 64. Future references are to this edition.

2. C. S. Lewis, *The Allegory of Love* (New York: Oxford University Press, 1958), p. 334.

3. Of the Red Cross Knight's isolation, Isabel MacCaffrey writes he "has no elders; his truth is a woman, a passive and nearly helpless truth in bondage" (*Spenser's Allegory: The Anatomy of Imagination* [Princeton: Princeton University Press, 1976], p. 135).

· 4. Speaking of this sense of a resounding universe, Rosamund Tuve explains that events in *The Faerie Queen* are connected by "entrelacement":

> Events connected by *entrelacement* are not just juxtaposed; they are interlaced and when we get back to our first character he is not where we left him as we finished his episode, but in the place of psychological state or condition of meaningfulness to which he has been pulled by events occurring in following episodes written about someone else. Moreover, though the intervening episode will look like a digression from the line previously followed, it will transpire that that line could not go on without something furnished in the seemingly unrelated second line of the narrative, the digression. (*Allegorical Imagery* [Princeton: Princeton University Press, 1966], p. 363)

In cantos 4 and 5, "entrelacement" reflects on the fear of infanticide or patricide.

5. See Lewis, *Allegory of Love*, p. 313–316.

6. A. C. Hamilton, contrasting the end of book 1 with that of book 2, says that "when the Red Cross Knight marries, everything serves his pleasure . . . above all Una" (see *The Structure of Allegory in "The Faerie Queene"* [Oxford: Clarendon Press, 1961], p. 104). Similarly optimistic, James Nohrnberg writes:

> The end of Spenser's legend is the uniting of the faithful and the true. Truth, if she is going to prevail, needs a champion. And the champion, if he is going to prevail, needs to know what he is doing. Spenser's theme, though, is the establishment of faith, and to be a legend of faith the story must not end in marriage, but in troth plight or bethrothal; that is, in a renewed pledging of faith. (See *The Analogy of "The Faerie Queene"* [Princeton: Princeton University Press. 1976], p. 281)

In calling Spenser's theme the establishment of faith, and in seeing its objectives realized "in a renewed pledging of faith," Nohrnberg de-emphasizes the narrative structure in favor of a thematic concern. The theme may be satisfied with a pledge, but Una appears, without her champion, as she did in canto 1, in "mourning."

7. W. B. Yeats, "Edmund Spenser," *Essays and Introductions* (New York: Macmillan, 1961), p. 356.

7. Two Creations

1. W. B. C. Watkins, *Shakespeare and Spenser* (Princeton: Princeton University Press, 1966), p. 17. Watkins reads backward from the *Prothalamion* and *Epithalamion*, assuming that the Spenser of *The Faerie Queene* is identical to the creator of the marriage hymns. The thesis here is that the marriage and "large posterity" of the *Epithalamion* are problematic for the poet of *The Faerie Queene*. Donald Cheney emphasizes this point in a different context when he writes of the ending of the original book 3: "Spenser and his contemporaries share . . . a concern to compress as many supplementary and even conflicting meanings as possible

into the image of marriage" (see "Spenser's Hermaphrodite and the 1590 *Faerie Queene*," *PMLA* 87 [1972]: 199).

2. Humphrey Tonkin speaks of this sense of dissociation when he writes: "In the garden we do not actually find the creatures themselves but rather their potentiality—that contained within the garden is that which individualizes the creatures, but not the creatures themselves" (Spenser's Garden of Adonis and Britomart's Quest," *PMLA* 88 [1973], 410).

3. Nohrnberg, *The Analogy of "The Faerie Queene,"* p. 567.

4. Isabel MacCaffrey summarizes the critical agreement about the organic relationship between Britomart and Amoret: "As most readers have recognized, Britomart's character and adventures are illuminated by our understanding of what Belphoebe and Amoret embody" (*Spenser's Allegory*, p. 273).

5. Commenting on the parallels between Isis and Venus, Nohrnberg writes, "like Spenser's Venus, Isis is also said to be bisexual and to represent nature" (*The Analogy of "The Faerie Queene,"* p. 613).

6. Of the Temple scene, Angus Fletcher writes that it "bequeathes the air of expectant temporality, much as if it were a court masque celebrating a hymeneal rite" (*The Prophetic Moment: An Essay on Spenser* [Chicago: University of Chicago Press, 1971], p.276). Fletcher, interested more in the prophetic possibility than the narrative actuality, does not seem disturbed that the expectation remains unsatisfied. Reasoning that Britomart represents Gloriana, who is the queen of England, he speculates that

> Spenser does not mean that Elizabeth will have to marry and have a son for England to survive. He means that the spirit of such a procreative act will have to inspire whoever rules England, and to the extent that Gloriana sends her knights on good quests, she has sons, many lions to serve her court of Maidenhead. What may not exist in actual fact may still exist in visionary truth and the latter may do more good to the kingdom than the fragile permanence of mere physical rebirth. (*The Prophetic Moment*, p. 275)

7. Of Britomart's desertion, T. K. Dunseath argues that "after Artegall is sufficiently recovered from the debilitating effects of his long imprisonment and poor diet, he resumes his quest to free Irene and establish peace. . . . Britomart now has all the attributes of a perfect wife" (*Spenser's Allegory of Justice in Book Five of "The Faerie Queene"* [Princeton: Princeton University Press, 1965], p. 181). Dunseath fails, however, to acknowledge that Britomart never is given the occasion to enjoy that perfection.

8. Two Recreations

1. Richard Neuse argues that, in book 6, Spenser reaches "the limits of his epic enterprise" (see "Book VI as Conclusion to *The Faerie Queene*," *ELH* 35 [1968]: 353).

2. Humphrey Tonkin, *Spenser's Courteous Pastoral* (London: Oxford University Press, 1966), pp. 44–45.

3. Harry Berger, Jr., notes "a deliberate casualness in Spenser's treatment of narrative and character" (see "A Secret Discipline: *The Faeire Queene*, Book VI," in *Form and Convention in the Poetry of Edmund Spenser*, edited by William Nelson [New York: Columbia University Press, 1961], p. 38).

4. Suzanne Woods emphasizes, instead, what Colin Clout gets from the lady: "By a reciprocal action the poet, who has received an inspiring grace from the lady then uses it to translate her figure into a very Grace" ("Closure in *The Faerie Queene*," *JEGP* 76 [1977]: 207).

9. *Richard III* and Genesis 4

1. *The Standard Edition of the Complete Psychological Works,* translated by James Strachey and Anna Freud (London: Hogarth Press, 1973), 14:314–15.

2. Comparing Richard to Hamlet, Michael Neill writes that "Richard with none of Hamlet's moral sensibilities but poised on the edge of the same ontological abyss, sets out, rather, to create himself" ("Shakespeare's Hall of Mirrors," *Shakespeare Studies* 8 [1975]: 100).

3. In calling the play tragic, critics concur with Freud's interpretation. See, for example, Murray Krieger, who writes:

> In the ritual of lamentation and in the ritualistic curses which successive generations form in answer to one another, we are eventually carried back far beyond *Richard III,* in history and tradition back to those dramas of lust and blood and Nemesis and to those extended cycles about family and domain with which Western tragedy began. ("The Dark Generations of *Richard III*" in *The Design Within,* edited by M. D. Faber [New York: Science House, 1970], p. 366)

Lily Campbell argues that Shakespeare

> portrayed and analyzed the passion of ambition that caused Richard to sin and the passion of fear that at the same time punished him for his sins and forced him to wade still further in blood. . . . These are the common methods of Shakespearean tragedy and they justify those who hold *Richard III* to be a tragedy. ("The Tragical Doings of King Richard III," in *Richard III,* edited by Mark Eccles [New York: Signet, 1964], p. 227)

4. Richard Saccio writes that "no contemporary portrait attests to [the crookback] and the fact that [Richard] permitted himself to be stripped to the waist for annointing at his coronation suggests that his torso could bear public inspection" (*Shakespeare's English Kings* [London: Oxford University Press, 1977], p. 159). Speaking of Richard as an inventor, Bernard Spivack writes that his "essential relationship to [his] crimes is not moral but artistic" (see *Shakespeare and the Allegory of Evil* [New York: Columbia University Press, 1955], p. 44).

5. Antony Hammond defends his use of "I and I," arguing that

> the drift of the present passage seems to be that Richard, in what we would now call a schizophrenic vein, is distinguishing between aspects of his personality: the clever, witty, self-reliant villain, and the conscience-smitten coward he is just now discovering. The anguish of this passage, expressed in short, choppy rhetorical dialectic, is an attempt to represent verbally the mutual encounter and alternation of these two selves, I and I. (See *The Arden Edition of King Richard III,* edited by Antony Hammond [London: Methuen, 1981], p. 340)

6. Waldo McNeir maintains that Richard's "continuous play acting has fragmented his personality, so dividing him that he has disintegrated into the ineffectuality of one who has lost all cohesion as an individual. At least temporarily, he is potentially anyone and at the same time no one" ("The Masks of *Richard III,*" *Studies in English Literature* 11 [1971]: 184).

7. About Richard's decline from god to man, Jan Kott writes that "Richard has been making history. The world was for him a piece of clay to shape in his hand. And now he himself is a piece of clay shaped by someone else" (*Shakespeare Our Contemporary,* translated by Boleslaw Taborski [London: Methuen, 1965], p. 43).

8. E. M. W. Tillyard, *Shakespeare's History Plays* (London: Chatto and Windus, 1960), p. 204.

9. "Angel with Horns: The Unity of *Richard III*," in *Shakespeare: The Histories* edited by Eugene M. Waith (Englewood Cliffs, N.J.: Prentice-Hall, 1965), p. 82.

10. Romeo, Juliet, and the Art of Naming Love

1. Critics who see Mercutio as merely vulgar assign him the role of foil to Romeo. But such dismissals misconstrue the importance of his defense of reason and underestimate his role as spokesman for art.

Among those who cite his carnality are Harold C. Goddard, *The Meaning of Shakespeare* (Chicago: University of Chicago Press, 1951), 1 : 120–23; Harley Granville-Barker, *Prefaces to Shakespeare* (Princeton: Princeton University Press, 1947), 2 : 335–38; and J. Dover Wilson, "The Elizabethan Shakespeare," in *Proceedings of the British Academy* (London: Oxford University Press, 1929), p. 123.

2. Harry Levin makes a similar distinction between art and nature when he argues that "Juliet calls into question not merely Romeo's name but, by implication, all names, forms, conventions, sophistications, and arbitrary dictates of society, as opposed to the appeal of instinct directly conveyed in the odor of a rose" (see "Form and Formality in *Romeo and Juliet*," *Shakespeare Quarterly* 11 [1960]: 4).

3. On nature's callousness, Frederick Turner writes:

The lovers call their love infinite, but in the world of time there can be nothing infinite. Time itself turns against the lovers, and blindly ejects them from its system as incompatible with its texture and tissue. The lovers treat time subjectively . . . and time revenges itself blindly for such temerity. (*Shakespeare and the Nature of Time* [Oxford: Clarendon Press, 1971], p. 126)

4. Comparing the balcony scene to the aubade, Mark Rose writes:

The segments of the early scene are arranged to give the effect of the dream dominating "reality," the lovers overwhelming the outsiders as the short initial segment yields to the long lyric episode. The [aubade] suggests the dream dissolving into day, the magical world of the lovers literally overwhelmed before our eyes. (*Shakespearean Design* [Cambridge: Harvard University Press, 1972], p. 72)

Similarly, James Black counterpoints the two scenes:

The fact that in each of these scenes the setting is the same and the stage picture reduplicated lends emphasis to the pathetic alteration in the speakers' tones and circumstances.

The parallels emphasize the differences: things look the same but are painfully altered. Thus the audience is looking at what it saw before, but is being forced to see more intensely. ("The Visual Artistry of *Romeo and Juliet*," *Studies in English Literature* 15 [1975]: 247)

5. Commenting on the way nature retracts its support, Donald Stauffer maintains that "in no other play does Shakespeare envisage a general moral order operating with such inhuman, mechanical severity" (*Shakespeare's World of Images* [Bloomington: Indiana University Press, 1973], p. 55).

6. M. H. Mahood writes that "Romeo and Juliet 'cease to die, by dying'" (see *Shakespeare's Word Play* [London: Methuen, 1957], p. 72).

7. Northrop Frye's comments about the negative metamorphosis of nature into art are relevant to the tragedy here:

> Changing a person into a statue would be an image of metamorphosis or descent to a lower state of being: the "statuas moving" that Bacon mentions as frequent in masques . . . is an image of restored identity.

Using Frye's terms, the tragedy in *Romeo and Juliet* can be seen as a triumph of a deadening order over the lively art created by the lovers (see "Romance as Masque," in *Shakespeare's Romances Reconsidered*, edited by Carol McGinnis Kay and Henry E. Jacobs [Lincoln: University of Nebraska Press, 1978], p. 36).

11. Earned Reprieve

1. T. S. Eliot, *Collected Poems* (New York: Harcourt, Brace, 1958), p. 73.

2. *The Comedy of Errors* (New York: Signet, 1965), p. xxviii.

3. A. C. Hamilton speaks of this submergence in, and surfacing from, the sea in his essay on *Errors* (see *The Early Shakespeare* [San Marino, Calif.: Huntington Library, 1967], pp. 107–8).

4. E. M. W. Tillyard writes that the "root of [Adriana's] trouble is stupidity" (*Shakespeare's Early Comedies* [London: Chatto and Windus, 1960], p. 58). Thomas Mark Parrot, *Shakespearean Comedy* (New York: Russell and Russell, 1962), p. 107, calls Adriana "the possessive woman." Vincent Petronella accuses Adriana of being "a force that pushes domestic affairs towards separation and dissolution" (see "Structure and Theme through Separation and Union in Shakespeare's *The Comedy of Errors*," *Modern Language Review* 69 [1974]: 485).

5. Writing of *Comedy of Errors* as an expression "in utero . . . of the psychological themes of *Hamlet*," Avi Erlich argues that "an ambiguous father, sons lost in incest and inherent doubleness, and a powerful mother are elements basic to both *Hamlet* and *Errors*. . . . Identical twins are an early dramatic expression of a man confused because he does not know his other self" (*Hamlet's Absent Father* [Princeton: Princeton University Press, 1977], p. 269).

6. See 1.2.35–38:

> I to the world am like a drop of water
> That in the ocean seeks another drop,
> Who, falling there to find his fellow forth,
> (Unseen, inquisitive) confounds himself.

About the interconnectedness of these lines, W. Thomas MacCary writes:

> We are reminded of the Narcissus myth—since water can reflect as well as absorb and Antipholus of Syracuse seeks himself in his mirror image. The water here is ocean, is the overwhelming aspect of the mother, the mother from whom the child cannot differentiate himself. (*"The Comedy of Errors:* A Different Kind of Comedy," *New Literary History* 9 [1977]: 533)

7. Alexander Leggatt writes that *"The Comedy of Errors* is unusual in that mistaken

identity is itself a motif, not (as in *As You Like It* or *Twelfth Night*) a technical device to aid in the presentation of some other issue" (*Shakespeare's Comedy of Love* [London: Methuen, 1974], p. 3).

8. R. A. Foakes observes that "Adriana seems to desire to absorb her supposed husband's identity into her own" (see *The Comedy of Errors* [London: Methuen, 1969], p. 34).

9. Sidney, *The Countess of Pembroke's Arcadia*, p. 19.

10. C. L. Barber quips that Adriana may have learned something from the Abbess's lecture even though the "Abbess turns out to be her mother-in-law" (see "Shakespearean Comedy in *The Comedy of Errors*," *College English* 25 [1964]: 494).

11. Defending the restoration at the end, Leggatt argues:

> The emphasis is . . . not on the creation of a "new social unit" (as in Northrop Frye's theory of comedy), but on the renewal of an old family unit. . . .
> The final image of security is not a wedding dance but a christening feast, a family celebration. This may be because of the concern with identity; identity is surrendered in love and marriage, but when the original family is recreated the characters join a comforting social group which asks only that they be their old selves. After the challenges to identity throughout the play, the characters—and perhaps the audience—need this kind of comfort, a return to the old and familiar rather than the start of something new which marriage symbolizes. (*Shakespeare's Comedy of Love*, p. 17)

12. F. D. Hoeniger sees Marina as the protagonist, arguing that she, "aided by the grace of Diana, the play's presiding goddess, becomes the main instrument of the freeing of Pericles" (*Pericles* [New York: Methuen, 1963], p. lxxxv).

13. Of the peculiar circumstances of Marina's birth, Derek Traversi remarks:

> She is at once "mortal," the issue of Pericles' own flesh and blood and the instrument of entry into a new, transfigured life; the conditions of her birth both link her to mortality and so to strain and suffering symbolized in her past subjection to the elements and exalt her, through their very remoteness, to the spiritual freedom of a fresh creation. Through her, past and present, death and life, temporal servitude and spiritual freedom are fused in a single organic process tending to the affirmation of a new state of being. (*Shakespeare: The Last Phase* [New York: Harcourt, Brace, 1955], p. 37)

14. Annette C. Flower writes that "Marina, by refusing to state her identity, forces others to deal with her simply as a captive virgin" (see "Disguise and Identity in *Pericles*," *Shakespeare Quarterly* 26 [1975]: 40).

12. The Dream of a Better Life

1. John Holloway uses this sonnet to begin his discussion of *Antony and Cleopatra:*

> Sonnet 129 helps the reader of *Antony and Cleopatra*. . . . It shows Shakespeare speaking of the experience of lust in a very remarkable way. Ferocious as is his condemnation of it in the earlier lines of the poem, and sorrowful as is his portrait of what follows after it is sated, for all that he calls it nothing less than "a bliss in proof." (*The Story of the Night* [Lincoln: University of Nebraska Press, 1961], p. 100)

Holloway's emphasis is on the connection between lust and bliss, opposites in the poem that parallel contrasts in the play. He does not refer, as does the discussion here, to the dream as vanishing prospect.

2. *Sonnets*, edited by William F. Burto (New York: Signet, 1964), p. 169.

3. See ibid.

4. Carol Thomas Neely says that the line characterizes a shift in tone from that of one both "ideally repulsive and hence ideally repulsible to something mixed, ambiguous. The emphasis is now on the dual pleasures of anticipation and satisfaction; even the aftermath of lust is no longer poisoned but is, more mildly, 'a very wo' and a 'dreame' " (see "Detachment and Engagement in Shakespeare's Sonnets 94, 116 and 129," *PMLA* 92 (1977): 91). For Neely, as for most critics, the "dream" represents the pleasant epilogue, not the evanescent quality, of experience.

5. See David Young, *The Heart's Forest* (New Haven: Yale University Press, 1972), p. 42.

6. On the darkness of the forest, Jan Kott writes:

> At all times . . . the Forest of Arden is a real world, always the same, bitter, cruel and fascinating; the world which one cannot accept but from which there is no escape, a world for which there is no justification except that it is the only one that exists. (*Shakespeare Our Contemporary*, p. 229)

7. Of Rosalind's preventive worrying in these speeches, C. L. Barber similarly argues "love has been made independent of illusions without becoming any the less intense; it is therefore inoculated against life's unromantic contradictions" (*Shakespeare's Festive Comedia* [Cleveland: Meridian Books, 1959], p. 236).

8. Rosalie Colie, *Shakespeare's Living Art* (Princeton: Princeton University Press, 1974), p. 189.

13. Hamlet's Story

1. Ernest Jones uses the Jephthah reference to demonstrate that through it "we see Hamlet's fundamental attitude towards moralizing elders who use their power to thwart the happiness of the young" (see "*Hamlet:* The Psychoanalytical Solution," in *Hamlet and Oedipus* [New York: Norton, 1976], p. 87). Jones fixes Hamlet's happiness on a liaison with his mother, an argument that allies him with his uncle in that Claudius incorporates Hamlet's own desires. The contention here is that Hamlet resents his elders, particularly his father, for imposing their failures on him. Hamlet's anger is directed at both his parents for having passed on—through original sin and their own weakness—a burden of evil.

2. Frederick Wertheim speaks psychologically to the point when he argues that "Hamlet the child was as surely put to death by Denmark as was Denmark put to death by Hamlet the prince" (see "The Matricidal Impulse: Critique of Freud's Interpretation of Hamlet," *Journal of Criminal Psychopathology* 2 [1941]: 463). J. Philip Brockbank compares the sacrifice of *Hamlet* to that of *Oedipus-Rex:*

> Claudius looks like the agent as well as the victim of a continuing and universal sacrificial process. In the *Oedipus-Rex* the king is guilty but . . . blameless; in *Hamlet* the king is culpable but so, in the operation of the play's language, are we all. ("Hamlet the Bonesetter," *Shakespeare Survey* 30 [1977]: 106)

3. Jean Kerr, "My Own Hobgoblin and How it Grew," *New York Times*, 5 January 1983.

4. W. L. Godshalk says, of Hamlet's immersion in his father's mire: "If Hamlet's father has been literally poisoned through the ear, so, figuratively has been Hamlet" ("Hamlet's Dream of Innocence," *Shakespeare Studies* 9 [1976]: 224).

5. Richard Sewall uses this phrase to describe the way tragedy "sharpens the issues" (*The Vision of Tragedy* [New Haven: Yale University Press, 1962], p. 44).

6. Of the sense of past innocence and present corruption, Maynard Mack writes, "Time was, the play keeps reminding us, when Denmark was a different place" (see "The World of *Hamlet,*" *Yale Review* 41 (1952): 517). But Mack does not deal with the interval in the play where Hamlet's dark vision erases from view that different place.

7. Describing Hamlet's transformation, Don Parry Norford argues that "Hamlet becomes transformed by his father's poison, becoming 'the vicious mole of nature . . . that burrows within'" ("Very like a Whale: The Problem of Knowledge in *Hamlet,*" *ELH* 46 [1979]: 570).

8. D. G. James writes of Hamlet's thinking that "*Hamlet* is a tragedy not of excessive thought but of defeated thought" (*The Dream of Learning* [Oxford: Clarendon Press, 1951], p. 42).

9. Those critics who say that Hamlet is here debating over Claudius's death include Davis D. McElroy, "'To Be or Not to Be'—Is That the Question?" *College English* 25 (1964): 543–45; Alex Newell, "The Dramatic Context and Meaning of Hamlet's 'To Be or Not to Be' Soliloquy," *PMLA* 80 (1965): 38–50; and Irving Richards, "The Meaning of Hamlet's Soliloquy," *PMLA* 48 (1933): 741–66.

Those who say Hamlet is contemplating suicide include A. C. Bradley, *Shakespearean Tragedy* (London: Macmillan, 1904), p. 111; Harry Levin, *The Question of Hamlet* (Oxford: Oxford University Press, 1957), pp. 67–75; Maurice Charney, *Style in "Hamlet"* (Princeton: Princeton University Press, 1969), p. 303; Vincent Petronella, "Hamlet's 'To Be or Not to Be' Soliloquy: Once More into the Breach," *Studies in Philology* 71 (1974): 72–98; and Harley Granville-Barker, "A Soul Adrift," in *Prefaces to Shakespeare* (London: Sidgwick and Jackson, 1937), pp. 322–23.

10. David Young describes Hamlet's conundrum: "To be and not to be would be more to the point, given the tendency for opposite states to exist simultaneously within characters, situations, and the meanings of spoken lines" ("Hamlet, Son of Hamlet," in *Perspectives on Hamlet,* edited by William G. Holzberger and Peter B. Waldeck [Lewisburg, Pa.: Bucknell University Press, 1975], p. 196).

11. Richard Helgerson comments on the word "nobler":

Hamlet's very sense of what it means to be derives from his paternal heritage. He wonders whether it is "nobler" to do one thing or another. He thinks in terms of a caste concept of virtue, of nobility, the particular virtue of the warrior, not goodness. ("What Hamlet Remembers," *Shakespeare Studies* 10 [1977]: 82)

12. Of the links between Hamlet and his father, Stephen Booth writes that "though the speech is a summary of the pains of life . . . its particulars introduce the ideas of duty. Heir is particularly relevant to the relationship and duty of Hamlet and his father; it also implies a continuation of conditions from generation to generation that is generally antithetical to any assumptions of finality in death" ("On the Value of *Hamlet,*" in *Reinterpretations of Elizabethan Drama,* edited by Norman Rabkin [New York: Columbia University Press, 1968], p. 166).

13. Barbara Everett underlines Hamlet's recovery: "Beyond a certain point, Hamlet didn't delay in revenging his father; in the end, he revenged only himself. The ghost is a presence that fades" ("*Hamlet:* A Time to Die," *Shakespeare Survey* 30 [1977]: 118).

14. A World Within

1. Among the critics who cite the pastoral qualities in *King Lear* are Nancy R. Lindheim, "*King Lear* as Pastoral Tragedy," in *Some Facets of "King Lear,"* edited by Rosalie

Colie and F. T. Flahiff (Toronto: University of Toronto Press, 1974), pp. 169–84; Maynard Mack, *King Lear in Our Time* (Berkeley and Los Angeles: University of California Press, 1965), pp. 63–66; and David Young, *The Heart's Forest*, pp. 73–103.

2. Paul Jorgensen argues that Lear's belief that "nothing can be made out of nothing" opposes the Judeo-Christian ideal of God's seminal organization of chaos: "Lear's confident reply would . . . have struck original audience as seriously, even ironically wrong. In its pagan doctrine it opposed a vital Christian tenet" ("Much Ado about Nothing," *Shakespeare Quarterly* 5 [1954]: 287). Jorgensen suggests that the speeches imply Lear's early paganism rather than his initial self-idolatry. The argument here is that when Lear says "nothing can be made out of nothing," he assumes an originating image in the human mind rather than an energizing force in the deific cosmos.

3. Jerry Wasserman cites another version of this ascendance in " 'And Every One Have Need of Other': Bond and Relationship in *King Lear,*" *Mosaic* 9 (1976): 21.

4. Of the sense of retrospective relief, Paul Jorgensen argues, "it may well have been the unwise decision that saved Lear in the fullest sense" (*Lear's Self-Discovery* [Berkeley and Los Angeles: University of California Press, 1967], p. 5).

5. Citing the rhetorical nature of this speech, Stanley Cavell maintains:

[Lear's] tone is not: we will love even though we are in prison; but: because we are hidden together we can love. He has come to accept his love not by making room in the world for it but by denying its relevance to the world. He does not renounce the world in going to prison but flees from it, to earthly pleasure. (*Must We Mean What We Say?* [New York: Scribners, 1969], p. 297)

15. Becoming the Story

1. Carol Thomas Neely writes that in *The Winter's Tale*, "Time . . . the gods . . . nature . . . or art . . . work their miracles only through the play's characters, particularly its women" (see "Women and Issue in *The Winter's Tale,*" *Philological Quarterly* 57 [1978]: 181).

2. At one extreme, Barbara Adams Mowatt ignores this speech when she says that "we are immediately struck by the absence of any attempts to raise the tale to tragic heights" (see "A Tale of Sprites and Goblins," *Shakespeare Quarterly* 20 [1969]: 38). Conversely, James Edward Siemon underestimates its rhetoric: "The emotional force of Paulina's outburst can only be taken to mean that Hermione is dead and that Paulina knows it" (see "But It Appears She Lives: Iteration in *The Winter's Tale,*" *PMLA* 89 [1974]: 14).

3. William Matchett suggests that the bear

is a way of making the audience aware of the medium, like Rodin's 'Hand of God' emerging from the rock of which it is a part, so that one must experience not only the realized form but its relationship to the inchoate rock, or like those canvases of Van Gogh which remind us constantly that whatever has been achieved has been achieved with paint—not with magic but with material. ("Some Dramatic Techniques in *The Winter's Tale,*" *Shakespeare Survey* 22 [1969]: 99)

4. Ben Jonson, "The Induction," in *Bartholomew Fayre*, edited by Alvin B. Kernan and Richard B. Young (New Haven: Yale University Press, 1963), p. 32.

5. Northrop Frye, "Recognition in *The Winter's Tale,*" in *Fables of Identity* (New York: Harcourt, Brace, 1963), p. 113.

6. See G. Wilson Knight, *The Crown of Life* (London: Oxford University Press, 1967), p. 105.

7. Harold Wilson, "Nature and Art," in *The Winter's Tale: A Casebook,* edited by Kenneth Muir (New York: Macmillan, 1968), pp. 151–58.

8. Knight, *The Crown of Life,* p. 105.

9. L. C. Knights speaks of Perdita's vitality: "Lost children are found again and attention is directed not to the "generation gap" (as in *King Lear*) but to the positive effect of young people in bringing some renewal of life to the world of the middle aged or old" ("Integration in *The Winter's Tale,*" *Sewanee Review* 84 [1976]: 577).

10. Peter Berek also writes about the mockery theme, but his emphasis is on artistry:

In *The Winter's Tale* . . . Shakespeare wittily acknowledges the two meanings mock can have—scorn and imitation—and uses the second to celebrate the necessity of man-made artifice in human life. Hermione's appearance as a statue, in which Paulina tells Leontes he will "see the life as lively mock'd as ever / Still sleep mock'd death" (V.iii.18–20) can thus be seen as the emblem of mankind perfected through the agency of art. ("'As We Are Mock'd with Art': From Scorn to Transfiguration in *The Winter's Tale,*" *Studies in English Literature* 18 [1978]: 304–5)

16. Telling the Story

1. On the influence of the Joseph story see James Hoyle, "The Joseph Story and the Cannibals," *Shakespeare Quarterly* 28 (1977): 358–62.

2. John Cutts writes that "Prospero's manipulation of Gonzalo is the most artfully and deliberately concealed of all." Cutts maintains that Prospero orchestrates not only the events on the island but the thoughts of his captors so that at the end he might have them, both physically and psychologically, where he wants them. See *Rich and Strange* (Pullman: Washington State University Press, 1968), p. 93.

3. Philip Sidney, *An Apology for Poetry,* edited by Geoffrey Shepherd (London: Thomas Nelson, 1967), p. 113.

4. Critical opinion about the speech varies from Robert G. Langbaum's optimism that "it is like Miranda's exclamation an expression of the marvelous quality of life" ("Introduction," *The Tempest* [New York: Signet, 1964], p. xxxiii) to Jan Kott's pessimism that "there is in it . . . the great anxiety of Hamlet's soliloquies and one more warning to the young lovers on the frailty of all human endeavor" (*Shakespeare Our Contemporary,* p. 275).

Most readers side with Langbaum, emphasizing the ways in which Prospero combines appearance and reality. Reuben Brower writes that it "presents a sort of Proustian merging of icon and subject. . . . We experience the blending of states of being, of substantial and unsubstantial, of real and unreal, which is the essence of *The Tempest* metamorphosis" (see "The Mirror of Analogy" in *The Tempest,* edited by Robert Langbaum, p. 199).

Similarly, David Young (*The Heart's Forest,* p. 174) argues that "to say there is a stuff of which dreams are made is to give them a certain palpability and substance; to say that all life is no more than the same substance and character is to radically alter basic notions of shadow and substance, illusion and reality."

The supposition that the speech makes palpable the illusory and impalpable the substantive misses, in its inclusiveness, Prospero's fear. He does not utter a benign philosophy, calmly smoothing over philosophic opposites. His agitated disposition indicates that he here contemplates something that had never occurred to him: the possibility of complete disappearance—of absorption so total that talk of fusion is absurd.

A still further ramification of the argument is that of George Slover, who finds the disappearing vista an analogue for a theologically greater vision: The "revels speech raises theological issues . . . [bringing] to the surface the play's underlying theology." It opens up a "horizon of consciousness into which it is possible to enter only by belief itself" (see

"Magic, Mystery and Make-Believe: An Analogical Reading of *The Tempest*," *Shakespeare Studies* 11 [1978]: 196).

5. Karol Berger writes that "Prospero's despair is not over the unreality of man but over his mortality" (see "Prospero's Art," *Shakespeare Studies* 10 [1977]: 233). Berger's argument does not coincide with Prospero's later acceptance of human limitations. The disappearance into nothingness is qualitatively different from death—when human mortality is viewed in terms of a natural cyclical pattern supported by the procreative process.

6. While he "cleaves" to Prospero's thoughts here, Ariel later undergoes the same transformation that Prospero experiences. Once freed from the task of giving substance to thought, Ariel will cling to forms that already have shape, finding his security at the end in the same way that he felt it in the beginning—by attaching, almost gluing, himself to the surest things he knows:

> Where the bee sucks, there suck I:
> In a cowslip's bell I lie;
> There I couch when owls do cry.
> On the bat's back I do fly
> After summer merrily.
> Merrily, merrily shall I live now
> Under the blossom that hangs on the bough.
>
> (5.1.88–94)

"Sucking" the flower as he formerly clutched Prospero, Ariel finds freedom "in," "on," and "under" the same eternally recurring objects upon which his master will come to depend. Both move from what can no longer be the enduring monument of art to what they surmise to be the stable pattern of nature.

7. Of the contrast between Prospero's dream and Hamlet's, D. G. James writes:

> Hamlet had thought he stood upon a firm ground of reality and feared the dreams of a sleep to come but now, true being is not here: we have only a dreaming life. 'The day it is that dreameth.' (*The Dream of Prospero* [Oxford: Clarendon Press, 1967], p. 138)

8. Northrop Frye, *The Secular Scripture* (Cambridge: Harvard University Press, 1976), p. 60.

9. John Armstrong cites this passage, also noting the connections between Arthur and Prospero. See *The Paradise Myth* (London: Oxford University Press, 1969), p. 95.

10. Malory, *Works*, edited by Vinaver, p. 1240.

11. In the *O.E.D.*, *sometime* means both "a particular occasion in the past" and "the possibility of recurrence." Thus, the phrase is similar to "*Hic iacet Arthurus, Rex quondam Rexque futurus.*"

12. Wallace Stevens, "A Collect of Philosophy," *Opus Posthumous* (New York: Knopf, 1957), p. 199.

The Findings of Loss

1. Jean Valentine, "Susan's Photograph," in *The Messenger* (New York: Farrar, Straus, Giroux, 1978), p. 4.

2. Joyce Carol Oates, *New York Times Magazine*, 1980, July 27, p. 46.

3. Peter Coveney, *Images of Childhood* (Baltimore: Penguin Books, 1967), p. 29.

4. Leslie Fiedler, "On Infanticide," *Journal of Popular Culture* 14 (1981): 676.

5. Ibid., p. 676.

Bibliography

References to Shakespeare's plays are from the New Arden editions, unless otherwise indicated.

Adelman, Janet. *The Common Liar: An Essay on "Antony and Cleopatra."* New Haven: Yale University Press, 1973.

Adelman, Janet, ed. *Twentieth-Century Interpretations of "King Lear."* Englewood Cliffs, N.J.: Prentice-Hall, 1978.

Alexander, Nigel. *Poison, Play and Duel.* London: Routledge and Kegan Paul, 1971.

Alpers, Paul. "Narration in *The Faerie Queene.*" *ELH* 44 (1977): 19–39.

———. *The Poetry of "The Faerie Queene."* Princeton: Princeton University Press, 1967.

Amos, Arthur K., Jr. *Time, Space and Value: The Narrative Structure of "The New Arcadia."* Lewisburg, Pa.: Bucknell University Press, 1977.

Anderson, Judith H. *The Growth of a Personal Voice: "Piers Plowman" and "The Faerie Queene."* New Haven: Yale University Press, 1976.

Armstrong, John. *The Paradise Myth.* London: Oxford University Press, 1969.

Ascham, Roger. *The Schoolmaster.* Edited by Lawrence Ryan. Ithaca: Cornell University Press, 1967.

Babington, Gervaise. *Certaine Plaine Briefe and Comfortable Notes upon Everie Chapter of Genesis.* London: Thomas Charde, 1592.

Barber, C. L. "Shakespearean Comedy in *The Comedy of Errors.*" *College English* 25 (1964): 493–97.

———. *Shakespeare's Festive Comedies.* Cleveland: Meridan Books, 1959.

Becon, Thomas. *Prayers and Other Pieces.* Edited by John Ayre. Cambridge: Cambridge University Press, 1864.

Bennett, J. A. M., ed. *Essays on Malory.* Oxford: Clarendon Press, 1963.

Bennett, Josephine Waters. *The Evolution of "The Faerie Queene."* New York: Burt Franklin, 1960.

Benson, Larry P. *Malory's "Le Morte d'Arthur."* Cambridge: Harvard University Press, 1976.

Berek, Peter. " 'As We Are Mock'd with Art': From Scorn to Transfiguration in *The Winter's Tale.*" *Studies in English Literature* 18 (1978): 289–305.

Berger, Harry, Jr. *"King Lear:* The Family Drama.*" Centennial Review* 23 (1979): 348–76.

———. "Miraculous Harp: A Reading of Shakespeare's *Tempest,*" *Shakespeare Studies* 5 (1969): 253–83.

———. "A Secret Discipline: *The Faerie Queene,* Book VI.*" In *Form and Convention in the Poetry of Edmund Spenser,* edited by William Nelson. New York: Columbia University Press, 1961.

Berger, Karol. "Prospero's Art.*" Shakespeare Studies* 10 (1977): 211–39.

Berry, Ralph. "To Say One: An Essay on *Hamlet.*" *Shakespeare Survey* 28 (1975): 107–15.

Black, James. "The Visual Artistry of *Romeo and Juliet.*" *Studies in English Literature* 15 (1975): 245–56.

Booth, Stephen. "On the Value of *Hamlet.*" In *Reinterpretations of Elizabethan Drama,* edited by Norman Rabkin. New York: Columbia University Press, 1969.

Bradbrook, Muriel. "Romance, Farewell: *The Tempest.*" *English Literary Renaissance* 1 (1971): 239–49.

Bradley, A. C. *Shakespearean Tragedy.* London: Macmillan, 1904.

Brockbank, J. Philip. "Hamlet the Bonsetter.*" Shakespeare Survey* 30 (1977): 103–15.

Brower, Reuben. *Hero and Saint: Shakespeare and the Graeco-Roman Heroic Tradition.* New York: Oxford University Press, 1971.

Campbell, Lily B. *Shakespeare's Tragic Heroes.* Cambridge: Cambridge University Press, 1930.

Cavell, Stanley. *Must We Mean What We Say?* New York: Scribners, 1969.

Charney, Maurice. *Shakespeare's Roman Play: The Function of Imagery in the Drama.* Cambridge: Harvard University Press, 1961.

———. *Style in "Hamlet."* Princeton: Princeton University Press, 1969.

Cheney, Donald. "Spenser's Hermaphrodite and the 1590 *Faerie Queene.*" *PMLA* 87 (1972): 112–200.

Colie, Rosalie. *Paradoxia Epidemica.* Princeton: Princeton University Press, 1966.

———. *Shakespeare's Living Art.* Princeton: Princeton University Press, 1974.

Colie, Rosalie, and F. T. Flahiff. *Some Facets of "King Lear."* Toronto: University of Toronto Press, 1974.

Connell, Dorothy. *Sir Philip Sidney: The Maker's Mind.* Oxford: Clarendon Press, 1977.

Coverdale, Miles. *The Christen State of Matrimony* (Translation of H. Bullinger, *Der Christlich Eestand*). London, 1541.

Curtius, Ernst Robert. *European Literature and the Latin Middle Ages.* Translated by Willard R. Trask. New York: Pantheon Books, 1953.

Cutts, John. *Rich and Strange.* Pullman: Washington State University Press, 1968.

Davis, Walter. *"A Map of Arcadia," Sidney's Arcadia.* New Haven: Yale University Press, 1965.

Dipple, Elizabeth. "Metamorphosis in Sidney's *Arcadias.*" *Philological Quarterly* 50 (1971): 47–62.

Driscoll, James. "The Vision of *King Lear.*" *Shakespeare Studies* 10 (1977): 159–89.

Dunseath, T. K. *Spenser's Allegory of Justice in Book Five of "The Faerie Queene."* Princeton: Princeton University Press, 1965.

Eliot, T. S. *Collected Poems.* New York: Harcourt, Brace, 1958.

Elton, William R. *King Lear and the Gods.* San Marino, Calif.: Huntington Library, 1966.

Erlich, Avi. *Hamlet's Absent Father.* Princeton: Princeton University Press, 1977.

Evelyn-White, Hugh G., trans. *Hesiod, the Homeric Hymns and Homerica.* Cambridge: Harvard University Press, 1914.

Everett, Barbara. "*Hamlet:* A Time to Die." *Shakespeare Survey* 30 (1977): 117–23.

Faber, M. D., ed. *The Design Within.* New York: Science House, 1970.

Fiedler, Leslie. "On Infanticide." *Journal of Popular Culture* 14 (1981): 676–78.

Fletcher, Angus. *The Prophetic Moment: An Essay on Spenser.* Chicago: University of Chicago Press, 1971.

Flower, Annette C. "Disguise and Identity in *Pericles.*" *Shakespeare Quarterly* 26 (1975): 30–41.

Freud, Sigmund. *Moses and Monotheism.* New York: Vintage Books, 1962.

———. *The Standard Edition of the Complete Psychological Works.* Translated by James Strachey and Anna Freud. London: Hogarth Press, 1973.

Frye, Nothrop. *The Anatomy of Criticism.* Princeton: Princeton University Press, 1957.

———. *Fables of Identity.* Harcourt, Brace, 1963.

———. "Romance as Masque." In *Shakespeare's Romances Reconsidered,* edited by Carol McGinnis Kay and Henry E. Jacobs. Lincoln: University of Nebraska Press, 1978.

———. *The Secular Scripture.* Cambridge: Harvard University Press, 1976.

Frye, Northrop, ed. *The Tempest.* Baltimore: Penguin Books, 1959.

Goddard, Harold C. *The Meaning of Shakespeare.* Chicago: University of Chicago Press, 1951.

Goldberg, Jonathan. "The Mothers in Book Three of *The Faerie Queene.*" *Texas Studies in Literature and Language* 17 (1975): 5–26.

Godshalk, William L. "Hamlet's Dream of Innocence." *Shakespeare Studies* 9 (1976): 221–32.

Granville-Barker, Harley. *Prefaces to Shakespeare.* London: Sidgwick and Jackson, 1937.

Hamilton, A. C. *The Early Shakespeare.* San Marino, Calif.: Huntington Library, 1967.

———. *Sir Philip Sidney.* Cambridge: Cambridge University Press, 1977.

———. *The Structure of Allegory in "The Faerie Queene."* Oxford: Clarendon Press, 1961.

Hamilton, A. C., ed. *Essential Articles for the Study of Edmund Spenser.* Hamden, Conn.: Archon Books, 1972.

Hammersmith, James P. "*Hamlet* and the Myth of Memory." *ELH* 45 (1978): 597–605.

Hankins, John E. "Spenser and the Revelation of St. John," *PMLA* 60 (1945): 364–81.

Hardison, O.B. "Myth and History in *King Lear.*" *Shakespeare Quarterly* 26 (1975): 227–42.

Helgerson, Richard. "What Hamlet Remembers." *Shakespeare Studies* 10 (1977): 67–96.

Heliodorus. *An Aethiopian History.* Translated by Thomas Underdowne. London: David Nutt, 1895.

Hinton, Stan. "The Poet and His Narrator: Spenser's Epic Voice." *ELH* 41 (1974): 165–81.

Holloway, John. *The Story of the Night.* Lincoln: University of Nebraska Press, 1961.

Holzberger, William G., and Peter B. Waldeck. *Perspectives on Hamlet.* Lewisburg, Pa.: Bucknell University Press, 1975.

Honig, Edwin. *Dark Conceit: The Making of Allegory.* New York: Oxford University Press, 1962.

Hoyle, James. "The Joseph Story and the Cannibals." *Shakespeare Quarterly* 28 (1977): 358–62.

Hurstfield, Joel. *The Queen's Wards.* London: Longmans, Green, 1958.

James, D. G. *The Dream of Learning.* Oxford: Clarendon Press, 1951.

———. *The Dream of Prospero.* Oxford: Clarendon Press, 1967.

Jones, Ernest. *Hamlet and Oedipus.* New York: Norton, 1976.

Jonson, Ben. *Bartholomew Fayre.* Edited Alvin B. Kernan and Richard B. Young. New Haven: Yale University Press, 1963.

Jorgensen, Paul. *Lear's Self-Discovery.* Berkeley and Los Angeles: University of California Press, 1967.

———. "Much Ado about Nothing," *Shakespeare Quarterly* 5 (1954): 287–95.

Jung, Carl, and C. Kerenyi. *Introduction to a Science of Mythology.* Translated by R. F. C. Hull. London: Routledge and Kegan Paul, 1951.

Kalstone, David. *Sidney's Poetry.* Cambridge: Harvard University Press, 1965.

Kermode, Frank. *Shakespeare, Spenser, Donne.* London: Routledge and Kegan Paul, 1971.

Knight, G. Wilson. *The Crown of Life.* London: Oxford University Press, 1947.

———. *The Wheel of Fire.* London: Methuen, 1949.

Knights, L. C. *An Approach to Hamlet.* Stanford: Stanford University Press, 1969.

————. "Integration in *The Winter's Tale.*" *Sewanee Review* 84 (1976): 595–613.

Kott, Jan. *Shakespeare Our Contemporary.* Translated by Boleslaw Taborski. London: Methuen, 1965.

Lambert, Mark. *Style and Vision in "Le Morte d'Arthur."* New Haven: Yale University Press, 1975.

Lang, Berel. "Nothing Comes of All: Lear Dying." *New Literary History* 9 (1977–78): 537–59.

Langbaum, Robert, ed. *The Tempest.* New York: Signet, 1964.

Lanham, Richard. *"The Old Arcadia," Sidney's Arcadia.* New Haven: Yale University Press, 1965.

Lawry, Jon S. *Sidney's Two Arcadias.* Ithaca: Cornell University Press, 1972.

Leggatt, Alexander. *Shakespeare's Comedy of Love.* London: Methuen, 1974.

Levin, Harry. "Form and Formality in *Romeo and Juliet.*" *Shakespeare Quarterly* 11 (1960): 3–11.

————. *The Myth of the Golden Age in the Renaissance.* Bloomington: Indiana University Press, 1969.

————. *The Question of Hamlet.* Oxford: Oxford University Press, 1957.

Lewis, C. S. *The Allegory of Love.* New York: Oxford University Press, 1958.

————. "Hamlet: The Prince or the Poem." In *Studies in Shakespeare: British Academy Lectures,* edited by Peter Alexander. London: Oxford University Press, 1964.

Lifton, Betty Jean. *Twice Born: Memoirs of an Adopted Daughter.* New York: McGraw-Hill, 1975.

Longus. *Daphnis and Chloe.* Translated by Paul Turner. Baltimore: Penguin Books, 1966.

Lovejoy, Arthur O., and George Boas. *Primitivism and Related Ideas in Antiquity.* New York: Octagon Books, 1965.

Lumiansky, R. M. *Malory's Originality.* Baltimore: Johns Hopkins University Press, 1963.

MacCaffrey, Isabel. *Spenser's Allegory: The Anatomy of Imagination.* Princeton: Princeton University Press, 1976.

MacCary, W. Thomas. *"The Comedy of Errors:* A Different Kind of Comedy." *New Literary History* 9 (1977): 525–36.

McElroy, Davis D. " 'To Be or Not to Be'—Is That the Question?" *College English* 25 (1964): 543–45.

McNeir, Waldo. "The Masks of Richard III." *Studies in English Literature* 11 (1971): 167–86.

Mack, Maynard. *King Lear in Our Time.* Berkeley and Los Angeles: University of California Press, 1965.

————. "The World of *Hamlet,*" *Yale Review* 41 (1952): 502–53.

Mahood, M. H. *Shakespeare's Word Play.* London: Methuen, 1957.

Mallette, Richard. "Poet and Hero in *The Faerie Queene* VI." *Modern Language Review* 72 (1977): 257–67.

Malory, Thomas. *Works*. Edited by Eugène Vinaver. London: Oxford University Press, 1967.

Matchett, William. "Some Dramatic Techniques in *The Winter's Tale*," *Shakespeare Survey* 22 (1969): 93–107.

Moorman, C. S. *The Book of King Arthur*. Lexington: University of Kentucky Press, 1965.

Muir, Kenneth. *"The Winter's Tale": A Casebook*. New York:. Macmillan, 1968.

Neely, Carol Thomas. "Detachment and Engagement in Shakespeare's Sonnets 94, 116, and 129." *PMLA* 92 (1977): 83–95.

———. "Women and Issue in *The Winter's Tale*." *Philological Quarterly* 57 (1978): 181–94.

Neill, Michael. "Shakespeare's Hall of Mirrors." *Shakespeare Studies* 8 (1975): 99–129.

Neuse, Richard. "Book VI as Conclusion to *The Faerie Queene*." *ELH* 35 (1968): 329–53.

Newell, Alex. "The Dramatic Context and Meaning of Hamlet's 'To Be or Not to Be' Soliloquy." *PMLA* 80 (1965): 38–50.

Nohrnberg, James. *The Analogy of "The Faerie Queene."* Princeton: Princeton University Press, 1976.

Norford, Don Parry. "Very like a Whale: The Problem of Knowledge in *Hamlet*." *ELH* 46 (1979): 559–76.

Ovid. *Metamorphoses. The Arthur Golding Translation*. Edited by John Frederick Nims. New York: Macmillan, 1965.

Parker, Robert W. "Terentian Structure and Sidney's Original *Arcadia*." *English Literary Renaissance* 2 (1972): 61–78.

Parrot, Thomas Mark. *Shakespearean Comedy*. New York: Russell and Russell, 1962.

Pauphilet, Albert, ed. *La Queste del Saunt Graal*. Paris: Librarie Ancienne Honore Champion, 1949.

Petronella, Vincent. "Hamlet's 'To Be or Not to Be' Soliloquy: Once More into the Breach." *Studies in Philology* 71 (1974): 72–98.

———. "Structure and Theme through Separation and Union in Shakespeare's *The Comedy of Errors*." *Modern Language Review* 69 (1974): 481–88.

Pinchbeck, Ivy, and Margaret Hewitt. *Children in English Society*. London: Routledge and Kegan Paul, 1969.

Poulet, Georges. *Studies in Human Time*. Translated by Elliot Coleman. Baltimore: Johns Hopkins University Press, 1956.

Rank, Otto. *The Myth of the Birth of the Hero and Other Writings*. Edited by Philip Freund. New York: Vintage Books, 1959.

Reibetanz, John. *The Lear World*. Toronto: University of Toronto Press, 1977.

Rogers, John. *The Glasse of Godly Love*. Edited by Frederick J. Furnivall. London: Ludgate Hull, 1876.

Rose, Mark. *Shakespearean Design*. Cambridge: Harvard University Press, 1972.

————. *Spenser's Art*. Cambridge: Harvard University Press, 1975.

Rosinger, Lawrence. "Gloucester and Lear: Men Who Act like Gods." *ELH* 35 (1968): 491–504.

Rudenstine, Neil. *Sidney's Poetic Development*. Cambridge: Harvard University Press, 1967.

Saccio, Richard. *Shakespeare's English Kings*. London: Oxford University Press, 1977.

Salter, F. R., ed. *Some Early Tracts on Poor Relief*. London: Methuen, 1926.

Scudder, Vida. *"Le Morte d'Arthur" of Sir Thomas Malory*. New York: Dutton, 1917.

Sewall, Richard. *The Vision of Tragedy*. New Haven: Yale University Press, 1962.

Sidney, Philip. *An Apology for Poetry*. Edited by Geoffrey Shepherd. London: Thomas Nelson, 1967.

————. *The Countess of Pembroke's Arcadia*. Edited by Jean Robertson. Oxford: Clarendon Press, 1973.

Siemon, James E. "But It Appears She Lives: Iteration in *The Winter's Tale*." *PMLA* 89 (1974): 10–16.

Slover, George. "Music, Mystery and Make-Believe: An Analogical Reading of *The Tempest*." *Shakespeare Studies* 11 (1978): 175–206.

Speaight, Robert. *Nature in Shakespearean Tragedy*. New York: Collier Books, 1966.

Spenser, Edmund. *Poetical Works*. Edited by J. C. Smith and E. de Selincourt. Oxford: Oxford University Press, 1964.

Spivack, Bernard. *Shakespeare and the Allegory of Evil*. New York: Columbia University Press, 1955.

Stauffer, Donald. *Shakespeare's World of Images*. Bloomington: Indiana University Press, 1973.

Stevens, Wallace. *Collected Poems*. New York: Knopf, 1961.

Stone, Lawrence. *The Family, Sex and Marriage in England, 1500–1800*. New York: Harper and Row, 1977.

Tayler, Edward. *Nature and Art in Renaissance Literature*. New York: Columbia University Press, 1964.

Tillyard, E. M. W. *Shakespeare's Early Comedies*. London: Chatto and Windus, 1960.

————. *Shakespeare's History Plays*. London: Chatto and Windus, 1961.

Tobias, Richard C., and Paul G. Zolbrod, eds. *Shakespeare's Last Plays*. Athens: Ohio University Press, 1974.

Tonkin, Humphrey. *Spenser's Courteous Pastoral*. London: Oxford University Press, 1966.

————. "Spenser's Garden of Adonis and Britomart's Quest." *PMLA* 88 (1973): 408–17.

Toole, William B. "The Motif of Psychic Division in *Richard III*." *Shakespeare Survey* 27 (1974): 21–32.

Traversi, Derek. *Shakespeare: The Last Phase*. New York: Harcourt, Brace, 1955.

Tufte, Virginia, and Barbara Meyerhoff. *Changing Images of the Family*. New Haven: Yale University Press, 1979.

Turner, Frederick. *Shakespeare and the Nature of Time*. Oxford: Clarendon Press, 1971.

Tuve, Rosamund. *Allegorical Imagery*. Princeton: Princeton University Press, 1966.

Uphaus, Robert W. "The Comic Mode of *The Winter's Tale*." *Genre* 3 (1970): 40–54.

Valentine, Jean. *The Messenger*. New York: Farrar, Straus, Giroux, 1978.

Waith, Eugene M., ed. *Shakespeare: The Histories*. Englewood Cliffs, N.J.: Prentice-Hall, 1965.

Wasserman, Jerry. " 'And Every One Have Need of Other': Bond and Relationship in *King Lear*." *Mosaic* 9 (1976): 15–30.

Webster, John. *The Duchess of Malfi*. Edited by Fred B. Millet. Northbrook, Ill.: AHM Press, 1953.

Wells, Stanley, ed. *Shakespeare: Select Biblioigraphical Guides*. London: Oxford University Press, 1973.

Whitaker, Muriel. "Christian Iconography in the Quest of the Holy Grail." *Mosaic* 12 (1979): 11–19.

Williams, Kathleen. *Spenser's World of Glass*. Berkeley and Los Angeles: University of California Press, 1966.

———. "Vision and Rhetoric: The Poet's Voice in *The Faerie Queene*." *ELH* 36 (1969): 131–44.

Wilson, J. Dover. "The Elizabethan Shakespeare." In *Proceedings of the British Academy*. London: Oxford University Press, 1929.

Wilson, Rowdon. "The Way to Arden: Attitudes towards Time in *As You Like It*." *Shakespeare Quarterly* 26 (1975): 16–24.

Woods, Suzanne. "Closure in *The Faerie Queene*." *JEGP* 76 (1977): 195–216.

Yeats, W. B. *Essays and Introductions*. New York: Macmillan, 1961.

Young, David. *The Heart's Forest*. New Haven: Yale University Press, 1972.

Index

226